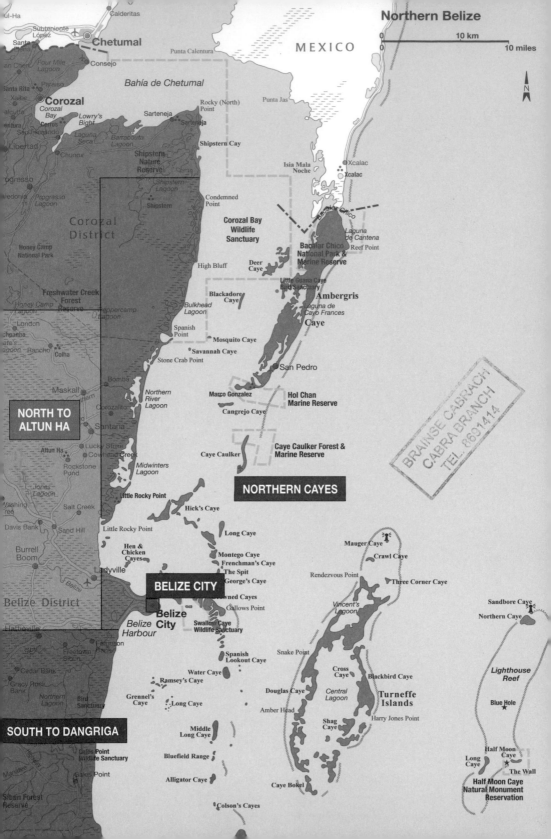

INSIGHT ◉ GUIDES

BELIZE

PLAN & BOOK
YOUR TAILOR-MADE TRIP

BRAZIL CHILE ECUADOR

TAILOR-MADE TRIPS & UNIQUE EXPERIENCES CREATED BY LOCAL TRAVEL EXPERTS AT INSIGHTGUIDES.COM/HOLIDAYS

Insight Guides has been inspiring travellers with high-quality travel content for over 45 years. As well as our popular guidebooks, we now offer the opportunity to book tailor-made private trips completely personalised to your needs and interests. By connecting with one of our local experts, you will directly benefit from their expertise and local know-how, helping you create memories that will last a lifetime.

HOW INSIGHTGUIDES.COM/HOLIDAYS WORKS

STEP 1
Pick your dream destination and submit an enquiry, or modify an existing itinerary if you prefer.

STEP 2
Fill in a short form, sharing details of your travel plans and preferences with a local expert.

STEP 3
Your local expert will create your personalised itinerary, which you can amend until you are completely satisfied.

STEP 4
Book securely online. Pack your bags and enjoy your holiday! Your local expert will be available to answer questions during your trip.

BENEFITS OF PLANNING & BOOKING AT
INSIGHTGUIDES.COM/HOLIDAYS

PLANNED BY LOCAL EXPERTS

The Insight Guides local experts are hand-picked, based on their experience in the travel industry and their impeccable standards of customer service.

SAVE TIME & MONEY

When a local expert plans your trip, you save time and money when you book, even during high season. You won't be charged for using a credit card either.

TAILOR-MADE TRIPS

Book with Insight Guides, and you will be in complete control of the planning process, from the initial selections to amending your final itinerary.

BOOK & TRAVEL STRESS-FREE

Enjoy stress-free travel when you use the Insight Guides secure online booking platform. All bookings come with a money-back guarantee.

WHAT OTHER TRAVELLERS THINK ABOUT TRIPS BOOKED AT
INSIGHTGUIDES.COM/HOLIDAYS

Trip to Portugal

Every step of the planning process and the trip itself was effortless and exceptional. Our special interests, preferences and requests were accommodated resulting in a trip that exceeded our expectations.

Corinne, USA   ★★★★★

Trip to Vietnam

The organization was superb, the drivers professional, and accommodation quite comfortable. I was well taken care of! My thanks to your colleagues who helped make my trip to Vietnam such a great experience. My only regret is that I couldn't spend more time in the country.

Heather   ★★★★★

DON'T MISS OUT
BOOK NOW AT
INSIGHTGUIDES.COM/HOLIDAYS

CONTENTS

Travel tips

Maps

LEGEND
⚲ Insight on
◉ Photo story

THE BEST OF BELIZE: TOP ATTRACTIONS

△ **Ambergris Caye**. Soak up the rays on this island – made famous by Madonna's 'La Isla Bonita,' Ambergris is lined with beaches and offers superb snorkeling and diving. See page 126.

▽ **Blue Hole Natural Monument**. View the depths of the famous Blue Hole from the air or underwater. This sinkhole includes tropical fish, swaying corals, and amazing drop-off walls. See page 131.

△ **Caye Caulker**. 'Go slow' is the apt motto at Belize's sleepy backpacker island, which has sandy lanes, excellent snorkeling and diving, the finest lobster in the country, and cheap accommodations. See page 125.

△ **Caracol**. The largest Maya site in Belize, Caracol features massive temples with sweeping views of the surrounding Chiquibul forest. See page 167.

△ **Placencia Peninsula**. The best beaches in the country. Relax on white-sands and snorkel and dive the Barrier Reef. See page 197.

◁ **Cockscomb Basin Wildlife Sanctuary**. The world's only jaguar reserve – a tropical forest, crisscrossed with hiking trails, waterfalls, and rocky pools. See page 191.

▷ **Mountain Pine Ridge**. Explore fragrant pine forests, thundering waterfalls, and ancient caves in the lush Mountain Pine Ridge in western Cayo. See page 164.

△ **Belize Zoo**. Come face-to-face with Belize's iconic creatures, from screeching howler monkeys to scarlet macaws to iguanas at one of the finest zoos in Central and South America. See page 119.

▽ **Lamanai**. The boat journey to Lamanai, along the New River, is as memorable as the site itself, which was the largest in the entire Maya world when it was built around 100 BC. See page 141.

△ **Punta Gorda**. A charming base for exploring the Toledo District – a mix of Maya villages, caves, and marine reserves. See page 207.

THE BEST OF BELIZE: EDITOR'S CHOICE

BEST ADVENTURES AND OUTDOOR ACTIVITIES

Snorkeling. The longest barrier reef in the Western Hemisphere affords spectacular snorkeling, particularly around the cayes, where you'll see everything from bright tropical fish to swaying coral. See page 130.

Diving. From the inky depths of the Blue Hole to the crystal waters of the Turneffe Atoll, Belize has some of the finest diving in the world – keep a watch for manta rays, turtles, hammerhead sharks, and more. See page 131.

Kayaking. Glide across the Caribbean Sea in a kayak, exploring the Belize Barrier Reef, mangrove islands and coral atolls. Numerous tour outfitters offer guided kayak trips or rentals. See page 236.

River tubing. Get an adrenalin rush as you go tubing down rivers and through elaborate cave systems, which the Maya considered a sacred underworld. See page 195.

Hiking. Explore Belize's lush interior on a hike through jungles and rainforests, such as Mountain Pine Ridge, where you can embark on everything from guided walks along medicinal plant trails to sweaty multiday treks. See page 164.

Fishing. Belize is a top fishing destination, and many lodges and local guides offer fishing trips that include catch-and-release fly-fishing on shallow flats off the cayes, as well as fishing for tarpon and other sportfish. See page 209.

Exploring Belize's beautiful coastline.

Temple of the Green Tomb, Altun Ha.

BEST JUNGLE LODGES

Chaa Creek. 'Wildly civilized' is the motto at Chaa Creek, an elegant lodge set on a 365-acre nature reserve in Western Belize, with treetop suites with outdoor Jacuzzis, a breezy spa, an excellent restaurant, and an infinity swimming pool. See page 163.

Sweet Songs. Experience the jungle first hand at this nature lodge on the teeming banks of the Macal River, which has bungalows with screened porches strung with hammocks, in addition to a huge variety of outdoor activities, from horseback riding to strolling through the adjoining Belize Botanic Garden. See page 163.

Blancaneaux. This 20-room luxury resort, owned by the famed film director Francis Ford Coppola, is surrounded by the mighty Maya Mountains, and features riverfront thatched-roof cabanas with views of thundering waterfalls. See page 167.

Chan Chich. Few lodges combine comfort and conservation like this highly-regarded lodge, which includes elegant thatched cabanas and suites with airy verandas and hammocks, all set in the grassy plaza of the Classic Maya site of Chan Chich ('little bird'). See page 147.

Hidden Valley Inn. Soak in a hot tub under the starry sky at this intimate inn, which is surrounded by pine forests and tumbling waterfalls, with colorful birds darting through the air. See page 166.

BEST FESTIVALS AND EVENTS

Lobster Festivals: Mid-June. Feast on fresh lobster made every which way – grilled, skewered, in a tangy ceviche, barbecued – at the country's trio of lobster festivals, on Ambergris Caye, Caye Caulker, and Placencia. See page 233.

Garífuna Settlement Day: November 19. Pay tribute to Belize's rich Garífuna heritage during this colorful festival in Dangriga, which includes lively parades, dancing, drumming, Garífuna church services, and more. See page 188.

Crooked Tree Cashew Nut Festival: Early May. Celebrate the famous nut, amid Crooked Tree's flourishing cashew trees, with traditional music, dance, storytelling, and tastings, from cashew jams to cakes to wines. See page 233.

La Ruta Maya Belize River Challenge: Early March. This perennially popular annual four-day canoe race, from San Ignacio to Belize City, is accompanied by celebratory events along the way, with local music, cuisine, and dancing. See page 233.

BEST MAYAN TEMPLES

Altun Ha. This beautifully preserved site encompasses two massive plazas and numerous Mayan treasures, including a jade head, which is the largest carved jade piece that has ever been discovered from the Maya era. See page 137.

Cahal Pech. Perched on the highest hill overlooking the town of San Ignacio, Cahal Pech dates back to the Classic Period and encompasses temples, ball courts, and stelae scattered across two acres. See page 162.

Caracol. The pyramid of Canna (44 meters/143ft),

the tallest man-made structure in Belize, presides grandly over this superbly preserved site in the Chiquibul Forest Reserve. See page 171.

Xunantunich. This Classic Period site, whose name translates as 'Maiden of the Rock,' includes the mighty El Castillo temple and well-preserved stucco friezes. See page 167.

Lamanai. Northern Belize's most impressive Maya site, rising over the New River, features numerous depictions of crocodiles – its name means 'submerged crocodile' in the original Maya. See page 141.

A TASTE OF BELIZE

Lobster. Feast on fresh, sweet lobster (in season, mid-June–mid-Feb) throughout the cayes and coast – try it simply grilled with a drizzle of butter, tossed in a salad, or piled high on a soft roll.

Gibnut. Feeling adventurous? Sample gibnut, a nocturnal rodent (also called *paca* elsewhere in Central and South America) that's hunted in the northern and western jungles of Belize. On the plate, gibnut looks like pork – slightly fatty, and often tender enough to tease apart with a fork; on the tongue, its wild, gamey nature comes through.

Belikin. Toast the night with Belize's local beer, which comes in many varieties, including a dark stout and the sparkling, golden Lighthouse.

Chan Chich jungle lodge.

Rum. The country's finest rum is Travellers One Barrel Rum, made by Belize's oldest distillery. Rich and dark, with hints of tropical fruit, this rum goes down well on its own – or mixed into cocktails.

Marie Sharp's pepper sauce. Dining tables across Belize have one important thing in common: bottles of Marie Sharp's beloved – and fiery – pepper sauce, made in a factory near Dangriga in the south.

Garífuna cassava bread. Sink your teeth into this traditional Garífuna favorite: a crispy bread made with cassava, which is similar in taste and texture to sweet potato. For more about Belizean food and drink, see page 71.

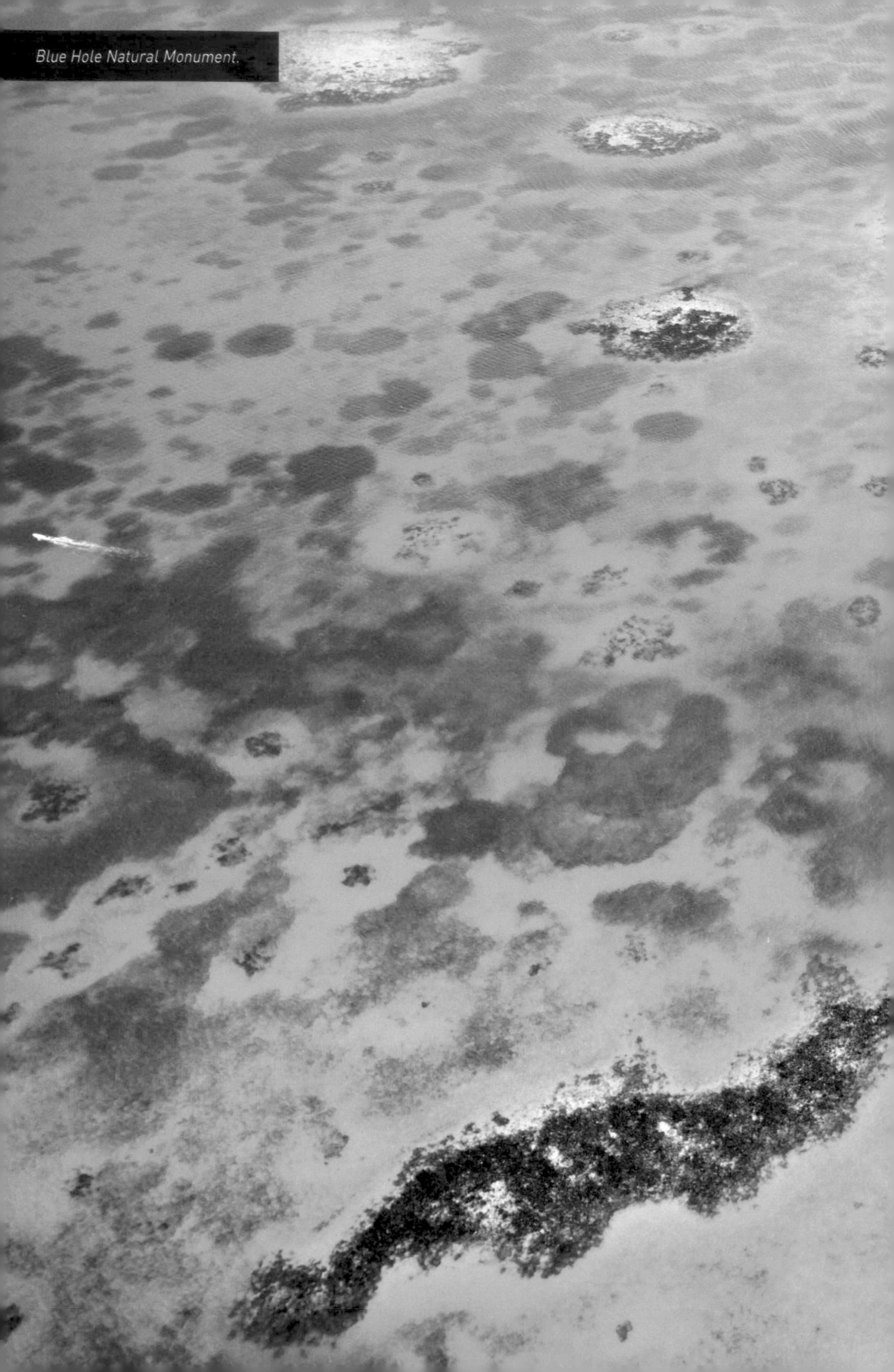

Blue Hole Natural Monument.

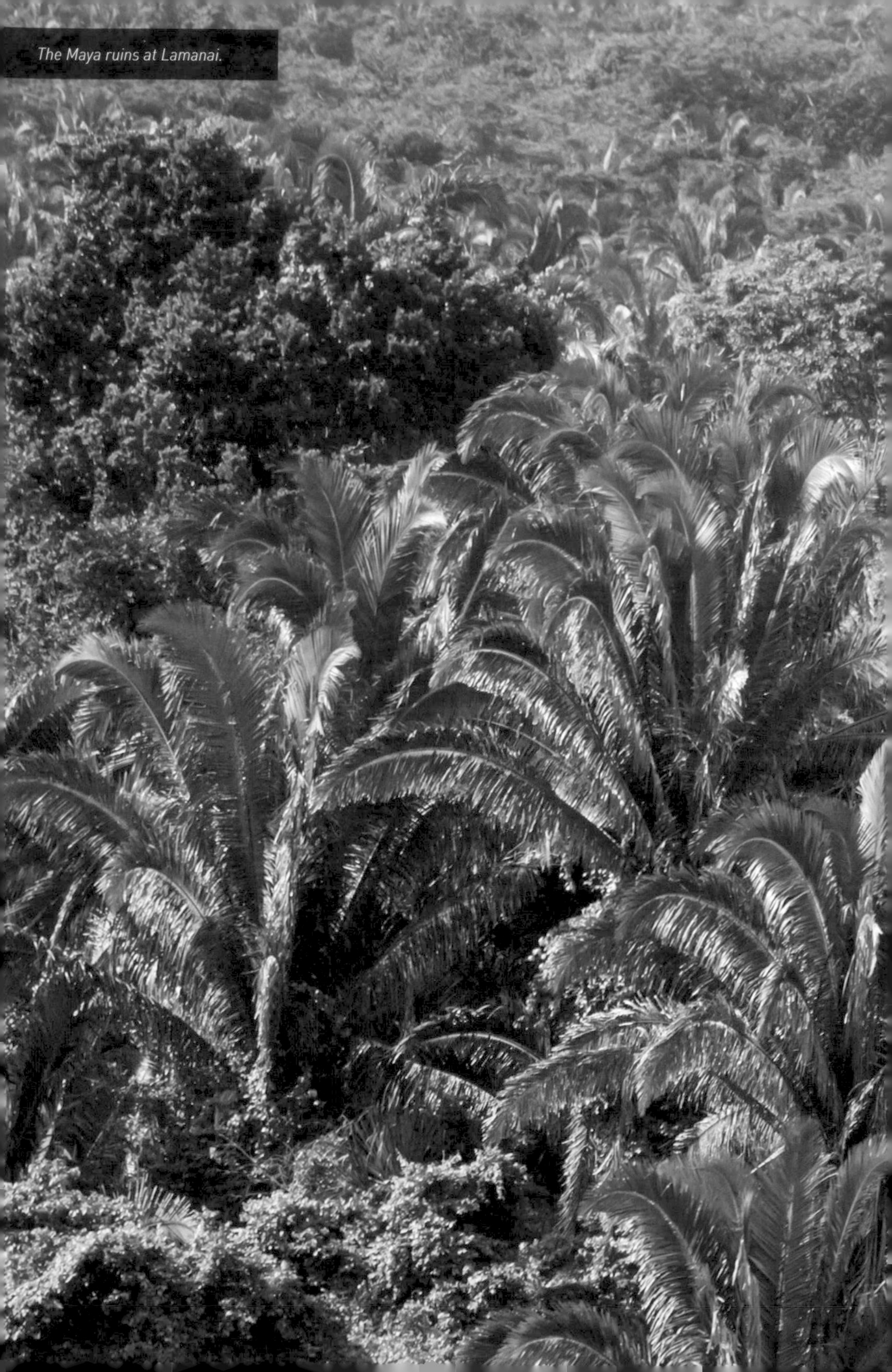

The Maya ruins at Lamanai.

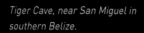
Tiger Cave, near San Miguel in southern Belize.

Laughing Bird Caye National Park.

CAYE ATTRACTIONS

Belize may be tiny, but it's bursting with cultural and natural wonders that rival its Central American and Caribbean neighbors.

Belize's national bird.

'If the world had any ends,' wrote Aldous Huxley in *Beyond the Mexique Bay* (1934), 'Belize would certainly be one of them. It is not on the way from anywhere to anywhere else. It has no strategic value. It is all but uninhabited'. Huxley's off-hand observation remains among the most famous made by a foreign writer about Belize, if only because he was one of the few to visit what was at the time a largely irrelevant corner of the British Empire.

Indeed, Belize's sheer obscurity had been the country's defining trait for centuries: first settled by English and Scottish pirates in the 17th century, it soon became a secret haven for loggers and their African slaves who operated under the noses of the Spaniards. By the 19th century, British Honduras (the name Belize was only taken in 1973) had become the ultimate backwater, an English-speaking, largely black Creole outpost in Central America.

In an irony that Huxley might have appreciated, Belize's centuries of under-development have guaranteed the country's greatest resource: nature. Belize has long been squarely on the map as one of the world's leading eco-tourism destinations. Contained within its borders are vast swathes of untouched rainforest, endless savannah and mangrove coasts, all containing the greatest variety of animal habitats north of the Amazon basin. Offshore, Belize's coral reef is the most splendid in the Western hemisphere, second in size and grandeur only to Australia's Great Barrier Reef, with more than 200 small islands or cayes (pronounced 'keys') dotted around it. Add to that

Kayaking at Caye Caulker.

the 900-plus ancient Maya sites scattered around the country and you begin to see why Belize has firmly taken its spot on the tourist circuit.

Even so, Belize's most beguiling attraction remains its old world eccentricity. It's a place where villages are named Double Head Cabbage and Bound To Shine. With a population that hovers around 390,000, Belize remains as relaxed and intimate as a small country town; yet, while everyone seems to know everyone else, it is one of the most culturally diverse places on earth – a mixture of black creoles, Spanish-speaking mestizos, Maya, East Indians, Syrians, Mennonites, Chinese, and North Americans, all getting along in a far more amicable fashion than most of its Central American neighbors.

Young Belizeans.

THE BELIZEANS

In spite of the influence of US culture and the economic lure of emigration to North America, Belizeans of all racial origins remain loyal to their own small country.

For most Belizeans, the presence of many different ethnic groups in the country is as much a national treasure as the Barrier Reef or Maya ruins. Belize is not so much a melting pot of cultures as a salad in which each element lends a certain flavor to the mix.

From an early age, Belizeans are encouraged to feel proud of their own racial traditions and appreciate those of others. 'Cultural presentations,' displaying the music, dance, and dress of the elements of Belizean society, are a regular part of grade school activities, community celebrations, and political rallies. In the words of Belizean artist Phillip Lewis, '*A tink a si wan new Belize weh di creole man, di mestizo, di Garífuna, an di Maya, no separate as a lis dem but instead all da Belizeans.*' – 'I think I see a new Belize where the creole, the mestizo, the Garífuna and the Maya, are not separated as I have listed them, but united as Belizeans.'

Or, as the creole saying goes, '*All a we mek Belize*' – 'we all make up Belize.'

Generations of racial mixing have made it impossible to describe the 'typical' Belizean – only a typical room full of Belizeans, whose physical characteristics range from the very darkest to the lightest skin tones, and every imaginable hair and eye color. Even within a single family there is likely to be considerable variation, since the grandparents usually have ancestors from several continents. But, despite the blurring of racial lines, most Belizeans identify themselves with a particular ethnic group.

THE SEARCH FOR IDENTITY

Belizeans have long described themselves as 'a Caribbean nation in Central America,' for

Local man in Punta Gorda.

they have more in common with the distant islands of the Caribbean than their next-door neighbors. This is because Belize has a British rather than Spanish heritage; English is the official language and much of the population is black creole, descended from African slaves and British settlers. There have always been the Maya and mestizos (those of mixed Indian and Spanish descent) as in the rest of Central America, but historically the creole culture has been dominant – making Belize's legal, political and educational systems closer to those of the English-speaking Caribbean, while its music, dance, and folklore share many African elements found dotted around the islands.

Things are changing, however. Creoles now make up less than 25 percent of the total population and the ethnic balance has shifted in favor of the mestizos, who represent almost 50 percent of all Belizeans. Large numbers of Creole Belizeans have been leaving for the United States, while mestizo refugees and immigrants flooded in from war-ravaged Central America in the 1980s. Although peace was restored in the 1990s, immigration from other parts of Central America has continued – with the immigrants seeking jobs and land for *milpa* (small-scale cornfield) farming.

lineage back to Belize's original inhabitants. There are three distinct Maya groups, the largest being the Mopan, the Kekchi, and the Yucatec. But, like many indigenous people elsewhere, the Maya are on the lowest rungs of Belize's socio-economic ladder. Most are subsistence farmers who live in remote villages and maintain a traditional lifestyle. Many exist outside the official economy, without access to national health care services or education.

The Garífuna were greeted with prejudice and suspicion when they first arrived in Belize

Much of Belize's population is black Creole.

These incomers have been adding to the numbers of Spanish speakers who settled in northern Belize in the 1860s, fleeing the bloody Caste Wars in Mexico. The mestizo families who are longer established in Belize mostly live around Orange Walk Town and Corozal and speak both Spanish and creole, or a Spanish that is heavily creolized. Some creoles are concerned that the increase in mestizos will mean the erosion of creole culture; others believe the new arrivals will adopt the creole language and traditions just as many other immigrant groups have in the past.

in the early 1800s. A mixture of escaped African slaves and Carib Indians, they ended up in Dangriga on the south coast after an epic 200-year persecution by European powers (see page 189). They make up only 7 percent of Belize's population, yet they have had a great impact on the country, figuring prominently in the professions and the arts.

Adding to the mix are East Indians, Syrians, Lebanese, Chinese, and Taiwanese, in addition to the distinctive Mennonites from the USA and Canada.

ANCIENT AND NEW INHABITANTS

Although they represent only 8 percent of the population, the modern-day Maya trace their

IMPERFECT HARMONY

Belize is not free from racial prejudice. A visitor might be told by creoles that the Central

American 'aliens' are very violent and therefore responsible for Belize's rise in crime; mestizos often dismiss creoles as lazy folk who would rather steal than work for a living. There is also resentment in some quarters towards Taiwanese and Hong Kong nationals, who some claim are 'taking over Belize.' But these same people who have bad-mouthed other ethnic groups will, moments later, proudly tell the visitor that, unlike other places in the world, there is no prejudice in Belize and everyone lives together in peace. In hard to keep things private and gossiping is a favorite pastime. But for most Belizeans, their small society is an advantage: it guarantees them a warm welcome wherever they go in Belize.

HOME AND ABROAD

Even so, many Belizeans have never left their villages, and residents of Belize City rarely go out to the cayes or neighboring districts. Because of this, they tend to be very absorbed in local happenings, and almost everything in Belize has a

From an early age, Belizeans are encouraged to feel proud of their cultural heritage.

short, like most countries that have absorbed multiple ethnic groups, there are times of great challenge with integration – and times of great harmony.

In the end, most Belizeans celebrate racial diversity. Being creole, Maya, mestizo, or even Taiwanese is still second to being Belizean, and everyone has the sense that they are helping to 'build the nation.' With a national population of only 390,000, tolerance is not only desirable, it is absolutely necessary.

Belize has the intimate, personal feel of a small town. Even in Belize City, strangers usually ask each other how they are related to friends with the same name, or where they attended school. Such familiarity makes it

⊘ INDIANS FROM THE EAST

East Indians comprise only 3.5 percent of the population of Belize, but like the Garífuna they have enjoyed disproportionate success, becoming prominent in Belizean business. They first arrived in the 1860s as indentured laborers on sugar plantations established by former Confederate Americans; their cultural identities soon dwindled, but East Indian physical traits are visible in almost every ethnic group in Belize. A second wave of East Indians arrived in the 1970s and set up as shop-owners in Belize City; this group still makes every attempt to preserve its customs, including traveling back to India to arrange suitable marriages.

political significance. Party affiliation is important, since everything from buying land to being hired for a job may depend on which political party you supported in the last election.

But not everyone sees Belize as the perfect home. An unemployment rate of close to 20 percent, low wages and a high cost of living have prompted many people – mostly creoles – to head north in search of a better life. Over the past two decades, thousands of young Belizeans have emigrated, both legally and illegally, to major cities in the United States. Many of them

More than 50 percent of the population are under 25.

have left small children behind to be raised by grandmothers or aunts. The majority of emigrants are skilled workers and professionals, including teachers and nurses, whose departure is a 'brain drain' from Belize that leaves it the poorer.

Almost everyone in Belize has relatives in the United States who send home money, clothing, and other goods. Access to American television has made Belizean young people crave not only US fashions and music, but a lifestyle well beyond their means. Belizean youths have also been influenced by the US street gang mentality, and local gangs modeled on those in urban America have sprung up around Belize City, complete with drug trafficking and drive-by

shootings. Many wonder whether the search for a better life has cost too much.

THE BEL-AMS

Belizeans living abroad don't always have it easy either. Although there are now more Belizeans living in the US than in Belize, they are still small minorities in the cities where they live. They may have to decide for the first time to which ethnic group they belong. Are they African Americans? Latinos? Are they 'Mixed' or 'Other?' If they stay in Belizean communities there is pressure to conform; if they strike out on their own they feel cut off from the homeland. And no matter how well Belizean-Americans do financially, or how well they adapt to the North American lifestyle, Belize always calls them home eventually. They generally make the pilgrimage for the September Independence celebrations, Christmas, or Easter. Even youngsters and teens born and raised in the US know there is something special about their parents' homeland; just give them a week and they will be trying to learn creole and asking for hot johnny cakes.

A RELAXED LIFESTYLE

Despite the recent influence of American culture, most Belizeans are still proud of their own culture. Belize's work environment is generally much more relaxed than in the US, and people think nothing of dropping by a friend's workplace to chat for a few minutes or stepping out of the office to run errands or to go to the bank. Offices and schools close for lunch, when many families sit down together for the big meal of the day.

Belizeans value leisure time and there is no shortage of public and bank holidays. Friday is the preferred night to go out, and any excuse is enough for a get-together. House parties with lots of food and drinks rave on until early the next morning and usually don't end until the liquor runs out.

Sundays are still sacred in Belize. The dominant religion is Catholic, although other evangelical Christian denominations have established a following in almost every town and village. While some reserve the day for worship, for others Sunday is a time for family or a trip to the cayes. For creoles, no Sunday is complete without the traditional stewed chicken, rice and beans, and potato salad.

VERBAL CULTURE

Belizeans don't read much, perhaps because only a few local authors and poets have published slim volumes of their works, but this doesn't mean Belizeans don't like words (see page 64). It is because Belize creole still has no standardized written form – although the 'Bileez Kriol Projek' has produced a dictionary and translated some folk tales and books of the Bible – that people tend to rely on their ears rather than their eyes for information. As a result, Belizeans are often capable of memorizing astonishingly large amounts of information.

gives him any of her food, or how he has something which could help relieve her headache, and from there the repartee begins.

A WORLD OF SUPERSTITION

In Belize, there are beliefs and omens pertaining to just about every aspect of life. Those who are having a hard time, or who face numerous disappointments, often fear they have been '*obeahed*' (fallen victim to someone's black magic), and people in love often consult tarot card readers or write their beloved's name on candles.

Education is compulsory between the ages of 6 and 14.

Belizeans also like to invent names for each other. Some people are so well known by their nicknames that their real names are unknown to their friends. Some reflect the person's appearance ('Big George,' 'Lagrahead,' like the loggerhead turtle, or 'Red Boy'). Others, like 'January Baboon,' seem downright insulting, although they are meant to express affection.

Belizeans also delight in giving ordinary conversations sexual connotations. What North Americans might denounce as sexual harassment is viewed as great fun by most Belizeans, and women see it as their obligation to put any man making unwanted advances in his place. A man might suggestively comment on how delicious a woman's meal looks, how she never

The survival of such Africanisms as black magic (*obeah*) and the folklore of both the Maya and European peoples have given Belize a rich variety of magical explanations for everyday events. Not only are Belizeans wary of ladders and black cats, but they also look out for Tataduhende, the little bearded bushman who has his feet on backwards (so that you'll think he's coming when he's really going) and Llorona, the weeping woman who lures drunken men to their death.

A wealth of pseudo-scientific beliefs relate to medical conditions, pregnancy, and birth, and even the most common household activities have magical overtones. Most housewives, for instance, will never sweep all the dirt out of the house (thereby losing all their luck) and a dropped spoon or fork means that visitors are coming. A guest who overstays his welcome can be made to leave by turning a broom upside down behind a door. Good fortune is continually being sought and dreams are considered a reliable source for lucky *boledo* (lottery) numbers.

MALE AND FEMALE ROLES IN THE FAMILY

Belizeans have a fairly loose definition of family. While there are many families that are made

degrees and becoming managers, or entering the legal and medical professions.

LOOKING TO THE FUTURE

Belize is a remarkably youthful country, with more than 50 percent of the population under the age of 25. This has translated into a vigor and flexibility that bodes well for the future. Although far too many young Belizeans stay in the US after graduating because of higher salaries and better opportunities, the enthusiastic desire to 'build Belize' pulls quite a few

Mennonite children in Spanish Lookout.

up of the traditional husband, wife, and two children, it's also not uncommon for married men to work to support more than one family or numerous 'sweethearts.' Plenty of Belizean women accept common-law marriages or spend years being a married man's sweetheart. Fifty percent of all children in Belize are born outside of wedlock and a single mother may have several children by different fathers. When fathers are absent from the domestic scene, grandmothers and aunts help with childcare, and cousins are often raised as closely as siblings.

Women make up a large percentage of the workforce. Although they tend to occupy traditional jobs like teaching, nursing, and secretarial work, increasing numbers are obtaining

back. Belize celebrated its 30th birthday in 2011, under the proud theme of: 'Honoring our History. Celebrating our Cultures. Uniting for Peace.' And indeed, Belize is going forth with those tenets in mind, while also maximizing its natural resources and courting tourist dollars. But, above all, it's doing so responsibly: over the years, there have been many detractors who believed that Belize's commitment to eco-friendly practices and sustainability would eventually wither away. That hasn't happened. In Belize, a natural wonder is only as valuable as the ability to preserve it – and it's this belief that may be its greatest insurance for a successful future. As the Belizeans like to say, 'You better Belize it!'

THE MENNNONITES

Belize's Mennonite community is a resilient, religious sect that traces its roots to the 16th-century Netherlands.

They stand out in any Belizean crowd: blond, blue-eyed men in denim overalls and cowboy hats; modestly dressed women whose home-made outfits – ankle-length, long-sleeved frocks and wide-brimmed hats tied down with black scarves – defy the tropical heat. Polite and reserved, they talk quietly among themselves, not in Spanish, English, or Creole, but in guttural German.

These are part of Belize's Mennonite community, who take their name from a Dutch priest, Menno Simons. Mennonites live in isolated farming communities, calling themselves *die Stillen im Lande*, the Unobtrusive Ones. They reject state interference in their affairs and are committed pacifists.

Belize is the latest stop in a three-century odyssey – their beliefs have often led to persecution, driving them from the Netherlands to Prussia in the 1600s, to southern Russia, and, when the Russian government suggested military conscription in the 1870s, to Canada.

After World War I, the Canadian government demanded that only English be taught in Mennonite schools and, spurred on by anti-German feeling, reconsidered conscription. Again, many of the Mennonites moved on, this time to Mexico – only for the Mexican government then to try to include them in a new social security program.

Around 80,000 Mennonites remain in Mexico, including a community in Campeche, but others have moved to Belize, where their farming skills have proved successful. In colonial times few Belizeans farmed the land – even eggs were imported from abroad.

FARMSTEADS IN THE JUNGLE

In 1958, the first of 3,500 Mennonites arrived, to begin hacking roads through the forest, clearing a vast wilderness of land to create their farmsteads in the jungle. But, after centuries of traumatic upheaval, though the Mennonite religion's core had survived intact, deep cultural divisions had opened up. Conservative groups spoke German and used only farming implements available in the early 1900s, while progressive Mennonites had learned English in Canada, and were happy to use tractors and fertilizer.

Settlements spread throughout Belize reflecting this cultural diversity: the progressive 'Kleine Gemeinde' (Small Community) settled around Spanish Walk near San Ignacio; the conservative 'Altkolonier' (Old Colonists) opted for the wilderness at Blue Creek on the corner of Mexico and Guatemala. Another contingent settled near Orange Walk Town at Shipyard and Richmond Hill.

A member of the Mennonite community in Spanish Lookout.

The Mennonites are today the most successful farmers in Belize. They supply much of the country's food, including chicken, dairy products, and eggs, and make most of the country's furniture. The modern Mennonite town at Spanish Lookout would not look out of place in the US.

Typical of more conservative Mennonites is Barton Creek, a breakaway group from Spanish Lookout's progressive ways. Here families live in wooden houses without electricity, linked to the highway by a rough dirt road.

Despite the isolation, Friesen and others are happy to meet interested visitors. There is one caveat: strict Mennonites object to having their photographs taken, believing no memory should be left of a person after they die.

DECISIVE DATES

Carved stone mask, Lamanai.

THE ANCIENT MAYA

*C.*2000 BC

Evidence of fixed Maya settlements in Mexico.

600 BC

First major evidence of the Maya in Belize.

500 BC

First monumental Maya buildings at sites like Tikal (in modern-day Mexico) and Dzibilchaltún (the Yucatán); style influenced by the Olmec culture of the north.

300 BC

Izapa-type pottery and hieroglyphs first appear. Beginning of the Classic Period when the most important ceremonial centers were built.

AD 100

Cities of El Mirador and Cerros founded.

AD 550–800

Maya civilization at its peak, spreading through southern Mexico, Guatemala, parts of Honduras, and El Salvador, and Belize.

900

Decline of the Classic Maya civilization. Sometimes (controversially) termed the 'Collapse'; this attributed to increased competition for resources leading to interstate wars following several prolonged periods of drought. Other influences begin to be felt.

1000

New civilizations compete for dominance in Central America (still including some Maya).

1250

Mayapan is the center of influence in the Yucatán Peninsula. Trading contacts between the Maya in Belize and the Yucatán.

THE SPANISH CONQUEST

1512

Two Spanish shipwreck survivors arrive in the Yucatán. First European contact with the Maya world.

1519

Spanish conquest of Mexico begins. First Mass held in Mexico.

1520

Smallpox, hookworm and malaria brought from Europe by conquerors begins to spread through remaining Maya communities. Spanish influence is felt throughout Central America.

1562

Maya in Yucatán are persecuted by Friar Diego de Landa who orders burning of Maya books and sculptures.

ARRIVAL OF THE BRITISH

1600S

Settlement of the first 'Baymen' around the mouth of Belize River. Trade in logwood for dyes.

1634

Captain Peter Wallace – after whom Belize, corrupted from Wallace, could have been named – sails into Belize Harbour

1638

The territory of Belize is founded by a group of British seamen, who name their settlement St George's Caye.

1670

Treaty of Madrid between Britain and Spain to end piracy in the Caribbean.

1697

Conquest of the Itzá of Noh Petén, an island in Lake Petén Itzá, Guatemala – the last Maya stronghold.

1700S

Start of mahogany trade, which brings the first influx of black slaves from Jamaica to Belize.

THE MAKING OF BRITISH HONDURAS

1765

'Burnaby's Code' drawn up as first constitution for territory to be known as British Honduras.

1779

Spanish force burns down St George's Caye and Belize Town.

1786

Convention of London allows 'Baymen' to cut wood but not establish a government; British settlers from the Bay Shore of Honduras evacuated to Belize.

1787

First British-appointed administrator arrives in British Honduras.

1798

Defeat of Spanish fleet in the Battle of St George's Caye establishes British rule more firmly.

1802

Spain acknowledges British sovereignty in Belize at the Treaty of Amiens. First Garífuna people arrive in Belize from Honduras; more arrivals follow in 1823, with the majority arriving in 1832.

1820S

British start extracting large amounts of mahogany from Belizean forests.

The Encounter Between Hernando Cortes And Montezuma II Mexico 1519.

1821

Mexico and Central American nations win independence from Spain. El Salvador and Honduras from Central American Federation and try to claim Belize. British settlers occupy three times the amount of land awarded in Treaty of Amiens.

1823

Central American leaders agree to abolish slavery at a time when slaves constitute a large part of the workforce in Belize.

1826–39

War culminating in the break-up of the United Provinces of Central America.

1847

The War of the Castes in Yucatán, a 50-year Maya revolt. Many Yucatec Maya flee to Belize.

1859

Convention between United Kingdom and Guatemala recognizes boundaries of British Honduras – something that has been disputed by Guatemalan governments ever since.

THE BRITISH COLONY

1862

British Honduras is officially declared a British colony.

1866–70

Influx of Confederate supporters from southern US found town of New Richmond.

The transporting of mahogany from the forest to the river, Belize, Honduras.

1871

Belize becomes a crown colony of the British Empire, ruled by a governor and legislative council appointed by the British Government.

1893

Mexico renounces its claim to British Honduras and signs a peace treaty. Guatemala still claims sovereignty.

1919

Riots started by Belizean soldiers over their bad treatment during World War I. Belize City is looted by 3,000 people, including police.

1921

United Negro Improvement Association is set up, marking the rise of black consciousness.

1926

Death of Baron Bliss, benefactor of Belize.

1931

Twin disasters of Great Depression and hurricane, killing 2,500 people, hit Belize.

1931–35

First written account of the colony's history, *Archives of British Honduras*, is compiled.

GROWTH OF PEOPLE'S POLITICS

1939

'Natives First' movement wins seats on Belize Town Board.

1941

Belizean Labour Party is set up.

1950

People's United Party (PUP) is founded.

1952

Radio Belize, the nation's first radio station, begins transmission.

Cyclone disaster in the city of Belize.

1954

Universal adult suffrage is introduced.

1958

Arrival of first members of Mennonite community from Mexico.

1961

Hurricane Hattie hits Belize's eastern shoreline, destroying most of the buildings in Belize City.

1964

Self-government granted to Belize. George Price is First Minister in the new system.

1970

New administrative capital of Belmopan is officially inaugurated.

1973

British Honduras is renamed Belize.

George Price (left) with Prince Michael, Duke of Kent, on Independence Day, 1981.

Belize became independent at midnight on September 20, 1981.

that gives them all but three seats.

2002
Proposal to settle border dispute with Guatemala subject to a referendum in both countries.

2003
People's United Party (PUP) win an unprecedented second term.

2006
Belize begins commercial drilling for oil.

2008
A landslide victory for the United Democratic Party (UPP) ends 10 years of PUP rule. Dean Barrow becomes the country's first black prime minister.

1980
United Nations passes unanimous resolution, calling for the independence of Belize.

INDEPENDENT BELIZE

1981
Belize becomes independent.

1984
United Democratic Party (UDP) wins general election for the first time.

1991
Guatemala recognizes the self-determination of the people of Belize in return for Caribbean coastal waters. Belize becomes a full member of the Organization of American States (OAS).

1992
Guatemalan Congress ratifies its decision to recognize Belize.

1993
Final British garrison leaves.

1995
Maya groups protest sale of land in the Southern Columbia Forest Reserve to logging companies.

1998
People's United Party (PUP) return to power in a victory

2015
Dean Barrow starts his third term.

2018
Belize bans offshore oil and gas drilling to protect its coral reefs.

2019
A referendum on the ongoing territorial dispute with Guatemala will be held.

Dean Barrow during the XLIII Ordinary Meeting of the Central American Integration System.

THE ANCIENT MAYA

Little remained of a highly creative and ritualized Maya society by the time of the Spanish conquest, but site excavations have gradually yielded its secrets.

When the Spaniards arrived in Mesoamerica in the early 16th century, they found the Maya living in scattered groups, with no central organization. They were not unified in any great political or ceremonial centers, and did not seem to the Spaniards to belong to any great civilization, in contrast to the Aztecs, farther north in Mexico, or the Incas of Peru. Although in some places, such as Tulum on the Yucatán Peninsula or Lamanai in Belize, the local Maya were still living in some of the ancient centers, they were apparently unable to explain who had built them, and could not read the inscriptions on the monuments.

In their search for riches, the Spaniards rapidly destroyed much of what remained of the ancient Maya culture. As they colonized the lands of the Maya in Mexico and Central America, they brought Christianity with them. The Franciscan friars, who were distributed throughout the Yucatán and Guatemala, were often the people who accumulated most knowledge about the religion and customs of the Maya. And it was one of them, the Spanish friar Diego de Landa, who helped later generations piece together an understanding of the ancient Maya.

NOTES OF THE ENEMY

De Landa, who was sent to the Yucatán to convert the Maya, committed barbarous attacks against Maya culture in the 16th century, the most famous being the auto-da-fé in 1562 at Mani, where he destroyed the last known hieroglyphic Maya texts (although at least four have been discovered since). Upon his recall to Spain to face legal charges brought against him for his actions, he wrote *Relación de las Cosas de Yucatán*, containing a virtual ethnography of the

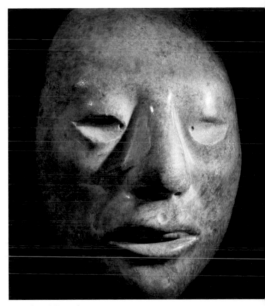

Jade head from Copan.

Yucatán Maya used for his legal defense. The ancient cities of the Maya had been abandoned long before de Landa's arrival, but his detailed accounts of 16th-century Maya life have proved, with archeological confirmation, that it was very similar to that of their more famous ancestors, whose culture reached its apex from around AD 250–900 (the Classic Period).

As the Spaniards consolidated their rule, interest in the lives of the ancient Maya diminished. Occasional explorers stumbled on ruins in the jungles of Central America, but no real effort was made to uncover or assess them for several centuries. It was only at the end of the 18th century that the Spanish king ordered Captain Antonio del Río to make a thorough investigation into the site at Palenque in southern Mexico.

When del Río's findings were published in Europe in 1822, they immediately aroused great curiosity. But del Río was one of the first of many Europeans who refused to believe that natives of Central America could have been responsible for such splendid architecture and sculptures. Many researchers tried to prove that the Maya must have been influenced by the great Classical civilizations of the Greeks, the Romans or the Egyptians,

Ceramic artifact, Museo Tikal.

rather than having created the riches of the jungles themselves. This kind of explanation has survived to the present day, with some writers still arguing that the Maya must have been visited by 'superior beings' from outer space, or that their land was host to the lost civilization of Atlantis. But, as more evidence of the growth and development of Maya centers throughout the region is uncovered, these fanciful theories have gradually given way to more rigorous explanations.

Unlike those of the Aztecs or Incas, the Maya civilization was never unified and controlled by a single ruler. Instead, the region was controlled by competing cities, rather like Greek city-states. Yet the whole region was unified through common cultural beliefs, technologies, languages, and trade.

THE MAYA WORLD VIEW

At the core of ancient life was a belief that everything – animate and inanimate – had a place in a cosmic order, and that everything contained some form of spirit or power. This ideology contradicts the Western notion of separation between the natural and the supernatural or unexplainable. The Maya attributed special powers to time, stars, stones, trees, and other natural phenomena.

They believed they lived in a Middle World, beneath the 13 levels of the Upper World and above the nine levels of the Lower World, or Xibalba. They believed in an after-life or a paradise, to which ruler, priests and those who die by sacrifice, suicide, in battle or in childbirth gain automatic entrance. And they believed in the destruction of an earlier world by flood.

A string of gods, often with good and evil sides, represented the power held by all objects, but found in various forms: they appeared as different dates, days and colors. Rituals and offerings to the gods insured the continuance of the basic needs of life, health and sustenance. A complex procedure of sacrifices, fasting, feasting and incense-burning was held on annual occasions, including New Year, and also used to induce rain, and for success in hunting, fishing, honey-collecting, and war.

The most powerful offering was blood – especially the blood of a king, who was considered a kind of god. The ruler would use an obsidian blade made from volcanic rock or a stingray spine to pierce his penis, lip, tongue or earlobe and use the blood to anoint an idol. During the blood-letting, the king would hallucinate and visualize a famous ancestor who would validate his power.

HUMAN SACRIFICES

The ritual significance of blood was such that the Maya indulged in human sacrifice on a regular basis. Friar Diego de Landa, despite his cultural ignorance, gives a vivid account:

'If [the victim's] heart was to be taken out, they conducted him with great display and concourse of people, painted him blue and wearing his miter, and placed him on the rounded sacrificial stone, after the priest and his officers had anointed the stone with blue and purified the temple to drive away the evil spirit. The *chacs* then seized the poor victim and swiftly laid him on his back across the stone, and the four took hold of his arms and legs, spreading them out. Then the *nacon* executioner came, with a flint knife in his hand, and with great skill made an incision between the ribs on the left side, below the nipple; then he plunged in his hand and like a ravenous tiger tore out the living heart, which he placed on a plate and gave to the priest; he then quickly went and anointed the faces of the idols with that fresh blood...'

In many rituals the Maya would ingest special concoctions like *balche*, a mixture of fermented honey and bark from the balche tree, to enable them to meet with ancestors or other powers. Special tobacco leaves were used to make cigars; some scholars speculate about the use of hallucinogenic mushrooms, peyote, water lilies, morning glory, and glands from tropical toads (occasionally a quick ingestion by means of an enema). Incense was another mainstay at ceremonies – usually copal, which would be formed into small cakes.

THE MAYA TIMELINE

It was during the Middle and Late Preclassic periods (roughly 800 BC to AD 250) that the Maya developed systems of agricultural terraces, raised fields and irrigation channels. The staple food was corn, or maize, which

was controlled by its own god, Yum Kaax (also known as God E). Farmers would also allow wild trees and plants to grow, termed 'Forest Garden' agriculture.

The apex of Maya culture was the Classic Period (roughly AD 250–900), when trade and the arts flourished. During this period the great cities were rebuilt, and it is Classic Period remains that survive at the major archeological sites today. The men of conquered cities possibly spent one month a year in work tribute to the victor, building *sacbeob*, the raised roads,

Human sacrifice was an important Maya ritual.

◉ MAYA CALENDARS

The ancient Maya had a complex system for measuring time. Many sites, such as Chichén Itzá in the Yucatán, are thought to have contained observatories where skilled astronomers checked the path of the stars and calculated dates. Their motivation was their belief in the delicate balance of the universe, and that, unless it was protected, the Maya world could end in death and destruction. The Maya evolved two separate but interconnected calendar systems. The first was based on a 'month' of 20 days that were connected like a wheel with the numbers one to 13, giving a complete cycle of 260 days. This calendar was used for ceremonial life and giving-birth dates.

The second system was based on the movement of the sun. This calendar had 18 months of 20 days, making a cycle of 360 days to which were added an extra five days so that the period more or less coincided with the annual solar cycle. The time of greatest uncertainty for the Maya was during these five extra days at the end of the cycle. This was when they sacrificed humans to the sun god.

The two calendars were thought to operate independently of each other, but they coincided every 52 years. This was a time of even greater uncertainty for the Maya, and some experts believe they may have abandoned some of their cities during this crucial period.

or public architecture such as pyramids, temples and palaces. Otherwise, the local residents might have undertaken the construction themselves, for the labor-intensive process of cutting, transporting (without the assistance of pack animals or wagons) and placing the stones required a mind-boggling number of man-hours.

At some point in Maya history, there was an increase in the number of human sacrifices – possibly as natural resources diminished and the gods demanded extra blood in return for

the ocean of green rainforest with wide open areas of farmland, roads, and public plazas, with stone buildings plastered and painted white or in various colors. The average family would have lived in a thatched hut located on the outskirts of a city and a few miles from the family's maize field.

The Maya life cycle was carefully regulated. Upon a child's birth, the family and perhaps the shaman would look at the 260-day almanac to determine the destiny and character of the baby. The ancient Maya probably conducted

Detail from the Madrid Codex, one of three surviving pre-Columbian books.

their blessing. Prisoners were sought from neighboring cities, so confrontations snowballed. During the Early Postclassic Period (AD 900–1200) Maya culture collapsed quickly and mysteriously, and most of the great cities were abandoned. The causes of the apocalypse are still hotly debated, with everything from earthquakes to famine and disease thrown into the theorizing. However, a few cities – including Lamanai in modern-day Belize – survived until the arrival of the Spanish.

EVERYDAY LIFE

At their cultural apotheosis, the Maya cities would have looked very different from the skeletons one sees today. Imagine replacing

something similar to the modern Maya naming or *hetzmek* ceremony in which two godparents carry the child and circle nine times around a table holding nine symbolic objects the child will use in adult life. The child receives three or four names – a *paal kaba* or given name, the father's family name, the *naal kaba* or father's and mother's family names combined, and the *coco kaba* or nickname.

At age four or five, a small white bead was fastened to a boy's hair and a girl had a red shell hung around her waist. These remained in place until a puberty ceremony when, before a public audience in a sponsor's house, priests recited prayers and the youths were anointed. After a gift exchange, the children could abandon the beads and shells. Young unmarried men lived together and helped their fathers in farming, while the young women were instructed in cooking, weaving and housekeeping.

Most adult men continued to work in agriculture, though other occupations were permitted – pottery, stone cutting, mining, salt- or shell-collecting, and trading. The Maya used cacao beans and other natural items like red shells for money.

Matchmakers negotiated with parents and

vaulted tombs – often with food and pieces of carved jadeite as currency, as well as idols and tools, which the deceased would need in the afterlife.

Contrary to earlier belief, Maya cities were not solitary ritual centers for peace-loving priests; they were lively centers of art, commerce, and political power.

Mask Temple at Lamanai.

young couples to arrange marriages. The groom's family would give a dowry of dresses and other articles. The marriage ceremony was brief, followed by a small feast for the families and special guests. The son-in-law lived and worked for six or seven years with his in-laws. It is thought that divorce was simple: the Maya were monogamous, but men would often leave their wives for other mates.

In death, relatives would silently mourn by day and wail in sorrow at night. The family often buried the deceased inside or near their home, and unless the family was very large, they would abandon the house soon afterwards. More important people were either cremated or buried in elaborate

HIGH FASHION, MAYA STYLE

The ancient Maya had some unique concepts of beauty. A good-looking Maya aristocrat would have had his or her forehead well flattened (the parents bound their children's heads between a pair of wooden boards). He or she might also have been cross-eyed (parents dangled balls between their baby's eyes). All Maya men had a bald spot burned into their pates. And some men filed their teeth to a point and inlaid them with pyrite or jadeite.

Not all Maya fashions were so dramatic. Common Maya men wore a loincloth, or *ex*, wrapped around the waist and often decorated with feathers, abstract designs and representations of faces. Covering their shoulders was a square cotton *pati*, decorated according to their position in society. Women wore a variation of the *huipil* still worn today in Mesoamerica – often a white dress or blouse with a square cutout for the head and holes for arms – along with a *booch*, a strip of material thrown over the head that acted as a headdress and scarf. Both men and women wore double-thonged leather sandals that were bound to their ankles with rope; their black hair was worn long and often braided.

The upper classes wore more colorful costumes with intricate woven designs, animal

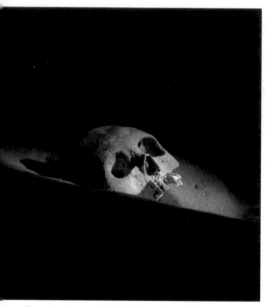

Remains of a sacrificial victim at Actun Tunichil Muknal, near San Ignacio.

skins and feathers (including the quetzal). Priests wore jaguar skins. High-ranking Maya wore a dazzling range of jewelry – bracelets, necklaces, earrings, nose rings, lip plugs, and pendants made from jade, shell, teeth, claws, wood, and stone. Every few days, men and women also anointed themselves with a red, sweet-smelling ointment. The men often painted their bodies: unmarried young men black, warriors black and red, priests in blue (the color associated with sacrifice).

MYTH AND HISTORY

The intimate connection between daily life and the supernatural is shown by the role of a ball game that was played in every Maya city. The game was also played to re-enact parts of the creation myth, the *Popul Vuh*, in which the Ancestral Hero Twins trick and defeat the Lords of Death of Xibalba (the Underworld). In Maya legend, the ball court was where the legendary Twins actively challenged and outwitted the gods.

The basic rules were simple enough. Two teams, using only particular body parts (usually hips or knees), tried to send a rubber ball through a hoop sticking out of a wall or atop a post in a playing field between two parallel buildings. The rules, team size and court size varied by region and changed through time. The game often held ritual significance when played by nobles or rulers, or with captives (who, when they lost, were sacrificed and sometimes bound up like a ball and rolled down pyramid steps). A later, post-conquest tradition held that, upon shooting the ball through the hoop, the successful player could claim the jewelry of the spectators unfortunate enough to witness the event.

The Maya living in Belize today speak three Mayan languages: Yucatec, Mopan and Ketchí. In ancient times there were also many varieties, but only one form of written hieroglyphs, a standard used throughout the civilization.

A key source of surviving hieroglyphs are the stelae, tall needles of stone planted to resemble ceiba trees. They were commissioned to commemorate important anniversaries, bloodlettings, conquests, and coronations. The messages solidified the power of the ruling lineage over the people, and let visitors know whose land they were entering. It is uncertain how many people could actually read these messages, however. For the illiterate masses, the designs found on pottery, clothing, stelae, and architecture may well have communicated the same propaganda as the hieroglyphs.

SITES CONTINUALLY DISCOVERED

Over the years, our knowledge about the Maya has increased dramatically. Great strides have been made in interpreting the stelae, other monuments and the written codices. New sites are continually being found and scientifically explored. In Belize, for example, Maya population centers have been uncovered in the northern lagoons at Chac Balaam. Here it is thought that as many as 10,000 ancient Maya lived, trading in salt and pottery with the inhabitants of other centers farther north on the Yucatán coast.

In 1957, one of the most important rediscoveries was made when a bulldozer clearing a track through the jungle north of Belize City crashed into the Maya city of Altun Ha (see page 137). Scientific excavation of the site began in 1963, and was rewarded with the discovery of many jade artifacts, including the famous jade head of the sun god Kinich Ahau, now kept under strict security in the vaults of the Belize Bank in Belmopan.

pyramids at Nohmul, in northern Belize while extracting rock for a road-building project. Both the Belizean government and international organizations were swift to condemn the company and hold it responsible; it was later charged with 'willfully damaging an ancient monument.' Local and international organizations are now assessing the damage to see what kind of historical data can be salvaged – and are also developing guidelines and regulations to guard against the wilful destruction of ancient monuments in future.

Temple at Altun Ha.

Another important center that has yielded its secrets is La Milpa (see page 146), which is thought to have rivaled the famous city of Tikal in northern Guatemala during the Classic Period. And in the last couple of decades, a number of exciting finds have been made in the Maya Mountains in the south of Belize. All of these suggest that the Maya population of the country was once much greater than that of today.

PRESERVING HISTORY

Maya sites are often being unearthed, but equally important is the preservation of them, which continues to pose a challenge. In 2013, for example, a construction company effectively destroyed one of the country's largest Maya

⊙ THE MAYA UNDERWORLD

In the Maya world, caves held sacred status and were considered entrances to the underworld, called *Xibalba*, the 'place of fright.' In spite of this, caves also allowed access to the dwelling of gods, ancestors, and spirits. Thanks to the country's porous karst limestone, cave systems form an extensive network under much of inland Belize. There have been numerous unique discoveries throughout these systems, including wall paintings and pottery shards. The Maya gods had to be placated with sacrifices, so the caves are also littered with altars. One of the best caves to visit for is Actun Tunichil Muknal (see page 165), which has some of the most intact artifacts in the country.

📷 UNCOVERING THE MYSTERIES OF THE PAST

The Maya region is one of the world's most fascinating archeological areas, and ongoing discoveries are contributing to reboots in assessments about the early Maya.

A prime example? Dr Richard Hansen and his team, who have been working at El Mirador since the 1970s, have rewritten Preclassic history, proving that the great city of the Kaan dynasty was a superpower of its day, controlling vast swathes of the Petén, flourishing alongside and ultimately overpowering the Olmecs. A stunning stucco panel at El Mirador of the fabled hero twins, created around 200 BC, has proved a pivotal link between the Preclassic Maya and the Popul Vuh, the Maya creation myth. Other discoveries include a ball court dating back to 500 BC unearthed at Nakbé and even a complete 'lost city' – Wakná, located near El Mirador. Academics are now able to read Maya glyphs far more accurately, revealing the names of the rulers, their family lineages, and the key political alliances of the era. It is now clear that bloodletting and human sacrifice were pivotal to the Maya religion, governing ceremonies, and used in all aspects of life, from planning agriculture to warfare.

Today the texts written on tombs' interior walls help unlock Maya secrets, yet these texts are all too often destroyed by looters foraging for artifacts for the lucrative, illegal pre-Columbian art trade. But, things are changing: the Belizean government, as well as international organizations such as the Global Heritage Fund (GHF), are slowly gaining the upper hand. Scientists are turning to advanced technologies to find and protect Maya sites. For example, archeologists now use airborne sensors operated from aircraft and satellites. Landsat, a satellite that delineates natural and large, manmade features, helped uncover the astonishing murals at San Bartolo, Guatemala, and Wakná deep in the Petén forest.

Jade mosaic mask, Museum of Belize.

A reproduction of the colorful Rosalila Temple, found under Temple 16 at Copán. This true-scale replica is in the Museo de Escultura, Copán.

The magnificent carved stelae at Copán in Honduras are considered the finest in the Maya world. Stela A, below, can now be seen in the Museo de Escultura at Copán.

The vivid 19th-century drawings of Maya ruins by Frederick Catherwood captured the world's imagination.

Archeological Expeditions

The birth of modern Maya archeology traces its popular origin to the epic expeditions, between 1839 and 1842, of adventurers John L. Stephens and Frederick Catherwood. Their discovery of immense ruined cities among the tropical jungles of Mesoamerica caught the imagination of the academic world.

Catherwood's beautiful lithographs of the ruins of Chichén Itzá, Uxmal, Palenque, and Copán were widely published in Europe and North America. The intrepid explorers' tales of discovery were hailed as the greatest of the century.

Some 80 years later, archeologists such as Thompson, Morley, Tozzer, Joyce, and Maler led expeditions to the jungles of Central America to try to unlock the mystery of the Maya civilization.

But it was only in the 1970s, with the help of modern technology, that archeologists began to decipher more than dates and numerals. Today, archeologists concentrating on minor sites, such as La Blanca in Guatemala, have revealed convincing evidence that suggests the late Classic Maya rulers may have suffered a revolt at the hands of their own people, possibly due to failing harvests and drought, as the masses lost faith in the divine influence of their rulers. A series of reports published in 2014 suggested that climate change may have been a key factor in the demise of the Maya, causing food and water to become scarce.

Detail on Stela 32 from the Tikal ruins, held in Museo Tikal near the ruins in Petén, Guatemala.

The natural blanket of the jungle helped to preserve the Tikal ruins for the first explorers.

Stela P stands in front of Temple 16 at Copán and was constructed when the Rosalila Temple (now underneath Temple 16) was still being used.

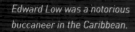

Edward Low was a notorious buccaneer in the Caribbean.

BUCCANEERS AND BAYMEN

Early Belize – called the Bay Settlement – was both a refuge for Maya escaping the Spanish in Mexico and a hideout for pirates, plundering galleons in the Caribbean.

For much of its early history, Belize existed largely under the radar. Well into the 17th century, when Spanish rule had been ruthlessly stamped on the rest of Central America, the colonial powers were only barely conscious of the region that now goes by the name of Belize. Spanish explorers avoided its coral reefs, and few conquistadors or missionaries ventured south of the Yucatán. Those who did reported none of the cities of silver and gold that would excite a conqueror's imagination, only murky swamps and mosquito-filled forests.

Nor were the local Maya inhabitants friendly. Their first encounter with Spaniards set the tone for relations, when a handful of shipwrecked sailors landed in northern Belize in 1511. Five were sacrificed, their still-beating hearts torn from their bodies, and the rest were made slaves. Most Spaniards decided to seek their fortunes elsewhere.

As a result, Belize became the first refuge crossroads of Central America. Thousands of Maya fled the Spanish subjugation of Mexico and Guatemala in the 16th century, which reached ferocious heights of cruelty. During Captain Alonso Pacheco's campaign against the Maya of Chetumal in 1544, for example, conquistadors routinely garotted men and women, tied them to weights, and threw them into lakes to watch them drown; chopped off their prisoners' noses, ears or hands, and had others dismembered alive by wild 'dogs of war.'

Those Maya who survived faced enslavement, the break-up of their families, and relocation. Little wonder that the Franciscan monks who brought the gospel (and demands for Spanish taxes) into the Belizean jungle in the early 17th century provoked instant rebellion. The few

The Welsh buccaneer known as Black Bart.

churches the missionaries managed to build were soon sacked and burned down.

LOGWOOD AND PIRACY

The Maya of Belize got on much better with a few motley Britons who turned up along the Bay of Campeche in search of logwood. The British were out simply to remove a few trees and make money, and showed not the slightest interest in taxing or converting anyone. Their small camps congregated in Belize's most miserable swampland, where the hard-as-stone logwood was to be found – its black, red, and gray dyes were essential for the woolen industry in Britain – which fetched £100 a ton, a small fortune in those days.

At first, the Spaniards ignored them. But before long, the barely inhabited coastline of Belize began to attract another kind of British entrepreneur: the buccaneer. It was a perfect hideout for a Caribbean freebooting operation. The buccaneers sailed fast, shallow draft ships that could chase down a heavily laden Spanish merchantman, capture the cargo, and out-pace the pursuing warships. Once inside the Belizean reef, with its low water, treacherous coral heads, and mud flats, they were safe. From there, the loot could be transported to the Bahamas, Bermuda or, after the British captured it, Port Royal in Jamaica, where the market for plundered goods was insatiable.

THE PIRATES' HONEST TRADE

Logwood was a valuable enough commodity that many buccaneers logged in their spare time. Some of the most famous names in Caribbean piracy – 'Admiral' Benbow, William Dampier, Bartholomew Sharpe, Edward Low, 'Blackbeard' Teach, Nicholas van Horn, William Bannister, and John Coxon – were all, at one time or other, involved in the trade. Together, they make up a Who's Who of 17th-century villainy.

THE LEGEND OF BLACKBEARD

None was as romantic, or enduringly remembered, as Edward Teach, better known as Blackbeard – who, according to local legend, spent a good deal of leisure time hiding out on Ambergris Caye. According to records of the day, Teach was such a terrifying sight that crews of enemy ships were known to throw down their arms without a fight. His huge black beard, one writer noted, was 'like a frightful meteor,' hanging down to his waist and twisted with colored ribbons. In battle he wore a leather holster with three pistols over each shoulder. More oddly, he 'struck lighted matches under his hat, which, appearing on each side of his face, his eyes naturally looking fierce and wild, made him altogether such a figure that imagination cannot form an idea of a fury from Hell to look more frightful.'

This archetypal pirate was born in Bristol, went into training in Jamaica, and embarked on his pirate career by pillaging the coasts of Virginia and the Carolinas. After capturing a large, 40-gun French ship, which he renamed *Queen Anne's Revenge*, Teach began to roam the Caribbean, often using the Belizean cayes off the Gulf of Honduras as a rendezvous (Ambergris Caye was one of his favorites, and fanciful tales of buried treasure are sometimes still trotted out in the bars of San Pedro).

A surviving fragment of his log shows a typical day under Blackbeard's command: 'Such a day, rum all out – our company somewhat sober – a damn'd confusion amongst us! Rogues a plotting – great talk of separation – so I look'd sharp for a prize – such a day, took one, with a great deal of liquor on board, so kept the company hot … then all things well again.'

Edward Teach, alias the pirate Blackbeard.

⊘ THE BUCCANEER GENTLEMAN

Captain Peter Wallace was the archetypal buccaneer. The Scottish sea captain, who served under Sir Walter Raleigh, was called one of the 'Gentlemen of the Coast.' In 1634, Wallace sailed his ship the *Swallow* into the harbor that would eventually become Belize City. To this day, Wallace remains a shadowy figure – he was reputed to be behind a fleet of ships pillaging the Caribbean. Whatever the truth, it is possible that Wallace gave his name, in corrupted form, to Belize. Others suggest it comes from the Maya word *beliz*, "muddy-watered," which accurately describes the Belize River for much of the year – but the Wallace connection is usually cited as more romantic.

As he captured more ships, several crews agreed to join Blackbeard in his expeditions, until he commanded a small fleet. Things were going so well that when one English captain informed him of a royal decree pardoning all pirates who ceased activities, he laughed in derision. The only major problem seemed to be venereal disease, which drove Blackbeard to lay siege to Charleston, Carolina until several hundred pounds' worth of medical supplies were obtained.

Finally, desperate merchants and shippers appealed for help to the Governor of Virginia, who hired Lieutenant Robert Maynard of the Royal Navy to hunt down Blackbeard in the heavily armed *Pearl*. They caught him off the North Carolina coast on 22 November, 1718, and the following dialogue was recorded:

Blackbeard: 'Damn you for villains, who are you? And whence came you?'

Maynard. 'You may see by our colors we are no pirates.'

Blackbeard demanded that Maynard come closer alongside, but Maynard replied: 'I cannot spare my boat, but I will come aboard of you as soon as I can with my sloop.'

Blackbeard (swilling a jug of rum and toasting his enemy): 'Damnation seize my soul if I give you quarter, or take any from you.'

Maynard: 'I expect none, and will give none.'

After this exchange, the two opened up cannons on one another. Maynard hid a number of his men below decks, tricking Blackbeard into boarding with only 13 men. Realizing his deception, Teach flew into a drunken rage. As the deck ran thick with blood, several guns were fired point-blank into Blackbeard's body, without obvious effect. He knocked down Maynard in a cutlass duel and received 20 sword slashes before suddenly dropping dead from blood loss. Maynard, wounded but not mortally, lopped off the pirate's head and hung it from his bowsprit.

Although feared for his ferocity, Teach earned the grudging respect of his enemies. He showed great tactical skill, fought to the death and never harmed his prisoners – a true 'Gentleman of the Coast.'

FROM LARCENY TO LOGGING

The death-knell for Caribbean freebooting was tolled in 1670, when a treaty between England and Spain pledged to suppress piracy on the high seas. Although it took a long time, the assorted captains and crews eventually realized that the hangman awaited, whoever captured them. Many decided to try logging full-time, and settled around the mouth of the Belize River – a humid, swampy delta chosen not for its setting, which was dismal, but because this was where the logwood trunks were floated from the many upriver camps.

The whole was referred to as the Bay Settlement, and its inhabitants, Baymen. By 1700, a

The fatal duel between Blackbeard and Maynard.

rough society of some 300 people was beginning to emerge, commuting to the logging camps, called Banks, upriver. Few English women dared settle here, although some loggers took Maya women as common-law wives, starting up the famous Belizean melting pot.

One upper-crust ship's captain who was wrecked here in 1720 was horrified by the lawlessness he found among its rowdy citizens: 'The Wood-Cutters are generally a rude drunken Crew, some of which have been Pirates; their chief Delight is in Drinking; and when they broach a Quarter Cask or a Hogshead of Wine, they seldom stir while there is a Drop left… keeping at it sometimes a Week together, drinking till they fall asleep; and as soon as they awake, at it again, without stirring off the place.'

THE ARRIVAL OF THE SLAVES

This small society of reformed pirates and drunkards was transformed when the world's best quality mahogany began to be pulled from the rainforests. Mahogany was much more valuable than logwood – the rich and powerful demanded it for their furniture in Britain and across the American colonies – and required a larger workforce to extract it. New fortune

Gun-toting Baymen in the swamps.

> The rough-and-tumble Baymen had quite the reputation, prompting one well-to-do captain, who was shipwrecked there in 1720, to lament, 'I had but little Comfort living among these Crew of ungovernable wretches, where there was little else to be heard but Blasphemy, Cursing, and Swearing.'

seekers arrived in Belize, bringing with them boatloads of slaves from Jamaica.

With names like Congo Will, Guinea Sam, or Mundingo Pope reflecting their African homeland, the slaves soon outnumbered white settlers by roughly ten to one. Belizean slavery wasn't as rigid as in the southern United States. Instead of tightly controlled plantations, a white slaver might take a handful of slaves up the river to set up a loosely structured logging camp. Every slave had a machete or an axe, and a few were given muskets and pistols for hunting and for defense against attacks by hostile Maya. Each slave had his own tent, wherever he wished to build it, and if the slavemaster had a whip, he probably used it on his mule.

Meanwhile, local slave laws baffled foreign visitors. For example, slaves only worked five days a week. If a slave worked on Saturday, he had to be paid. A slave could buy his freedom, and many did, and any male slave who turned up in Belize was declared free unless proven otherwise. Any female slave who was taken as a common-law wife or mistress by a settler was freed, and by the late 18th century a substantial portion of the settlement was recorded in the census as people of 'Mixed Colour.'

Nevertheless, slaves had few legal rights and slavery could be just as brutal in Belize as anywhere else. Several small-scale rebellions occurred in the bush, including one where six white men were murdered and a dozen slaves escaped to freedom in the Yucatán.

FRONTIER DEMOCRATS

The free Baymen ruled themselves by voting for magistrates at a public meeting – in much the same way that pirate captains had been freely elected by their crews. All free men could vote, regardless of property or color, to the disgust of visiting aristocrats from England (although women could only look on from the balconies, waving their handkerchiefs).

Meanwhile, Belize Town, as it was then known, was growing, filling up the swampland with wood chips, conch shells, and empty bottles of Santa Rita rum. The whites and 'free coloreds' lived on St George's Caye a few miles offshore, flanked by a small fortress, while on the mainland a warren of backstreets developed for the black population. As in other Caribbean outposts, African religious practices such as *obeah* were rife, despite attempts to control it. (Slave revolts in other islands had made the white settlers nervous, and the night-long playing of *gombay* drums was banned as they 'deprive the Inhabitants therein from their natural rest.')

A dozen or so of the richer, older white families became known as the 'Old Baymen' and made up a minuscule locally born elite. They made a half-hearted attempt to maintain their British way of life in this malaria-ridden outpost. A Presbyterian church service on Sunday, said under a canvas canopy with the congregation in stifling black coats, might be followed by an afternoon's fishing from a dory, or wooden dugout, and swimming in a remote river (after first digging about with your 'setting pole' to clear out the snakes and crocodiles). In the dry season, families headed upriver to their Banks, living in tents and eating 'bush stew' of gibnut, turtle, and peccary, spiced up with fried plantain and Johnny cakes ('No man should crave more toothsome food,' wrote a contemporary).

It was back-breaking work, but lucrative: one Scottish family who moved to Belize bought a moderate holding upriver and earned £5,700 in the first season.

TROUBLE WITH THE SPANIARDS

Although vast fortunes were to be made in the Belizean forest, the life of the loggers was desperately insecure. Apart from tropical diseases, poisonous snakes and clouds of mosquitoes, there was the Spanish threat. The Spaniards had never recognized the British presence, and the story of the 18th century is one of constant conflict between the settlers, cut off from Britain or any outside aid, and the surrounding enemy. (And since the majority of settlers were of Scottish origin, they saw an English prejudice in the authorities' indifference.)

Not that the Baymen were blameless. Although a treaty was fleshed out in 1765 to limit their activities, loggers continually crossed into Spanish territory, bribing frontier guards and customs officials, and smuggling anything they could into Mexico. Meanwhile, bandits based in the Yucatán made continuous forays into Belize, often storming the isolated logging banks. One chronicler records how his young fiancée, fresh off the boat from Scotland, was kidnapped by a bandit named Diego Bustamente while she was paddling a canoe near the camp. Friendly Indians led the

Baymen to a remote Maya ruin, where Diego had holed up and was preparing to force himself upon his captive. The settlers were able to surprise the bandit and his men, and rescued the distraught woman – who, despite her ordeal, chose to remain in Belize.

Throughout the 18th century, the Spanish kept up raids on the lumber camps, but the Baymen could always slip away into the forest. The conflicts with Spain might have remained petty and limited except for the American War of Independence. The Baymen first learned

Nineteenth-century engraving of logging in the Belizean rainforest.

about it when a strange ship, *The George Washington*, pulled into St George's Caye. A few citizens went out in their dories to meet Captain Hezikiah Anthony of the United States Navy, only to be immediately imprisoned as ransom for rum.

Unfortunately for the Baymen, the American struggle prompted Spain to declare war, yet again, on Britain, and use it as an excuse to wipe out Belize. A sizeable Spanish force attacked St George's Caye in 1779, burning it and Belize Town to the ground. Most of the Baymen escaped into the forest, but the unfortunates on the Caye were captured and sent on a forced march 300 miles (480km) into the Yucatán.

One Bayman, Tom Potts, was captured with his wife Charlotte and daughter. The hard-bitten couple survived the forced march, and had a second child in a dungeon while awaiting trial. After several more years in a prison in Cuba, they were released and headed back, by sea and land, to Belize – and Potts eventually became Belize's chief magistrate.

RENEWED HOSTILITY WITH SPAIN

The Bay Settlement was rebuilt, logging recommenced and new arrivals of British set-

A British colony in the Bay Islands.

tlers, forced by treaty to leave the Mosquito Shore of Honduras and Nicaragua, boosted the numbers back to more than 3,000 souls. Then, in 1796, Britain and Spain started squabbling again in Europe: this time the battle for Belize would be for good.

News of an imminent invasion caused a commotion amongst the Baymen. Public meetings turned into riots over the question of whether to stay and fight. Running away from the Spaniards was an old and honorable tradition in Belize, and many favored it now. After all, the British authorities offered no protection other than a single gunship from Jamaica.

Others were adamant that they would defend the colony: it had grown too large to

abandon, there were too many fine buildings and too much equipment could be lost. Tom Potts, the chief magistrate who had personal experience of Spanish dungeons, wanted out, but Thomas Paslow, a fiery Irishman, thundered that 'A man who will not defend his country does not deserve to reap the benefits of it.'

In a close vote – 65 to 51 – the majority elected to remain. Many of the deciding votes were cast by a group of free slaves led by Adam Flowers. Despite the acrimony, however, everyone stayed to fight: not a single Bayman left.

THE FINAL CONFLICT

The Baymen spent the next couple of years preparing for an attack. Finally, on September 3, 1798, a Spanish force of 32 ships, including 16 heavily armed men o'war and 2,000 troops, bore down on the Baymen. They had managed to dig in on St George's Caye and had armed all the slaves, but their rag-tag naval force consisted of only one Royal Navy battleship, the *HMS Marlin*, five schooners and seven logwood barges fitted out with a single cannon each. But the Baymen had geography on their side: when the Spaniards advanced, four ships were bogged in mud flats and blown out of the water.

Every day, the Spanish advance party was pushed back. Then, on September 10, the Spaniards made a major effort to land on St George's Caye, sending fourteen of their largest ships close to its shore. This time they were caught in a narrow channel and ravaged by the Baymen's fire. The British naval officers attempted to coordinate an attack on the foundering ships, but the boatloads of slaves and free men attacked without orders (and with great success – the sight of the huge slaves, with machetes in their teeth and a pistol in each hand, was terrifying). The Spaniards withdrew, this time ending their claims to the territory forever, and the settlement, for the first time, was secure.

More than a century later, September 10 was declared a national holiday in Belize, and the battle of St George's Caye is still celebrated as National Day throughout the country to this day.

THE CHICLEROS

That stick of gum in your pocket has a fascinating history – and the Belize *chicleros* played a key role, traveling deep into the country's tangled jungles to gather chicle gum.

Perhaps the strangest figures in the history of Belize were the *chicleros* – the men who went into the jungles of Belize, the Peten region of Guatemala, and Mexico's Yucatán Peninsula to gather chicle gum.

The tree that provides the sap that is made into chicle is the *chicozapote* (*Manilkara zapota*), also commonly known as the *sapodilla*, whose rot-resistant wood was used by the Maya for lintels in their temples. There is evidence that they also cultivated the tree for its fruit in nearby plantations.

The medicinal uses of the *chicozapote* have long been known to the peoples of Mexico and Central America, where the tree is native: various parts have been used as treatments against a range of ailments, from dysentery to coughs and colds, kidney stones, snake bites, and insect stings; the latex was even used as a temporary filling for tooth cavities.

The first commercial use of the chicle gum as chewing gum, however, dates back to the late 19th century. In 1866, New York dentist Thomas Adams was given a kilogram (2.2lbs) of chicle gum by Mexican general, Antonio Lopez de Santa Ana. A year later, after a series of tests, Adams produced the first commercial chicle-based gum, and – so the story goes – the chewing gum industry began.

The role of the *chicleros* remained pivotal to the commercial success of chewing gum. Many of these men were Maya or Waika indigenous people, who had come to Belize from the Mosquito Coast, in present-day Honduras. They obtained the chicle by making slashes in the trunks of the *chicozapote* tree during the rainy season. The latex sap would drip down the slashes and collect in containers at the foot of the tree. They would then heat up the liquid latex and form it into solid blocks weighing some 4kg (10lbs), which were then shipped to factories in the United States. At its peak productivity in 1930, more than 6.3 million kg

(14 million lbs) of chicle was exported from Belize and other Central American countries.

As a result of their expeditions into little-known territory, the *chicleros* also acquired intimate knowledge of the trails through the dense jungle where the Maya sites had been hidden for centuries. It was thanks to the chicle-hunters that the Austrian explorer Teobert Maler was able to find and photograph such important sites as Tikal, Yaxchilan, Piedras Negras, and El Naranjo.

As the industry boomed, many methods were employed to replace the costly collection techniques of the *chicleros*, who were running into problems such as over-tapped trees and deforestation. Plantations were

The chiclero's work has changed little in over a century.

started, but these did not prove to be a practical alternative and were abandoned. After World War II, however, business slumped, with cheaper synthetic substitutes for chicle being introduced, and increased competition from other parts of the world, particularly Asia.

The demand for natural chicle never totally disappeared, however, and today a few *chicleros* in Belize continue to gather the white sap in much the same way as their forefathers did in the 19th century. The largest market for the gum is Japan, and the rising interest in natural, organic products in Europe and the US is also keeping the latex business bouncing. Maya gatherers and others are again being employed in this unique trade, and stumbling on yet more ancient sites in the jungle not seen for hundreds of years.

Mahogany cutters, the source of continual conflict with Maya farmers and Mexican bandits.

BRITISH HONDURAS

After its historic defeat of the Spanish, the new British colony then lapsed into 200 years of lassitude.

As the smoke cleared after their victory at St George's Caye, the Baymen jubilantly looked forward to the 19th century as a new era of peace and prosperity. With the Spanish threat broken, it seemed that they could carry on making fortunes from logging and bathe in a glow of patriotic pride. 'Many colonies have been won for England by her brave soldiers and sailors,' crowed one Bayman in his memoirs, 'but British Honduras is, I believe, the only one in which a mere handful of settlers, without help from home, wrested the lands from a powerful foe and added them to the British Empire.'

R.N. Posnett, a former governor of British Honduras.

> Life for the Baymen in the logwood camps was rough, to say the least. They lived in rudimentary huts roofed with palm leaves (also called 'Bay leaf') and survived on basic provisions brought in from other parts of the Caribbean. The one nightly highlight? Caribbean rum, which they drank voraciously.

Things were not, of course, that simple. News of the great victory barely reached the halls of power in London, where the Napoleonic Wars were of far more immediate interest. As far as the British government was concerned, Belize was more of an irritation than a valued aquisition. It was not officially a part of the empire at all. The Baymen were not even British subjects – they were just an unruly bunch of loggers, working in a godforsaken backwater, entirely on Spanish suffrance.

It was not until 1862 that Westminster officially recognized Belize as the Colony of British Honduras, sending out a proper governor and ordering a colonial parliament. But Central America remained all but unknown to the outside world, and played next to no part in the great strategic struggles of the day. In short, British Honduras may have become a part of the empire, but to the politicians and traders who orchestrated it, the acquisition seemed almost an irrelevance.

AN AMERICAN IN BELIZE TOWN

One of the few who took an interest in Belize in this period was the American John L. Stephens, an amateur archeologist whose memoirs form the basis of modern research on the Maya world (they are still in print and widely read to this day). His account provides the classic view of Belizean society in the making.

Arriving in 1839, Stephens found Belize Town firmly established as the settlement's capital (during the battle with the Spanish, the Baymen had burned every building on St George's Caye, so they wouldn't fall into enemy hands). Indeed, when seen from a distance, the town was almost picturesque. Seeing several boats in dock and dozens of canoes plying the river, Stephens was moved to compare it to Venice or Alexandria. Equally impressive were the canoes that came out to his ship, made of single, huge mahogany trees that would have been worth a fortune in New York City.

A 19th-century engraving of Belize City.

A fine wooden Government House had been built by the shore, lined with groves of coconut trees, and a bridge had been erected over the river. Settlers imported bricks from London – the same used to build mansions on Regent Street, they noted with some pride – to build St John's Cathedral. It was Belize's first brick building, its first permanent church, and the perfect place for the British to crown the Indian 'Mosquito Kings' of the neighboring Mosquito Coast (present-day Honduras), ensuring their allegiance throughout the 19th century.

Once on shore, however, Stephens's favorable impression evaporated when he found that the 'town seemed in the entire possession of blacks.' A pre-Civil War American used to a strictly segregated society, Stephens confessed that he 'hardly knew whether to be shocked or amused' by the hubbub of African vendors, black soldiers from Jamaica in red uniforms and women in white frocks with ('I could not help remarking') nothing on underneath.

Slavery had been abolished in Belize in the early 1830s, although the position of the average logging worker was hardly much improved. Even so, Belize's racial melting pot was already well advanced, as Stephens discovered to his horror when invited to lunch one day, only to find British officers dining with mulattoes: 'By chance a place was made for me between the two colored gentlemen,' writes Stephens. 'Some of my countrymen, perhaps, would have hesitated about taking it, but I did not; both were well dressed, well educated, and polite. They talked of their mahogany works, of England, hunting, horses, ladies, and wine...' In Belize, Stephens mused, 'color was considered mere matter of taste.'

Just as baffling to Stephens was the operation of Belize's 'Grand Court,' where no lawyers argued cases because none of the judges had legal training. Two were merchants, one a mahogany cutter, and one, a mulatto, was a doctor. The eminent American left the settlement soon after to seek out the Maya ruins in Honduras (Belize's as yet being hardly discovered), with the soldiers from Jamaica providing a 13-gun salute.

BANDITS AND WARLORDS

Even as Belize was being drawn into the fold of British colonial rule, the surrounding Spanish Empire in Central America was breaking into independent republics – creating waves of civil war, frontier disputes, and domestic chaos that spilled over into Belize. Just as the Baymen had had to defend themselves from the Spaniards, so the colonial Belizeans spent the entire 19th century fending off their new neighbors.

Raids by Mexican bandits made life out on the logging camps a constant peril. Worse came after 1847, when the Maya of the Yucatán rebelled against the ruling Mexican *ladinos* (mestizos) in the great Caste Wars. The conflict would continue until 1900, and spill over the borders into Belize.

At first, the British traders happily sold arms and supplies to the largest Mayan state, Santa

Cruz (so named because they worshipped a miraculous speaking cross). But this brought them into conflict with another Maya group, the Icaiche. What's more, British loggers were steadily intruding onto Mayan *milpa* or slash-and-burn lands (the Crown in Belize Town distributed permits to the countryside with little interest as to who was actually living there). Traditional good relations between British and Maya soured, and when the Icaiche rebel, General Marcus Canul, attacked Belize, most of the local Maya villages willingly supported him.

In 1866, Canul captured a British mahogany camp on the Río Bravo and held its members for $3,000 ransom. Next year, he attacked the sugar plantation of Indian Church near Lamanai, forcing local settlers to retreat to Belize Town. Matters were grave enough for the governor to order evacuation ships readied in the harbor, although the expected attack never came. In 1870, the Icaiche occupied the town of Corozal, and in 1872 besieged Orange Walk Town. Luckily for the inhabitants, a troop of US Confederate soldiers had settled nearby; fresh from the Civil War, their modern rifles devastated the Maya ranks. Canul himself was shot from his saddle, and later died, taking the wind out of the Icaiche rebellion.

THE LOST CONFEDERATES

How did the American soldiers happen to be there in the first place? When Lee surrendered to Grant at the Appomattox Court House, ending the American Civil War in 1865, many Southerners decided to escape Yankee rule forever and head for Latin America. Some 7,000 Confederates abandoned the United States for isolated colonies where they hoped to recreate the Old South – complete with plantation houses, belles in hoop skirts, gentlemen drinking iced tea and droves of black workers out in the fields. Most of these voluntary exiles went to Brazil, where slavery was still legal. But around 1,500 decided to try their luck in the wilds of British Honduras.

Southern curiosity in this obscure Central American republic had been piqued long before the Civil War, and when reconstruction began, the interest became intense. Emigration agents sprang up in every Southern city, and a fortnightly steamship service began from New Orleans to Belize in 1866. First reports from settlers were positive, and the British government

encouraging: import duties were waved for Confederate families, and London even promised that the young colony would soon be independent (broadly hinting that the Southerners could take the reins). The British governor even entertained new arrivals at state dinners, when the halls echoed with patriotic renditions of *Bonnie Blue Flag*, *My Maryland*, and *God Save the King*.

From 1867 to 1869, the *Trade Winds and the General Sherman* were bringing 100 settlers per trip. The majority were Confederate soldiers and their families, including many of high rank. The Ameri-

A large block of mahogany, 1850.

can consul in Belize noted with astonishment that 'generals and colonels meet one at every turn.'

Most of the new arrivals were appalled by Belize Town with its largely black population, and pressed on into the countryside. Some 300 followed the Reverend B.R. Duval of Virginia south to a spot near present-day San Pedro, setting up a town they named New Richmond (the whole colony was envisaged as 'Confederate County'). Another group from Louisiana – including Captain Beauregard, brother of the famed general, and a certain Colonel Benjamin, brother of the Confederate secretary of war – bought sugar plantations on the New River, south of Orange Walk Town. Other smaller groups of settlers scattered in remote pockets through the Belizean countryside.

The Confederates' stated aim was to withdraw from the rest of the world to recreate an antebellum fantasy. But the realities of Belizean frontier life caught up with them quickly. Conditions were much harsher than many had expected: apart from the constant heat, the rain and mosquitoes, settlers faced rampant diseases, problems with food supplies and incessant Indian raids in the north. Even more galling, black employees could simply walk away if pressed too far. Most Confederate exiles packed up and left Belize within a few years, returning to the United States poorer

Southern community soon lost any social cohesiveness. Children were sent back to the United States to be educated and find white spouses; many did not return. The families that remained in Belize were drawn into the more relaxed local attitude toward race, soon inter-marrying with members of the black and Hispanic communities.

TERRITORIAL CLAIMS

During the last quarter of the 19th century, the British were able to relocate demoralized Maya groups in towns, mixing their numbers with ref-

Belize City, 1914.

The border dispute between Belize and Guatemala has deep roots, going back to the mid-1800s, which partly explains why it has been so challenging to solve it. Local and international politicians and peacekeepers have extended huge efforts to resolve the issue, particular over the last decade.

but wiser. But others stayed on, using their skills and wealth to establish themselves in Belizean society, usually in the professions.

Although many Belizeans today can trace their lineage to former Confederate soldiers, the

ugees from Guatemala. Even so, the frontiers were not fully secure after the end of the Caste Wars until the late 1890s. In 1897, the Mexican and British governments signed a treaty, as a result of which Mexico formally renounced its claims on Belize.

Diplomatic problems with the neighboring Guatemalans were not so easily resolved. When it achieved independence in the 1820s, Guatemala picked up Spain's centuries-old claim to Belize, and pressed it enthusiastically. A treaty was signed between Britain and Guatemala in 1859 to settle the dispute, but Britain reneged on a key clause that entailed building a road between Guatemala City and the Atlantic coast (various routes were surveyed, but the price tag of £100,000 seemed a little steep just to secure Belize). Guatemala's threatened invasion and diplomatic pressure over the issue have recurred regularly throughout Belize's history right up to the present day.

HAGGIS IN THE TROPICS

As the 19th century drifted into the 20th, the racial amalgamation of Belizean society was proceeding apace. The Old Baymen families of landowners and merchants, with names like Hyde, Haylock, Usher, and Fairweather, had

had managed to convert almost the entire black population and replace many African rituals. But Christmas was the time when old traditions reasserted themselves in the slums of Belize Town's South Side: work was suspended for more than a week, rifles and pistols were shot off into the air and the drinking and dancing went on around the clock. Members of each African nation joined together to revive their homeland's dances and music. The excess of local energy was also channeled into an annual river regatta through Belize Town, in dories (dugouts) or larger pitpans, with

largely been 'creolized' through intermarriage. Although they lost their monopoly on land and trade, they went into the professions, training as barristers and doctors, as well as setting up the colony's first newspapers.

Meanwhile a steady flow of British expatriates formed a parallel high society, which ran local business. The majority of new arrivals were Scots, forming a clique with its own social clubs and considerable political clout. When a Scottish governor, Sir David Wilson, arrived in 1897, he was met by the local St Andrew's Club, who presented him with a haggis, sang Land o' Cakes and performed the highland fling. Every year, a Burns' Night was celebrated, reducing the congregation to tears.

For the bulk of the population, more humble celebrations were the norm. Anglican missionaries

crews of a dozen or so. Prizes and betting ran high, and the races had the advantage of improving crews' skills at bringing logs down-river.

DEMOCRATS AND RIOTERS

Although the remote society of British Honduras seemed to wallow in a heat-induced somnolence broken only by epidemics of yellow fever and cholera, social upheavals were brewing. The country was rapidly becoming the most backward in Central America. The alliance of white expatriates and old Creole families controlled political power in the form of a five-seat, appointed Legislative Council, often even out-voting the governor. There was no income or land tax in Belize, so no railroads were built. Roads were no better than mule trails: it would take weeks to get from San

Ignacio to Belize Town by land, so most commuters went by canoe. Agriculture, meanwhile, was in disarray or non-existent. Creoles traditionally disdained farming, and even the most basic foodstuffs needed to be imported.

A half-hearted attempt was made to include the masses in politics by electing a Belize Town Board in 1910. Unfortunately, thanks to a property qualification, only 282 of the 15,118 Belizeans were able to vote.

World War I brought matters to a head. In 1915 and 1916, some 600 loyal British Hondurans signed

A school in British Honduras, 1918.

up to fight in Europe. But, instead of being sent to cover themselves in glory on the Western Front, this predominantly black contingent was packed off to dig ditches in the Middle East. Protests were met with the news that 'it is against British tradition to employ aboriginal troops against a European enemy.' Worse, when they arrived in Cairo and marched in to camp whistling *Rule Britannia*, they were stopped by British officers. One black soldier reports being asked: 'Who gave you niggers authority to sing that? Clear out of this building – only British troops admitted here.'

Troops returning to Belize in 1919 brought back the weight of these insults and an awareness of the connections between race, class and empire. They could not help notice that no black soldiers

were invited to tea at the golf club after a sports event held by the governor in their honor. Tensions finally broke out in a riot two weeks later. Soldiers marched down Regent Street in Belize City (as the town was by then known), smashing shop windows. Unpopular employers were beaten up. News spread, and the whole population joined in, police included. Some 3,000 people looted the town until dawn the next day, when a gunboat was called in to quell the disturbance.

BETWEEN THE WARS

The riots led directly to the foundation in Belize City of a branch of the United Negro Improvement Association, and a visit in 1921 by its Jamaican-born founder Marcus Mosiah Garvey. A passionate orator and skilled mass organizer, Garvey traveled around the Caribbean raising black political consciousness. At meetings he was careful to have *God Save the King* sung so as not to concern the authorities unduly, but his speeches were sharp and damning. Black soldiers had fought to protect the empire, he said, and received in return 'a kick and a smile.'

But Belizeans were unable to sustain the momentum for very long, and, when Garvey visited again in 1929, he was easily outshone by a visit from the US aviator Charles Lindbergh, fresh from his solo crossing of the Atlantic.

Meanwhile, Belize was about to be hit by the twin disasters of the Great Depression, which put the fragile economy into a tailspin, and a devastating hurricane. For generations, the citizens of Belize City had thought that any approaching hurricane or tidal wave would be spent on the Barrier Reef. Nothing terribly damaging had happened since 1787, so when a fully-fledged hurricane finally arrived on the morning of Settlement Day, September 10, 1931, nobody took it seriously. Most of the population, including the governor, was involved in a commemorative parade, which was cut short by a deluge. Retiring to St John's College for patriotic songs, the Imperial Band was soon drowned out by the wind: velocity rose from 40 miles (70km) an hour at noon to a peak of 132 mph (210 kmh) at 3pm.

Within minutes the sky had cleared and grateful citizens went to check the wreckage of their homes. Tragically, few realized that this was only the eye of the storm, and many were caught when the hurricane returned with even greater force. Whole houses were picked up and smashed by the wind; the Poor House with 41 inmates inside was washed out to sea; the city was flooded and the air was thick with flying sheets of corrugated iron, decapitating passers-by. Some 1,000 people were killed in the disaster, made worse by years of bungled relief work.

A DEPRESSED NEW WORLD

The hurricane only added to Belize's growing economic mire. The chicle trade, which depended on a demand for chewing gum in the United States, was suffering; but, much more seriously, the mahogany trade had collapsed.

During his 1936 visit to Belize, the writer Aldous Huxley observed that a minor fluctuation in British middle-class taste had profoundly affected the lives of woodcutters in the remote forests. 'When I was a boy there was hardly a single reputable family which did not eat off mahogany, sit on mahogany, sleep in mahogany,' Huxley wrote in the slightly dotty book *Beyond the Mexique Bay*. 'Mahogany was a symbol of economic solidity and moral worth. Alas, how quickly such sacred symbols can lose their significance! [Today] my friends eat off glass and metal, sit on metal and leather, sleep on beds that are almost innocent of enclosing bedsteads. Mahogany, in a word, is now hopelessly out of fashion.' There, of course, Huxley's interest ended. He was no more interested in Belize than Stephens had been a century before, and headed straight for the Maya ruins in Guatemala.

THE RISE OF UNION ACTIVISM

Belizeans were starting to take a hand in improving their own affairs. The hurricane had left Belize City with a swamp-like appearance, its dirt streets looking like rivers, with sewers overflowing and water supplies regularly drying up. Dysentery, malaria and yellow fever returned as the colony's major causes of death. Social and economic conditions were so bad that Belize's first labor union was formed, although the leader, Antonio Soberanis, was promptly jailed by the British authorities.

Other political organizations followed, usually starting off as motley public rallies in the sandy Central Park (dubbed 'the Battlefield'). For the first time the possibility of independence from Britain was seriously discussed. A 'Natives First'

movement managed to gain seats on the Belize Town Board in 1939, and in 1941 a firebrand named Joseph Blisset formed a Belizean Labour Party. Among its more bizarre proposals was the expulsion of all whites, and Belize becoming the next state of the USA. This led to an all-out brawl on the Battlefield between Blisset's men and the largely white loyalist group called the Unconquerables. Blisset ended up in jail, as did several other more moderate nationalists.

Anti-colonialism was growing by the end of World War II and Governor Sir John Hunter,

British Honduras Volunteer Guard, 1972.

During British rule, a stream of UK artists and luminaries visited Belize, including Aldous Huxley, who came by in 1936, and wrote about the country's mahogany trade in the eccentric *Beyond the Mexique Bay*.

embarrassed by constantly having to throw Creole activists in prison, suggested to London that they give Belizeans the vote. The Colonial Office replied that they couldn't 'go handing out self-government to all and sundry,' and the scene for a long political struggle was set.

Supporters at a football match between Belize and Costa Rica.

MODERN BELIZE

Belize's unique identity – a colorful mix of Central America and the
Caribbean – has flourished since its long-awaited independence in 1981.

On September 21, 1981, the British Union Jack was lowered and the Belizean flag raised in its place. Belize had finally become an independent nation – but many Belizeans who attended the ceremonies or listened to them on the radio that night felt only apprehension at what the future would bring.

Many would have preferred to delay independence – not because they disagreed with the idea but because the 19th-century territorial dispute with Guatemala had not yet been settled. Despite assurances from the British government that they would maintain a garrison in Belize 'for an appropriate period,' Belizeans were nervous. Some even feared that, as soon as the international delegates and media left, Guatemalan troops would swarm over the nation's border.

LONG ROAD TO INDEPENDENCE

During World War II, many young Belizeans traveled outside their country for the first time. Several thousand fought with the British armed forces, and many more traveled to the United States to help in the war effort. When these young men returned to Belize after the war, they found there were no jobs for them, and that they had no say in running the colony's affairs. Thereafter anti-colonial feeling grew apace, fueled in 1949 when a currency devaluation in Britain resulted in the loss of half the value of the British Honduran dollar. The first serious political movements in favor of complete independence began to take shape. Prominent among them was the General Workers' Union, which, under the leadership of George Price, in 1950 became the People's United Party (PUP).

One of the first positive results of this new pressure for change came in 1954, when a new constitution for the colony was brought in. For the first time, this gave all literate adults in Belize

Prime Minister Dean Barrow meeting the Queen.

the right to vote. Previously, only some 3 percent of Belizeans had met the strict property qualifications required to vote; unsurprisingly, many felt that the country was being run like an enormous private plantation for the wealthy elite, many of whom were British or American expatriates.

The new constitution also set up a legislative council in which, for the first time, some of the members were elected by the populace, although the British-appointed governor continued to exercise final control. The PUP won eight of the nine elected seats in the first council. It was plain that the political make-up of the colony was changing fast.

Two events in the early 1960s further accelerated this process of change. The first was the natural disaster of Hurricane Hattie, which almost completely destroyed Belize City in 1961. Many Belizeans felt that the colonial authorities had not done enough either to prevent the disaster, or to assist the subsequent relief work. Plans were laid – and eventually realized – for the building of a new administrative capital in the interior, at Belmopan, on a site less likely to be affected by tropical storms. Nevertheless, the experience of Hurricane Hattie gave new impetus to the struggle for independence.

The second milestone of the decade was the constitutional conference held in London in 1963.

Former prime minister, George Price.

George Price led the Belizean delegation to the conference, and by 1 January, 1964 he had negotiated a new constitution which granted the colony full internal self-government. Price himself became the first minister. He officially renamed the colony Belize, and brought in a new flag and a national anthem.

GUATEMALA PROTEST OVERRIDDEN

Full independence was delayed by hesitancy on the part of the British government and aggressive noises from Guatemala. The latter had renewed its claims to British Honduras in the 1930s; in 1945, it had officially announced that 'Belice' (as it is called in Spanish) was a Guatemalan province. When Belize gained self-government, Guatemala's

Guatemala claimed Belizean home rule was 'a flagrant violation of the sovereign rights of Guatemala,' and threatened to go to war over the territory.

military government broke off diplomatic relations with Britain. Diplomacy was fruitless; twice in the 1970s, Guatemala moved troops to the border and threatened to invade, only being dissuaded by reinforcements of British troops.

The case for Belizean independence was taken to international forums and the turning point came in 1980 when a United Nations resolution supporting independence finally put the wheels inexorably in motion. But controversy lasted right up to the moment of the transfer of power. The 'Heads of Agreement,' a document outlining proposed points of negotiation with Guatemala, had caused rioting in Belize City in early 1981; Guatemala closed its border with Belize in protest against Belizean independence. Even so, the ceremony went ahead in September, and Belize became an independent part of the British Commonwealth.

POST-INDEPENDENCE

Yet again, it was George Price and the PUP who were the dominant force in Belizean political life. Price became the newly independent country's first prime minister, and his party had a big majority in the new assembly. During the 1970s, however, opposition groups, supported mostly by the business sector, had joined together to challenge the PUP's dominance, and in 1973 they had formed the United Democratic Party (UDP). In 1984, in the first elections after independence, the UDP won a majority in the national assembly. The party's leader, the former schoolteacher Manuel Esquivel, became Belize's second prime minister.

Meanwhile, the sovereignty issue with Guatemala had still to be settled. In 1986 civilian rule was finally returned to Guatemala, and the succeeding civilian regimes showed much greater flexibility on the Belize issue than their military predecessors. In 1991 President Jorge Serrano finally announced that Belize's sovereignty would be recognized. Direct diplomatic relations with Britain were also re-established. Belize responded by passing legislation that limited its maritime claims in the Southern Toledo area; this offered Guatemala access to the Caribbean, which had always been one of its key demands.

In 1993, because of the new atmosphere of co-operation, Britain finally withdrew the last of its troops from the Belize garrison. Defense of the country was left in the hands of the small British-trained Belize Defence Force. With only around 1,000 soldiers, the BDF cannot hope to resist a serious invasion attempt from its much larger neighbor, but Mexico and Britain continue to act as deterrents to any military venture of this kind.

The sovereignty dispute flared up again in 1999 and 2000. The Guatemalan Congress decreed that, although it recognized Belize's right to self-deter-mination, this did not mean it renounced its claim to almost half of Belizean territory. Both sides agreed, however, to continue talking in an attempt to resolve their historic dispute peacefully.

In 2008, Prime Minister Dean Barrow announced that resolving the border dispute was one of his chief goals while in office. In December 2008, Belize and Guatemala signed a special agreement to submit the border issue to the International Court of Justice (ICJ), but in October 2013, this agreement was suspended. In April 2018, however, a referendum on whether the Guatemalan government should ask the ICJ to resolve the territorial dispute was held in Guatemala and over 95 percent of voters said "yes." In 2019, at the time of writing, a refer-endum is expected in Belize to confirm that the Belizean people also agree that Guatemala should request the ICJ to resolve the dispute.

PARTY POLITICS

Despite the continuing nervousness about Gua-temala and numerous social and economic prob-lems, most Belizeans today feel that life is pretty good. Since independence, the democratic process has proceeded smoothly and voter turnout is gen-erally high. But Belizean politics remains a curious affair to outsiders.

Election campaigns operate at a personal level, with candidates handing out T-shirts and making small talk with their supporters. Politicians happily grant personal favors; many Belizeans think noth-ing of asking candidates for anything from a piece of land to schoolbooks for their children.

Politically, Belize has a two-party democratic system, with the People's United Party (PUP)

alternating with United Democratic Party (UDP) nearly every term. In 2003 the PUP, under Prime Minister Said Musa, proved an exception to the rule by winning an unprecedented second term. It didn't win a third term, however; following a spate of corruption allegations, the UDP was returned to power in 2008, under Dean Barrow, and was re-elected in 2012. The party made history in 2015 by winning a third consecutive term for the first time, with Dean Barrow continuing his term as prime minister. The next general election in Belize must be held in February 2021 at the latest.

Town hall, Orange Walk Town.

CULTURAL LOYALTIES

Following waves of immigration from other Cen-tral American nations in the 1980s and early 1990s, some creoles are deeply concerned about what they call the 'hispanicization of Belize.' As a result, there has been a fair amount of 'alien bashing' in the newspapers and on radio call-in programs. But most Belizeans continue to have a wait-and-see attitude, hoping Central American immigrants will follow the pattern set by previous immigrant groups who have embraced the Belizean way of life. Nevertheless, since it emerged that mestizos now outnumber creoles, the new demographic reality has shaken up Belize's traditional self-image as a Caribbean nation that is only geograph-ically part of Latin America.

In truth, Belize's ties to the islands of the Caribbean have been more a matter of tradition than substance. It shares a British heritage with other Caribbean islands. Cultural connections are also still strong: Belizean youth look to Jamaica in particular as a source of spiritual and musical inspiration.

TRADING PARTNERS

To promote integration, Belize became a member of the Caribbean Community (CARICOM), an alliance of Caribbean nations. But many complain that Belize benefits little: few of the other member nations are interested in Belizean goods, but Belizeans are still expected to 'buy Caribbean.'

THE POLITICS OF TOURISM

Belize may have embraced tourism long after its Caribbean neighbors, but today the tourist industry is booming. The numbers say it all: tourism brings in US$245 million a year out of Belize's US$1.9 billion GDP and is the mainstay of Belize's economy, pushing agriculture and fisheries into a close second place. Tourism is also responsible for employing nearly a third of the country's workforce. The quality and standards of hotels, restaurants, tour-guiding, and services have also been on a steady rise since the late 1990s, and Belize is frequently represented worldwide at international travel shows.

For the most part, government duty and tax exemptions have been aimed at attracting foreign investors. As a result, a huge number of the country's hotels and 'lodges' are owned by foreigners, especially North Americans.

Belizean nationalists are working hard to ensure that local operators benefit from tourism and tourist officials have placed emphasis on Belize as an eco-tourism destination. Another important initiative is the Mundo Maya project, an attempt to join forces with their counterparts in Central America on the basis of a shared Maya heritage.

But perhaps the biggest tourist trend to hit Belize since the mid-2000s is the phenomenal growth in the number of visitors who arrive by cruise ship.

A warm welcome.

⊘ THE RISE (AND RISE) OF THE CRUISE INDUSTRY

Gaze out to sea from Belize City, and you'll see sparkling waters, the blazing sun, seagulls swooping through the air – and a hulking cruise ship (or five). The rise in cruise ship passenger numbers in Belize is meteoric, from just a few hundred passengers per year in the late 1990s to around 700,000 yearly now. The growth of the cruise industry impacts the country's conservation efforts and, according to some, Belize's overall cultural philosophy as well. Since the early 2000s, tour operators have catered enthusiastically to cruise-ship day trippers, and you'll often see massive buses disgorging passengers at sights throughout the country. This can detract from the majesty of Maya temples and the country's once-undiscovered wilderness. On the other hand, proponents claim that the industry brings in the big bucks and, for many Belizeans, that's imperative to a rosy future.

So, what does the future hold? Many are looking at Norwegian Cruise Line (NCL) as an example of how the industry might unfold in Belize. In 2013, NCL purchased an island – Harvest Caye – from the Belizean government to develop its own resort-like cruise port. NCL invested US$50 million in the caye, which opened in 2016. The resort meets the highest eco-friendly standards, materials used to construct it were sourced locally and all stores and restaurants there are also locally owned. It also features a nature center, a zipline and 11 villas for rent.

⚲ REFUGEES

Throughout its history, Belize has welcomed newcomers, and even though it faces the occasional challenge and cultural rifts, it will likely continue to do so.

When Belize became independent in 1981, it was in a much more fortunate position than its Central American neighbors. In Nicaragua, soon after the Sandinistas had taken power in 1979, the country was riven by civil war – with the 'contra' counter-revolutionary forces, financed by the Reagan administration in Washington, trying to overthrow the Sandinistas. The Nicaraguan war spilled over into Honduras, creating instability there. Meanwhile, in El Salvador, guerrillas tried to repeat the Sandinista victory, but were resisted by the armed forces. And in Guatemala, where an armed struggle had been going on since the 1960s, the army took the war to the countryside. The main victims were the peasants, whose lives and livelihoods were threatened on all sides.

Inevitably, many of these people were attracted to the political and economic stability of Belize, and at first the refugees were given a warm welcome. In the 1980s, the Belizean economy was expanding out of its traditional sectors and there was a need for cheap labor in agro-industry in which urban creoles had little experience. Many refugees in Belize not only worked in agriculture, but managed to buy land or to set up in small businesses. Their children were offered free schooling and access to health care.

Many had crossed the border illegally, but there were few concerted attempts to send them home. However, when a national census in 1991 revealed that between 30,000 and 40,000 Spanish-speaking immigrants had arrived – almost a fifth of the total population – Belizeans were taken aback. More than three-quarters of the new arrivals were from El Salvador; most of the others were Guatemalans. For the first time in the history of the country, according to the census, Spanish speakers represented more than half of the nation, whereas creole Belizeans made up only a third.

This situation led to something of a backlash. The Belizean authorities made more of an effort to check up on immigrants, and to return those without papers to their own countries. The end of the civil wars in Nicaragua, El Salvador and finally Guatemala also meant that some of the newcomers willingly went back. But employment opportunities and wages remained considerably better in Belize, so they had little incentive to return home.

The influence of these newcomers is immediately obvious, particularly in the south of Belize. The people in the countryside are predominantly Hispanic; many shops have signs in Spanish, and most people listen to

Bilingual signs in English and Spanish

Mexican or Guatemalan radio. As creoles continue to emigrate to the United States, some politicians have called for Belize to recognize that it is only a small territory which needs to foster links with its immediate land neighbors rather than continue to think of itself as part of a community of Caribbean nations.

Others are still suspicious of Guatemala, which has always laid claim to the territory, and want to discourage any further immigration from there or other Central American countries. They stress that Belize should continue to strengthen its ties with the English-speaking world. But throughout its history, Belize has received and absorbed wave after wave of newcomers – from the Baymen to the Garífunas, from the British to the Mennonites – and it is likely to continue to do so.

Residential neighborhood, Dangriga.

CREOLE AS IT IS SPOKEN

Creole is not to be confused with pidgin English – it's a complex spoken language with grammatical rules and a fruity turn of phrase.

Belizeans have a proverb to describe a person who is self-important: *Fowl caca white an tink e lay egg* ('A chicken shits white and thinks it has laid an egg.') This illustrates that the official language of Belize may be English but, as any visitor soon realizes, the language of the street is rather different.

An example from everyday speech: *Da weh da lee bwai mi di nyam?* ('What was that little boy eating?') Here, *Weh da lee bwai* can be traced back to the English *'what that little boy,'* but the rest is unintelligible to English speakers. *Da* means 'is.' *Nyam* is an African word for 'eat,' from the vegetable yam, while *mi* and *di* are grammatical words indicating the past imperfect tense.

There was a time when the creole languages of the world (and there are dozens in the Caribbean region alone, as well as the version in Louisiana) were regarded as 'uncivilized' or 'broken' speech – imperfect, childish copies of the colonial languages from which they were derived, whether English, French, Portuguese, or Spanish. Today, with more scholarly and objective scrutiny, creole languages are being recognized for what they are: new linguistic creations with fully-fledged, highly nuanced grammatical systems. The process of standardization in many creole-speaking countries is well under way, with grammars and dictionaries being commissioned and panels of scholarly experts working on linguistic problems.

In Belize, the Bileez Kriol Projek has been developing standard spellings for all the words Belizeans toss into the air and catch again so freely. But, although it has produced a small glossary, translated several books of the Bible, and written down a few folk tales, its system is

Sign in a Caye Caulker restaurant.

not gaining widespread acceptance. Belizeans may speak creole, but they read English.

LINGUISTIC HYBRID

In Belize, the creole people are the products of centuries of inter-breeding between the British colonizers and their West African slaves. The language, Belize creole, is the linguistic result of this meeting: English (including many English and Scottish regional dialects) blended with the diverse language groups of West Africa.

Belize creole's nearest relative is Jamaican creole, also based on English, although the two are quite different. Adding to the Belizean mixture are words from Spanish (*goma* for a hangover, for example) and others from the language of the Miskito Indians of Nicaragua (*konka* for a house fly, amongst others).

Although Belize creole was the creation of the creole people, today it is far from their exclusive property. It is the country's *lingua franca*, spoken by mestizos, East Indians, the Maya, and Garífunas. To speak it is part of being Belizean – so much so that the US Peace Corps has decided to teach creole to its volunteers. Many travelers have also taken quick courses.

A good place to start solving the mystery of Belize creole – in which hundreds of English words lurk but meanings of phrases are lost in the different grammar – is a small book called *Creole Proverbs of Belize*. Proverbs are a storehouse of folk wit and wisdom in any language and Belize creole proverbs are an amusing way of getting to understand local cadences, as well as customs. For example, one translates: 'The man who has lifted his horse's tail knows that the bottom is red,' and another goes: 'The bull knows on what part of the barbed wire to rub its balls.'

> *Everyone in Belize understands English but it's fun to learn a bit of creole. After all, saying a person went 'bliggity blam boom, boff!' is so much more expressive than 'he slipped and fell.'*

Of course, there's another bonus to picking up a few words in creole: The smiles and delighted reaction that you'll receive by locals. A few useful phrases to know, when traveling around the country: *'Yu gat eni room fu rent?'* (Do you have any available rooms?), *'Weh di go aan?'* (What's up/How's it going?) and *'Ah mi gat wahn gud taim'* (I had a great time).

Some Belize creole words have infiltrated the standard English language. The word *jook*, for example, is used by all Belizeans to mean 'stick,' although its secondary meaning is 'copulate.' The term migrated to many southern black communities of the United States, where a brothel was often called a 'jook-house' – so that when music-playing boxes began to appear in nightclubs and whorehouses, they were naturally referred to as 'jook-boxes' or, as it is usually spelled,

'juke-boxes.' Another Belize creole word still current in the southern US is *pinda* (spelled 'pinder' in American English), an old African word for peanuts.

THE FUTURE OF CREOLE

There has been some debate about teaching Belize creole in schools, but the proponents seem to be losing the battle. Most of the parents surveyed by the Education Department, and even the children themselves, seem to feel their future success will depend on their

Creole remains a common dialect.

ability to converse in an internationally recognized language such as standard English. There is also increasing demand for Spanish courses, and Spanish has recently been put on the curricula of all grade schools. This is due, of course, to the increasing Hispanicization of the country.

Even so, creole seems destined to remain a common dialect: from the Mennonite carpenter to the Salvadorean fruit vendor, and even the new Taiwanese immigrant (after around three months), everyone knows how to 'wap wa li creole.' Ultimately, creole is a language at the heart – and soul – of Belize's history and therefore, while it may take a back seat to English and Spanish, it will never entirely die out.

Traditional dance performance.

HOLIDAYS AND MUSIC

Two national days in September, plus Garífuna Settlement Day and Carnival, are celebrated with music, dancing, and costume parades.

Belize may be best known for its natural wonders and Maya temples, but the country has an equally vibrant musical culture and history. From Garífuna drumming and punta rock to melodic Maya percussion, and jaunty marimba and mariachi to creole *brukdown*, Belize's musical traditions reflect its diverse population.

Punta rock, based on traditional Garífuna music and lyrics with some contemporary electronic alterations, has won the hearts of every ethnic group in Belize, and a number of artists have recorded albums and perform regularly in US and European cities. Like the older-style Garífuna music, punta rock lyrics cover topics from social commentary and humorous jibes at community members to the loss of a loved one. Reggae, soca, and several bands from Mexican-influenced northern Belize employ a salsa or merengue beat. Traditional music is still popular: creoles can claim *brukdown* and a large number of original folk songs, while the Maya and mestizos occasionally explore their musical roots in the few villages that still have a marimba band.

With so many holidays on the Belizean calendar, it's not hard for visitors to find a musical celebration during their stay – especially if they pass through in September.

PATRIOTIC PARTY TIME

September is the month when Belizeans are at their most patriotic and spirited, celebrating both St George's Caye Day on the 10th – marking the victory of the British Baymen and their slaves over Spanish invaders in 1798 – and, on September 21, Independence Day. Weeks on either side of these dates are filled with activities, most taking place in Belize City.

Drummers, Garífuna National Day.

Banners with patriotic slogans, red, blue, and white streamers, and twinkling lights festoon the streets, which are crowded with the Queen of the Bay beauty pageant, bicycle races, concerts, and military displays. Many 'Bel-Ams' (Belizeans residing in the US) choose this time to come home for a visit.

Music, both old and new, plays a vital role in the celebrations. Every year an assortment of favorite old 'tenth songs' – some patriotic march tunes, others sentimental ballads – hits the airwaves, while Belize's contemporary musicians try to release at least one new song, or perhaps an entire album, in honor of the season. And the party always features at least one calypso or soca band from the Caribbean to give the

Belizean crowds something to help them *wine dey waist* (wind their waists).

The Carnival Road March in Belize City has grown from a small children's parade to a full-fledged Caribbean extravaganza. Bands from the districts also head into town for the event, which usually occurs sometime around September 10. Junior and senior carnival bands spend weeks, even months, fundraising and making colorful costumes. Whereas the adult bands often have corporate sponsors, in the poorer neighborhoods junior band leaders will even pawn their gold

Carnival revelers.

jewelry or spend their office syndicate savings so that no child is without a costume for the big day. When the day comes, spectators get out early to find a spot at the side of the street, whose center becomes a mass of costumed dancers accompanied by music blasted from trucks.

Things are a lot more somber at the flag-raising at the courthouse on Independence Eve and the official ceremonies the next morning, but the party atmosphere is revived later in the day as people swarm the parks or main streets for the 'jump up' or street fair.

> *Andy Palacio, an award-winning Garífuna musician and composer, died in 2008, but his music lives on, particularly in his last album, Watina, which was awarded World Music Album of the Year in 2008 by the BBC. It's available at www.stonetreerecords.com.*

OLE TIME CHRISTMAS

Many of Belize's Christmas traditions go back to logging days, when slaves and apprentice wood-cutters got a break from life in the 'bush' to visit the town with family and friends. Everyone would celebrate the temporary reprieve with two solid weeks of drinking, dancing, singing, and parading through the streets.

As in the old days, most people still turn their houses inside out for a Christmas cleaning, hang new curtains and make *rum popo*. The traditional holiday meal, served on both Christmas and New Year's Day, is ham and turkey, rice and beans, and cranberry sauce.

In Dangriga, the Christmas season is greeted by Joncunu (John Canoe) dancers. Outfitted in a pink wire mask, white tunic with flowing ribbons, an elaborate crown with tall feathers, and hundreds of tiny shells attached to their knees, the dancers go from door to door dancing the *wanaragua*. Some say the dance is meant to be an imitation of white slaveholders and their behavior, which may be why it was popular at Christmas when normal master and slave relations were traditionally more relaxed.

New Year's Eve in Belize is less distinctive, really just a continuation of Christmas. People 'ring in' the coming year with parties and champagne, and then New Year's Day is usually spent quietly with family or friends.

⊘ BRAM AND BRUKDOWN

Though the creole celebrations of *bram* and *brukdown* are slowly being replaced by more modern traditions, you'll still occasionally find it in smaller villages around Belize. Bram is a Christmas ritual, where a group of revelers travel from house to house, pushing the furniture against the walls and using household objects as instruments to make *brukdown* music. Anything from a broom handle, washbasin, or a metal grater to drums, banjos, guitars, accordions, and cowbells can be used. The creole lyrics, invented on the spot, are about famous people or local village happenings. These days, there are still several 'Boom and Chime' bands and singers who are sought-after for private parties.

GARIFUNA CELEBRATIONS

Garífuna Settlement Day is anything but quiet. Celebrated on November 19, the day commemorates the 1832 arrival of the largest group of Garífuna to Belize's southern shores, and is a non-stop cultural fête.

The best place to witness this is in Dangriga, the town that accommodates the greatest number of Garífuna in Belize. As well as performing the *wanaragua*, or Joncunu, on the eve of Settlement Day, the Garífuna get the chance to show off their most popular dance, the punta. In what is supposed to resemble the courtship ritual, a couple circle each other shaking only their hips and plowing the earth with their toes as they alternately propel themselves toward and away from each other. The *hunguhungu* is also performed for Settlement Day, although it usually has a more ceremonial function as part of the *dugu* ritual (see page 183).

At dawn the next morning there is a re-enactment of the arrival of the early settlers in their dories. As they enter town from the mouth of the river, the travelers are greeted by women singing, drums beating, and the waving of cassava sticks and Garífuna flags. Everyone then proceeds to the church for a lengthy Thanksgiving Mass.

MESTIZO TRADITIONS

The religious celebrations of the mestizo communities of northern Belize are concentrated around Easter, though costume parades begin the weekend before Lent. In Orange Walk, *los mascaradas* wear scary disguises and drag chains through the streets, while others perform humorous skits or *comparsas* door to door. A dummy made of old clothes with a calabash head is dubbed 'Juan Carnival' and burned at sundown. In San Pedro, skits tell the story of the mestizos' arrival in the village in the 19th century. In both towns, children roam the streets carrying raw eggs, flour, and paint to ambush each other – and hapless adults – a tradition said to have been inspired by the mischievous Maya god, Momo.

Good Friday is often observed with a religious procession through the streets. Many Belizeans are superstitious about swimming or using boats on this day, while others joke that swimmers will turn into fish or mermaids. By contrast, the next day is filled with action for 'The Holy Saturday Cross Country' bike race. On Easter Sunday people attend sunrise services and the Easter Bunny has also hopped into the center of many festivities.

Most mestizo and Maya villages also have an annual *fiesta* in honor of the town's patron saint. The most prestigious of these is the Benque Fiesta held in July in Benque Viejo del Carmen near the Guatemalan border. The *Costa Maya Festival*, held in San Pedro during the third week of August, is a celebration of dance, music, and culture that attracts performers from Mexico and throughout Central America.

Live music.

IN MEMORY OF BARON BLISS

One of Belize's most popular holidays, held every March 9, celebrates the life of English aristocrat Baron Bliss, who spent two months fishing in 1926 before he fell ill and died on board. He enjoyed his stay so much that he left his estate to the country.

This gift made possible many of the public facilities Belizeans enjoy today, and helps finance the annual Baron Bliss Day Regatta in Belize City. Held off Fort George, this spectacle draws Belizean sailors piloting every form of craft. The waters are packed with fancy sailboats, working 'sandlighters', and brightly trimmed dugout dories. Meanwhile, the skies are filled with kites. Baron Bliss's legacy also lives on in the Bliss Centre for the Performing Arts (see page 115) in Belize City.

A hearty plate of chicken, rice and beans.

FOOD AND DRINK

Rice and beans with stewed chicken or beef are the local daily fuel, washed down with beer or rum – but Belizean seafood and fruits are tempting tropical treats.

Belizean cuisine is best described in the plural – cuisines. Wander through most any town or village, and you'll encounter a delightful and distinctive mix of Latin American, Caribbean, Creole, and Garífuna options, not to mention delicacies from farther afield – Taiwan, Thailand, Lebanon. And then there's the seafood: Fresh and plentiful, the fresh fish and shellfish – particular the succulent and mildly sweet lobster – is, not surprisingly, the highlight for most visitors. Happily, you'll find it everywhere: From the cayes to the coast to the inland communities. Just make sure to time your visit with lobster season (June 15–February 15).

But at the heart of Belizean cuisine is the ultimate comfort food: rice and beans. This is prepared in two ways: red kidney beans cooked together with rice; or beans and rice cooked separately, often with a piece of pigtail thrown in for extra zest. The best versions of both dishes use coconut milk in the rice. The traditional Sunday dinner consists of rice and beans, stewed chicken, potato salad, and fried plantain.

DOWN TO THE BONE

Chicken is certainly the Belizeans' favorite meat, and each bird is stretched to the limit. Except for the head, every bit of the chicken – including the feet – is stewed and served up. The bony, rather than meaty, pieces are considered the choicest, especially by those who like to suck out the marrow. Even the former Prime Minister, George Price, is said to always ask for the chicken neck.

But chicken doesn't just make an appearance in the national dish of rice and beans.

Mouthwatering ceviche.

You'll also see fried chicken sold at Chinese takeout windows throughout the country. You used to get a bag for as little as a dollar ('dolla chicken') and you can still get a quarter chicken and fries for Bz$5–10 from roadside stands. In true creole fashion, the more zany the nickname of the shop (like 'kick-down-fence' or 'fresh kill'), the more delicious the product is reputed to be. Also popular in Belize are weekend streetside barbecues, which are sometimes set up by fund-raising groups.

Belizean steaks are rarely worth the money, or the jaw-power they take to chew, but decent pork is plentiful. Almost all meat is generally served stewed and seasoned with red *recado*, a spice ball whose main ingredient is anatto seed. The classic dish 'bamboo chicken' is actually a type of iguana known for its tender white flesh. In an effort to conserve the species, the dish is banned during the February and March breeding season. Another game meat is armadillo, known locally as 'hamadilly,' but the most popular game is gibnut. This large rodent is considered so delectable that it was served to Queen Elizabeth on one of her visits. The British press had a field day, with headlines blaring Queen Eats Rat in Belize. Conservationists may frown on the custom of eating this wild animal, but gibnut remains popular, as does the story of its royal connections, and the animal is now referred to as 'royal gibnut.'

BOUNTIFUL WATERS

Seafood is abundant in Belize. The standards include red snapper, mackerel, grouper, shark, and barracuda (also called 'barro'), and fresh- and salt-water snook – a light-textured fish considered 'the steak of the sea.'

Yams and yucca.

⊘ MAYA SOUL FOOD

Perhaps the greatest contribution the Maya and mestizos have made to Belizean culture emerged from their fire hearths and kitchens. Traditional dishes have become so much part of the Belizean diet that many consider foods like *escabeche* and *panades* to be of creole origin. One creole restaurateur coined the phrase 'Maya Soul Food' to describe the Spanish heritage foods that he served.

Tamales can be obtained anywhere, anytime in Belize. They are made from ground corn meal, or *masa*, mixed with shredded chicken or pork, wrapped and steamed in a plantain leaf. *Tamales de chaya* are a spinach variation that may include cheese.

Many Belizeans also enjoy other corn-based, deep-fried Spanish foods. The nationwide favorites are fish or bean *panades* made from corn *masa*, folded over and fried until crispy, and served with an onion and vinegar sauce spiced up with habanero pepper. These can be quite small, so you may have to fill up on *garnaches* – crispy corn tortillas topped with refried beans, grated cheese, and tomato sauce.

Spanish soups are more substantial. *Escabeche* is a clear, tangy onion soup with large pieces of chicken; *chichac* is a clear broth that may be spooned over a whole fried fish or contain fish patties.

Besides being baked, barbecued, or stewed, fish often appears in soups, the richest of which is 'serre.' This traditional Garífuna dish requires numerous 'ground foods' such as yams, cassava, and okra, as well as plantains and lots of coconut milk; it is often served with thin, crispy cassava bread. The thinnest fish soup is called 'fish tea,' typically made by fishermen camped at the cayes. Its ingredients include only onions, black pepper, and live fish – they have to be still jumping when they hit the boiling water.

lime juice to make 'ceviche,' a dish common to many Latin American countries; it is also fried in batter as the 'conch fritters' sold on the streets.

Some seafood dishes are reputed to have special powers. If a woman wants to conceive a child, she and her husband are encouraged to eat *behave bruda* (behave brother), a soup made from snapper and ground foods with an entire grouper head thrown in (the eyes are said to be the most potent ingredient). If a man wants to increase his sexual prowess

Tequila-flamed shrimp steaks.

Shellfish, whose supply seemed limitless only a generation ago, now have strictly regulated harvesting seasons. Lobster, unavailable from mid-February to mid-June, has become a lucrative export and fetches handsome prices locally. Shrimp, with a closed season from mid-April to mid-August, is a little cheaper, especially the freshwater variety sold in Chinese restaurants, but is still a luxury for most. Shrimp farming is fast becoming a profitable business in Belize, but it is mainly for the export market. Conch (pronounced conk) is the most affordable and widely consumed shellfish, although unavailable from the beginning of July until the end of September. It is often chopped up and cooked in

or 'strengthen his back,' he should drink seaweed shakes or eat thick white conch soup. (Cowfoot Soup, which really is made of cow's feet, is another back-strengthening creation, particularly sought-after following a hard night of drinking – although the uninitiated may be put off by its gummy texture.)

FRUIT LOVER'S FANTASY

Some say it is because the colonial masters discouraged farming that the closest many creole families get to serving vegetables, even today, is from a can. If you are determined to taste a typical Belizean vegetable, however, try a wrinkled green squash called *cho-cho* (which is said to resemble a granny with her teeth out).

On the other hand, fresh fruit is everywhere in Belize. Street vendors sell everything from the familiar bananas, watermelon, papaya, and pineapples to exotica like *craboo* – small yellow balls that are often made into wine or ice cream – and hard little green plums topped with hot pepper and salt. Bags of pumpkin seeds, called *pepitos*, or macobi seeds are supposed to help keep your mind off a failed romance or absent lover.

Yellow cashew fruit is stewed with brown sugar (delicious!) or made into cashew wine.

fish' for evening 'tea.' Favorites include the small, flaky biscuits known as 'johnny cakes' (the original name for which may have been 'journey cakes,' because they travel well). These are best eaten hot with melting butter or slices of ham and cheese. 'Fry jacks' are also delicious. These are made of flour, lard, and baking powder – like a *tortilla*, then split in half and deep fried – good with refried beans and cheese.

You can't leave Belize without trying 'creole bread,' made in round dense loaves using

Freshly-harvested oranges.

During April and May, there are several varieties of mango, which can be eaten green (sliced and served with salt and pepper), served as chutney or eaten fresh when ripe and sweet. Plantains, rich in potassium, are often served with rice and beans or mashed to make Garífuna dishes like *fufu* or *matilda foot*. Coconut is also a key cooking ingredient, with every part used: the milk, the meat, the oil for frying and the husks for fuel.

BREADS AND SWEETS

Breads, buns, and other pastries are baked in Belizean kitchens almost daily, to be consumed in the morning with a cup of coffee or Ovaltine, or eaten with cheese, beans, or 'fry

coconut milk for extra flavor, and sometimes with a dash of cinnamon and a smattering of raisins. This is a favorite with hot tea in the evening.

Belizean desserts are rich, gooey and filled with calories. The sweetest of all is lemon pie, also known as 'merengay pie,' which has a rich filling of condensed milk and lime (not lemon) topped by light, fluffy meringue. There are coconut pies, tarts, and trifles, as well as coconut 'crusts,' made of grated coconut and brown sugar sealed in a flour shell and cooked over an open fire. Coconut candies include *cutubrut*, chopped coconut meat crystalized in brown sugar, and its cousin, *tableta*, made with shredded coconut. 'Stretch me guts' is a taffy-like confection created from a mixture of coconut water, lime, and sugar.

The British heritage emerges in desserts such as bread pudding, rice pudding, and 'potato pung,' a heavy cake made of grated sweet potatoes and sprinkled with brown sugar and ginger. Finally, Christmas is always greeted with rum-preserved fruit cakes and *rumpopo*, a sort of rum eggnog.

LIQUID REFRESHMENTS

Despite Belize's Central American location, Belizeans aren't great coffee drinkers. As you

corner shops. It comes in a variety of styles, from dark and rich to light and sparkling. Either way, you'll probably soon become a fan: There's nothing better than watching the sun set with your toes in the warm sand, reggae coming from the speakers, and a chilled Belikin in hand.

But the finest alcohol in Belize is undoubtedly rum. There are several local brands of rum, including Caribbean and Durleys (which is also called 'parrot rum' because of its company logo). One of the best, though, is Trav-

Cocktails in the Rum Bar at Copal Tree Lodge, Punta Gorda.

might expect in a former British colony, tea is the preferred hot brew, especially in the evenings. It is drunk with condensed milk and, although no one seems to know why, people traditionally knock the spoon against the side of the cup while stirring, to make a tinkling sound.

Many villagers pride themselves on their home-made wines – concocted from everything from berries and rice to cashew and sorrel. Wine making is becoming a thriving cottage industry, although locals generally drink wine only at Christmas.

The most successful Belizean beer, *Belikin*, with a Maya temple on the label, is consumed and sold everywhere, from local beach bars to

ellers One Barrel Rum. Travellers is Belize's oldest rum distillery, which was launched originally as a bar in 1953 by Jaime Omario Perdomo Sr. Why the name "Travellers"? Because, say the founders, the bar's customers were always traveling to somewhere else. For an overview of the rum's history (and, more importantly, a tasting), head to the Travellers Liquors Ltd. distillery just outside of Belize City (Mile 2.5 Philip Goldson Highway; www.onebarrelrum.com; Mon–Fri 8am–5pm), where you can peruse exhibits of old photos and vintage rum bottles, and observe the bottling factory. The tour also includes tastings of the famous One Barrel rum, along with flavored rums.

Diving amongst the coral and plantlife off Belize.

BENEATH THE WAVES

The Belize Barrier Reef is home to an underwater paradise of multicolored coral and a kaleidoscope of tropical fish.

At 185 miles (300km) in length, dotted with around 200 cayes, the Belize Barrier Reef is the second largest in the world after Australia's Great Barrier Reef. The variety of reef types and marine life within its borders is unequaled in the northern hemisphere.

Belizean waters are perfect for coral growth. Corals are surprisingly finicky, requiring warm, clear water, steady sunlight, and a shallow, firm foundation to grow on. The vast mass of marine life now following the Belizean coast actually grows on a prehistoric reef. This thrived more than a million years ago, when water was imprisoned in gigantic northern glaciers and sea levels were 300ft (90 meters) lower than they are today. The underlying Pleistocene reef structure contains many of the same coral species divers still see, as scientists found from cores drilled 175ft (53 meters) below the surface of present-day reefs.

Closer to the surface, at Reef Point on the northern shore of Ambergris Caye, lies further evidence of these ancient reefs. Here, portions of the Pleistocene coral reef intercept the shoreline in an area no larger than a football field. Sharp, skeletal remains of staghorn, elkhorn, and brain corals lie exposed, cemented together in a matrix of coral sands. During the winter, heavy surf pounds this coast, fracturing the ancient reef and tossing limestone fragments upon a 15ft (4.5-meter) rubble wall, but in calmer weather charter boats slip through a narrow channel from San Pedro. The eroding limestone and fossil corals conjure up images of prehistoric landscapes, but you don't have to go far to see the images come to life.

Big-eye squirrel fish.

DIVING ON THE REEF

South of Reef Point, the 'hard' coral begins to form a true barrier reef, snaking south into the Bay of Honduras. The reef is not one continuous wall of coral, but is splintered into segments separated by relatively deep channels. The oxygen and plankton carried by the Caribbean Sea flush the Belize coastal zone twice daily through these channels, feeding billions of hungry coral polyps and other reef creatures. Attracting large numbers of fish as a result, they are often excellent for diving and snorkeling (the most popular and accessible is Hol Chan Marine Reserve on Ambergris Caye).

There are more than 460 species of fish that a snorkeler or diver is likely to see while swimming over coral reefs. Though some look formidable, most fish are unconcerned by your presence. Barracudas for example, have an unnerving habit of approaching swimmers and following them about. This is pure curiosity – there has never been a report of an unprovoked attack by a barracuda, and they normally move away when approached. Eels have a nasty reputation, although they are generally non-aggressive. Alarmingly, they open and close their mouths as if preparing to bite, but they are merely pumping water through their gills.

But be careful: eels can inflict a painful bite if annoyed, especially the green moray eel.

Sharks are not commonly encountered in Belize, with the exception of the docile nurse shark. Chances are that sharks will sense you long before you see them, and move away. However, all sharks should be treated with caution. Even the normally docile nurse shark can become aggressive if harassed.

Probably the most serious underwater hazard is the long-spined urchin. Needlelike spines will pierce gloves or wet suits, and the tips easily

Turneffe Atoll.

⊘ ANATOMY OF THE REEF

The structural framework of a coral reef is limestone; upon this, billions of individual coral polyps form colonies, connected by living tissue. Each coral polyp essentially consists of a set of tentacles, a mouth, and a gut perched atop a limestone skeleton. The polyps have special cells on the outside of their bodies that secrete calcium carbonate.

As the colony grows, polyps build their skeletons from beneath, pushing themselves up or out into a myriad of sizes and shapes. Growth rates vary with different species and different conditions, but coral reefs in warm, tropical waters grow only about 5 ins (13cm) every century.

A coral reef, then, is actually a thin layer of life on top

of ever-growing pieces of limestone. When an inattentive swimmer or errant boat hits or brushes against a piece of coral, the damage may not be immediately apparent but the damaged piece of coral may allow disease or infection to develop. And since the entire colony is connected by living tissue, a small, seemingly inconsequential injury may eventually kill a whole colony that might have taken thousands of years to grow to its present size.

Other coral groups have forsaken a hard shell for a more flexible, internal skeleton. These 'soft' corals come in a range of hues – from yellows to reds and purples – and their trunks and branches create colorful underwater forests.

break off. Fire coral is a danger in shallow water: with a smooth surface and a uniform mustard color, it grows in two distinct forms, platelike or encrusting. Though it looks like one, fire coral is not a true coral. This hydrozoan has tiny silica needles that break off on contact and can cause intense stinging. Some sponges cause irritation, as do bristle worms.

The best way to avoid any potential problems when exploring the coral reef is never to touch anything – for your own safety and the health of the reef.

12 minor zones have been established along an east–west line north of Carrie Bow Caye. These zones include grass beds, where conch and striped grunts feed; reef flats, where crabs, small corals and anemones lie concealed among the rubble and sand; and spur and groove formations, where the coral grows in long linear mounds separated by coral sand gullies.

Moored as close as 10 miles (16km) off the Western Caribbean Barrier Reef lie three of the four coral atolls in the Caribbean:

Belize offers some fantastic snorkeling locations.

RESEARCH ON THE REEF

The basic structure of the Barrier Reef is similar all along its length. At Carrie Bow Caye, a marine lab perched atop the edge of the Barrier Reef, scientists from the Smithsonian Institution's National Museum of Natural History have divided the reef up into the basic zones, or habitats.

A zone is an area where local environmental conditions – temperature, sunlight, water movement – allow certain groups of animals and plants to exist together. Usually one or two species in the group are more abundant than the rest and are used to characterize a habitat. Starting from the shoreward, or western side of the Barrier Reef, four major and

⊘ PRESERVING THE REEF

Belize's astonishing marine environment – a colorful, living reef that stretches 185 miles (300km) from north to south – offers among the most exciting diving and snorkeling experiences in the world. Exploring the reef comes with responsibilities, however. Note, too, that the reef is more than just a fascinating glimpse into underworld flora and fauna – it's also vital to the country's survival. The Barrier Reef absorbs most of the surf shock from hurricanes, which annually sweep across the Caribbean, causing mass injury and devastation. To help preserve the reef, swim at least an arm's length away from coral and stay horizontal so as not to raise sediments, which may suffocate it or introduce diseases.

Turneffe Island, Glover's Reef and Lighthouse Reef. The origin of these atolls – shaped like underwater table-top mountains, with gardens of coral on the summit – is still a matter of speculation. Most geologists agree that the atolls grow over protrusions created by the movement of the tectonic plates of the region. The sequence of uplifting and sinking of the land masses has created magnificent underwater drop-offs, some plunging to depths of 10,000ft (3,000 meters) to the east of Lighthouse Reef.

Diving at Silver Cave, near Lighthouse Reef.

The reef systems surrounding these atolls rival the Western Caribbean Barrier Reef in length, with almost 140 miles (225km) of lush coral growth. Within the coral barrier surrounding the atolls lie thousands of patch reefs; in the case of Turneffe, the largest of Belize's atolls with an area of more than 200 sq miles (520 sq km), there are hundreds of small mangrovecovered islands. Together, these three atolls provide some of the finest wall diving in the world.

THE MANGROVE COASTLINE

Coral reefs do not exist in isolation. Mangroves line much of the Belizean coastline, the cayes and lower reaches of the rivers.

Seagrass beds, their blades swaying in the current like prairie meadows, blanket the sea bottom between reef and shore.

Mangrove and seagrass may not look as spectacular as coral reefs but, as giant marine nurseries, they form the foundation of the continuing long-term health of the Belize coastal zone. The quiet, protected water of the mangrove roots and grass blades provides plentiful food and shelter for countless juvenile marine organisms. In fact, most of the shellfish and the fish caught for food or sport off the Belize coast rely on mangroves for at least part of their lives.

Four different species of mangrove thrive in Belize – red, white, and black mangrove and buttonwood. As well as stabilizing the coastline against erosion and presenting a natural buffer against destructive hurricanes, mangroves link the rich nutrients on land with the billions of hungry mouths at sea. Every year, Belizean rivers transport tons of sediment to the sea from deep within the interior. The nutrients in these loads, deposited along the coast, are often in forms unavailable to marine life. But mangroves thrive on the frequent deposits, producing branches, leaves, and seeds.

When a mangrove leaf drops into the waters below, the process of decomposition begins. The leaf slowly releases thousands of minute particles, each coated with millions of voracious micro-organisms. Small invertebrates like worms, shrimp, and crabs begin to feed on the microbes; these small invertebrates are in turn eaten by larger creatures, until the nutrients in river silt are passed on through the food chain.

Many of these smaller fish also become prey for flocks of wading birds combing the surf line for food. Belize's coast has an abundance of water birds and nesting colonies, with more than 50 mangrove-covered cayes reported to have nesting sites on them. Roseate spoonbills, ibis, herons, and cormorants nest on many of the small mangrove islands in Chetumal Bay to the north. The magnificent frigate bird and brown boobies have established large nesting colonies on many cayes to the south. Man-O-War Caye, east of Dangriga, has one of the largest colonies of frigate birds in the Caribbean. Meanwhile, ospreys locate the highest trees on the cayes, usually black mangroves, to build their nests on top from piles of loose sticks.

A LIVING TREASURE

The entire coastal zone of Belize is a treasure of sea life, pristine and as yet mostly unexploited. Jewels of evolution are continually being found. For example, scientists from the Smithsonian Institution's marine lab on Carrie Bow Caye discovered a tiny bay that may be unique in the Caribbean – if not the world. A quirk of nature allows mangrove to grow on the edge of a series of deep sinkholes. Healthy colonies of lettuce coral carpet the steep slopes of the depressions. As the slopes rise into shallow water, the scene explodes

management of the area. The risk to any pristine environment cannot be overestimated. After all, these marine organisms evolved over millions of years within a stable or gradually changing environment. Any sudden stress – whether from pollution, siltation, overfishing or injuries from a careless diver – can be devastating. For a visitor, kicking a piece of coral is hardly noticed; for the coral it is a matter of life and death; for Belizeans it is slow destruction of a priceless resource.

The good news is that local and international organizations continue to monitor the reef, and

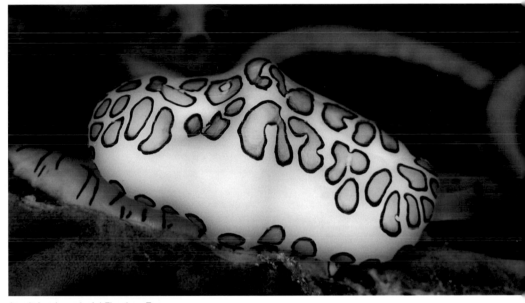

A weird and wonderful Flamingo Tongue.

into activity, with bright oranges and reds, deep purples and blues streaming past, and star and brain corals flourishing among seagrasses and mangrove trunks. Sponges, anemones, and tiny, barrel-shaped sea squirts cling to the prop roots, competing for the limited amount of space.

Smithsonian researchers have identified 43 different sea squirts in this one location, more than was previously known throughout the entire Caribbean. The fish are so abundant that they form layers, with the smaller fry near the surface, the larger ones a level down, and the fat-bodied herrings blanketing the carpet of lettuce coral. The location of this bay will stay a secret until scientists, the government and conservation groups within Belize can agree on the proper

are increasingly inviting volunteers to join in. A prime example: the non-profit Oceanic Society (www.oceanicsociety.org), founded in 1969 with the mission of preserving marine habitats worldwide, has set up a base in Turneffe Atoll. They offer 'volunteer vacations' where you can work alongside researchers to monitor and preserve the health of Turneffe Atoll's coral reefs. By day, you'll snorkel the reef and gather data on water quality and reef populations, and by night, take in lectures and presentations. The reef is the ultimate gauge of the environmental health of Belize, and in the end, it's organizations like this that will help ensure that visitors can enjoy Belize's astonishing natural bounty – while also doing their part to preserve it.

Red-eyed tree frog.

IN THE WILD

An abundance of exotic native species lives in Belize's vast areas of protected natural habitats.

For centuries, Belize's small population, limited agriculture and lack of industry doomed it to being a backwater of civilization. Today, it has the most accessible tropical wilderness in the Western hemisphere, and wildlife that lures travelers from around the world. Though not as biologically rich as the Amazon or Costa Rica, Belize, for its size, is unique in the number of different habitats and species within its borders.

The reason can be traced back to its climate and geological history. Set in the heart of Central America, Belize is part of a landmass bridging two great continents. This has not always been so. Around 100 million years ago, Belize formed part of an ancient archipelago, isolated from North and South America by primordial oceans. During this time of isolation, many animals evolved that were endemic, or native to the region.

Then, roughly 2 million years ago, giant continental plates began to grind against each other, thrusting up mountains. As water became imprisoned in the colossal ice sheets of the poles, the seas receded, exposing new land. Central America became a land bridge between North and South America, allowing a free flow of migration. The resultant mixture of endemic and immigrant creatures spawned one of the most varied faunas on earth.

Thanks to its complex geological history, Belize's landscape mixes mountains, savannahs, and coastal lagoons, while the tropical climate provides wet and dry seasons, hurricanes and heat. The resulting environmental mix creates an astonishing variety of animal and vegetable habitats: although only the size of New Hampshire in the United States, Belize has more than 4,000 species of flowering plants, including 250 orchids and more than 700 species of trees. In contrast,

Black panther.

the whole of the US and Canada supports only 730 species, giving Belize on average 1,000 times the diversity of trees per square mile.

Scientists have catalogued more than 70 kinds of forest in Belize, grouping them into three basic types: 13 percent are open forests of pine and savanna; 19 percent are mangroves and coastal habitats; and by far the largest type, 68 percent, is covered by broadleaf forests and cohune palms, the rainforests of Belize. This vegetation determines to a large extent what animals will thrive and where.

INTO THE RAINFORESTS

The broadleaf forests (rainforests) support by far the greater diversity of wildlife. They are the result of the most favorable possible conditions for life on land – abundant sunlight, warmth, and moisture. Most of the plants are trees, which grow to form a dense canopy overhead. Lower down are multiple layers of smaller trees and shrubs, tied together by twisting vines. Finally, leaves, fallen branches and fungi litter the forest floor, and are quickly broken down into minerals by soil decomposers and recycled through the forest. Each layer is an animal habitat in itself, allowing space for a multitude of creatures to evolve. The secret of the rainforest is that the majority of the nutrients are stored not in the soil at all, but in the biomass – the roots, trunks, leaves, flowers, and fruits, as well as the animals – of the forest.

Despite this, many visitors to the tropics are disappointed with the apparent lack of wildlife. Don't be. The animals are there. Most creatures of the rainforests perceive human intruders long before they themselves are noticed, and the seemingly solid wall of green provides innumerable hiding places. But to the patient, perceptive and informed visitor, the biological wealth of the forest eventually reveals itself.

Iguana and its offspring.

⊘ VITAL PRECAUTIONS

Though a naturalist's heaven, Belize can become purgatory for those ill-informed about the dangers of tropical wildernesses, so stay safe by following a few simple rules:

Don't go alone. All forests begin to look alike once you're off the trail, and if you chase a bird or a red-eyed tree frog into the forest, it can be very easy to lose your orientation. It's best to hire a licensed guide; carry a spare flashlight at night.

Stay on the trails. You are not only less likely to get lost, but also much less likely to stumble over nasties such as the deadly fer-de-lance and coral snakes that live among the litter of the forest floor. (Don't panic: most snakes are non-poisonous, and all will avoid you if they can.)

Watch where you place your hands and feet. Some palm trees have needle-like thorns sticking out horizontally from their trunks, which will cause a nasty wound. Avoid unexpected meetings with snakes by looking to see what's on the other side before stepping over fallen logs. And check for ants before sitting down.

Carry sunscreen. You need only leave the protection of the broadleaf canopy for a short time to get burned.

The multitude of insects in Belizean forests is generally more of a nuisance than a serious hazard; but see page 233 for information on how to avoid the more disagreeable species.

Midday is a poor time to visit the rainforest. The heat of the overhead sun and the stillness of the air force most creatures into the shade, and humans should probably follow suit: the chainsaw buzz of flies and cicadas, along with the heat and humidity, make walking hard work. For birdwatchers, the best time is sunrise, when the air is cool and filled with the sounds of birds feeding and declaring territories. (See page 95.)

On the ground, it's easiest to spot leafcutter ants, also known as 'wee wee' ants, carrying a load of leaves along the wide, clean highways they've cleared on the forest floor. The pieces of leaf are carried into huge underground chambers, where they are chewed and processed to grow fungus. The fungus in turn feeds the ants. This incredible relationship is so finely evolved that the fungus can no longer reproduce without the ants. Of the reptiles, the most easily spotted are snakes: of Belize's 54 species, 45 are harmless to humans, and even the most poisonous are as eager to avoid you as you are them. Staying on trails is probably the surest way to stay clear of snakes; unless you are sure of identification, do not attempt to handle them.

RAINFOREST NIGHTS

After the sun sets, the rainforests come alive with the creeping, the crawling and the jumping, making it the perfect time to scrutinize vegetation on well-marked trails. Red eyed tree frogs, gaudily colored lizards, and delicate salamanders awaken and roam the blackness.

Insects abound in an astonishing array of shapes and sizes. Spiders are one of the most conspicuous creatures encountered at night, the glinting reflections from their multiple eyes visible up to 50ft (15 meters) away. Delicate crickets, iridescent beetles, and mantis prowl the night in search of a meal. Many insects sport antennae two to three times their body lengths, using touch in the inky blackness to catch or avoid becoming prey.

Night is also the best time to view mammals. Bats dart above trails, gathering insects and startling hikers. Armadillos, opossums, and anteaters are nocturnal, foraging along the stream banks and fallen logs of the forest. Most nocturnal animals have large eyes to see by moon or starlight, so pointing a flashlight at rustling in the leaves often produces eyeshine.

The paca, known as gibnut in Belize, is a nocturnal rodent the size of a large rabbit, often heard chewing on cohune nuts and thrashing around the litter of the forest floor at night. It has a large head sprouting from a chestnut-colored body with four distinctive lines of white spots running along its back. This small animal, with enlarged cheeks, often gives out a hoarse bark or deep grumbling. Gibnut meat is a favorite item in traditional Belizean restaurants, and it is also a favorite prey of the five species of Belizean wildcats.

The reclusive jaguarundi.

FAMOUS FELINES

As Central America's largest spotted cat, the jaguar is probably the most celebrated creature of the rainforest, and Belize has created the world's first wildlife sanctuary specifically for the jaguar's protection (see pages 91 and 191). But roaming beneath the rainforest canopy and along the banks of mountain streams, four other wildcats share the same territory as the jaguar – the jaguarundi, the margay, ocelot, and puma. Though all are endangered throughout their ranges, Belize supports healthy populations of each. That five species of cat, so similar in their ecological needs, can coexist and thrive within the same rainforest is a tribute to the health of the Belizean habitat.

Smallest of the wildcats (and most abundant), the jaguarundi moves like a fleeting shadow. The long, lanky body, slender tail, and short legs make the jaguarundi unmistakable. No bigger than a house cat, this wildcat feeds mainly during the day on small rodents, birds and insects.

The margay is the most nocturnal of the cats: its large eyes and very bright, reflective eye-shine attest to its highly developed night vision. Superlative balance and great leaping ability – one researcher recorded a vertical leap of 8ft 2ins (2.48 meters) – make the margay ideally

Howler monkey.

The ocelot's name comes from the ancient Aztec word tlalocelotl, meaning 'field tiger,' although it generally prefers secondary growth or recently cut forests.

adapted for life in the forest canopy. Smallest of the spotted cats, the margay prefers primary or old growth forests and is rarely seen in the wild.

Known locally as the "tiger cat" (a name also used for the margay), the ocelot is about the size of a medium dog. It keeps to the forest floor, feeding occasionally on larger prey such as anteaters and brocket deer. Due to its

exceedingly soft and beautiful spotted pelt, the ocelot was hunted nearly to extinction around Central America to produce fur coats.

While the jaguar inhabits lowland forests near streams and swamps, the puma, known as cougar or mountain lion in the US, prefers the highlands and drier ridge areas of the forest. The puma is extremely shy and secretive and probably the least likely to be seen.

THE CALL OF THE WILD

Another celebrated inhabitant of the Belizean rainforest is the black howler monkey, whose guttural cry is often mistaken for the roar of a jaguar. "Baboons," as they are known in Belize, live in troops of four to eight, carving out a territory of between 12 and 15 acres (5–6 hectares). They defend their territories from intruding troops by using their remarkable voices to let other troops know their location. Howlers often begin and end their days by roaring, and the noise can carry for several miles.

The black howler monkey's range is limited to southern Mexico, northern Guatemala and Belize, but the populations are rapidly declining due to increasing deforestation throughout Central America. Belize supports one of the last strongholds of the baboon in the region: at the Community Baboon Sanctuary, a grassroots project where landowners agree to manage their properties to benefit the baboons, there are an estimated 2,000 monkeys. The roaring is deafening at sunrise and sunset around the sanctuary. A project is now underway to transfer howler monkeys from the sanctuary to some of their former homes, including the Cockscomb Basin Wildlife Sanctuary.

SAVANNAH AND PINE FORESTS

In contrast to the mountainous tumble of rainforests blanketing the interior of Belize are its many areas of flat, relatively dry savannah. With the exception of the pinelands covering the Mountain Pine Ridge in the Cayo District, much of the savannahs, locally referred to as 'broken ridge,' occur along the level lowlands of the north and the coastal strip east of the Maya Mountains.

The coastal road (also known as the Manatee Road), between Belize City and Dangriga meanders through some of the most beautiful savannahs in Belize, flanked on the coast by mangrove forests, and inland by some of the country's largest citrus fruit plantations. Islands of limestone, surrounded by oceans of wind-blown grasses and gnarled trees, attest to the harshness of the habitat.

Savannah flora in Belize evolved to take advantage of the extremes of climate and soil. The plants must deal with alternate water-logging during the rainy season and severe drought during the dry season. The savannah soils are generally acidic and nutrient-poor, allowing only hardy plants like craboo, oaks, and palmettos to flourish. (The craboo is a small tree with tiny, yellow flowers that turn red with age. The fruit – cherry-

plants are often referred to as pyrophytes, meaning they are adapted to frequent burning. However, not all fires start by natural causes. Though the practice is discouraged, hunters will often start fires to flush deer and other game. Fire is not the only threat. In the Mountain Pine Ridge Forest Reserve trees have been devastated by the Pine Bark Beetle – many have died, while others have been clear-cut to stop the spread of the infestation.

Despite the often scorched, inhospitable appearance of the savannahs, many species of mammal forage there. Most commonly seen is the

Baird's tapir.

sized and also yellow – is a favorite of Belizeans, used in jams, ice cream, and wine.)

As the name suggests, Caribbean pine is a prominent feature of pine and savannah woodlands. Driving along stretches of the Northern Highway, the new coastal road and much of the Southern Highway, formations of pine align themselves like silent sentries awaiting review. Many of these pines have scorched trunks, blackened by fire – usually lit by lightning strikes in the spring and early summer. The fires start atop dead pines or in the tinder-like grass and may burn and smolder for days. The thick bark of the pines allows many of the trees to survive, while the underground root system of the grasses and shrubs allow them to re-sprout. In fact, savannah

gray fox, one of the most abundant mammals in Belize, and one that often darts in front of cars or sprints along the side of the road before dodging into roadside vegetation. About the size of a house cat, with a large bushy tail, this member of the dog family feeds on small rodents and birds; it is an excellent climber, spending much of the hot midday in the shade and breeze of the upper branches of the forest. Often seen after a fire is the white-tailed deer, emerging during early morning and browsing for tender new shoots. Though some luck is required to spot mammals in the pine and savannah woodlands, the wide, open spaces are ideal for bird-watching – more than 100 species are common. The striking vermilion flycatcher, a sparrow-sized, bright-red bird, is often seen 'hawking' or making repeated sorties to nab flying insects on the wing. The fork-tailed flycatcher, another unmistakable inhabitant of the savannahs, has 10in (25cm) long tail feathers called 'streamers,' which provide increased maneuverability for catching insects flushed up by fires. Often, coveys of quail explode from the tall grasses lining roads in the broken ridge.

By far the most spectacular bird of the savannah and pine habitat is the jabiru, largest stork in the Americas. Standing nearly 5ft (1.5 meters) tall, the jabiru is entirely white except for a black head and

coastline and lower reaches of the rivers are lined by three different species of mangrove.

The most common and distinctive is the red mangrove, found in frequently or permanently saturated areas. Numerous stilt-like prop roots arch from the main trunk into the soft mud, while aerial roots drip down from the branches, providing additional support in the loose sediments. The red mangrove seed sprouts while still on the tree, forming a 10in (25cm) spear that, when released, embeds itself into the soft mud or sand below.

Three-toed anteater.

Saltwater crocodile.

a red band around the neck; it constructs a distinctive 8ft (2.4-meter) diameter nest atop a lone pine, often visible from a mile away. In pre-protection days, this exposed nest made the endangered stork easy prey for hunters, and jabiru meat was often peddled in Belize City markets. Now protected, the jabiru's figure graces the back of Belizean $20 bills.

MANGROVE AND COASTAL HABITATS

Near the coast, savannahs and pine woodlands often blend into brackish water swamps and lagoons shared by mangroves. Though not requiring saltwater to survive, mangroves grow better in salt and brackish water than other terrestrial plants. Long stretches of the Belizean

Swallow Caye Wildlife Sanctuary (www. swallowcayemanatees.org) has a healthy population of West Indian manatees, as well as bottlenose dolphins. The sanctuary is open to guided visits, some of which depart from Ambergris Caye and Caye Caulker.

The black mangrove is found in slightly drier areas. The soft sediment around the tree trunks is punctured with armies of spiky projections (pneumatophores) which rise above the soil or water to assist the plant with gas exchange.

Found on still drier ground are white mangroves, with oval leaves that sport a pair of salt glands for exuding excess salts at their stems. Bunches of wrinkled, grape-sized seeds crowd the outer branches. After dropping, the seeds are dispersed by currents.

The easiest way to see mangroves is by taking a short boat ride up the Belize River from Belize City, where they form a majestic, cathedral-like tunnel over Haulover Creek. But mangroves reach their greatest size along the lower reaches of the remote Temash River in the

Like most herbivores, they are normally slow and lumbering, but can exhibit tremendous bursts of speed when startled, leaving behind swirls of mud.

A long history of harvesting manatee has led to a general population decline. Manatee meat was once an ingredient in the diet and ceremonial activities of the Maya. In the 19th century, logwood cutters relished the manatee meat; the tails were reportedly pickled and eaten cold, while the tough skin was made into durable boot soles. As recently as the 1930s, manatee meat was sold in local markets.

Fer-de-lance.

Toledo District (see page 208). Here, red mangrove trunks send up 10–15ft (3–5-meter) high stilt roots, forming open forests of arches.

MANATEES AND CROCODILES

Compared to other ecosystems in Belize, mangrove wildlife is not diverse or abundant. In fact, few terrestrial animals are restricted only to mangroves. Yet two endangered animals, the American crocodile and the West Indian manatee, rely on the mangrove environment.

Manatees are vast, docile and amiable creatures that are found all along the Belizean coastline, in lagoons and brackish water. They can easily grow to 15ft (4.5 meters) and 3,500lbs (1,585kg), the only marine mammals that feed primarily on plants.

⊘ FOREST GIANT

Belize's national animal, Baird's tapir, known locally as the 'mountain cow,' is the largest creature in the forest. Although weighing up to 650lbs (300kg), tapirs can dissolve silently into the forest at the first sign of danger. A distinctive feature of these tapirs is their long prehensile lip, used to forage for leaves.

Tapirs prefer rainforest rivers and swamps, although they can survive in just about any other habitat. Despite their adaptiveness, the tapir is endangered throughout its range (Mexico to Ecuador) by hunting and deforestation. Belize is one of the last remaining strongholds of this magnificent mammal.

Today, manatees enjoy special protection, and the population is no longer declining: in fact Belize has the largest population in the Americas. But, while hunting has been controlled, water and noise pollution are taking their toll: increased boating and fishing activities have damaged the manatee's coastal habitat and are affecting their numbers.

The American crocodile feeds on fish, crabs, birds, and small mammals, and can grow to lengths of 22ft (7 meters). During the dry season, females build nesting mounds, depositing up to 60 eggs inside. The eggs hatch near the start of the

Nephila spiders (3ins/7.5cm long) spin golden webs to capture the abundant flying insects, while clouds of dragonflies dart through the open spaces as though locked in aerial combat. Fiddler crabs and 1ft (30cm) long great land crabs continually churn up the nutrient-rich soil. Though relatively poor in diversity, a mangrove forest remains a crucible of birth and decay.

SMALL BUT NASTY

Not all wildlife in Belize is a wonder to behold, in particular some of its insects, though they are not

Jumping spider.

wet season and the parents often feed and protect the newly hatched young for some weeks after.

The American crocodile is much less aggressive than its much-maligned cousin, the American alligator, which has overrun southern Florida. The crocodile typically shuns human activity. But despite its shyness and a thick hide which protects it from most natural predators, the American crocodile is threatened across its range by hunting and habitat destruction. The mangrove and coastal habitats of Belize are one of the last remaining strongholds of this magnificent reptile.

Other above-water life in the mangroves is not quite as spectacular. The mangrove warbler, a tiny yellow bird with a rust-colored head, hops from roots to branches, picking up ants and flies.

generally the holiday-destroying nuisance they can be in other parts of the tropics. Most insect problems are solved by applying insect repellent during the day and draping mosquito netting around you while sleeping. Lightweight, long trousers and shirts will protect you from insects and the occasional scrape – infections thrive in the humid tropics.

Finally, always check your shoes or boots and shake out your clothes before dressing: scorpions, though generally rare, can be locally common, especially around San Ignacio. Some of these are about 6ins (15cm) long and shiny, metallic black – but are not deadly. This may not be much comfort if one strolls into your room at night, and even the most avid eco-tourist has been known to pick up a heavy book and crush an intruding scorpion.

Belize's national reserves and parks make it an eco-tourism paradise.

Belize Audubon Society

The Belize Audubon Society (BAS; www.belizeaudubon.org), formed in 1969, is Belize's foremost environmental organization. It aims to maintain a balance between the needs of the nation's people and the environment through sustainable management of natural resources and public education programs. The society manages more than 192,000 acres (77,000 hectares) of protected land in nine separate areas, including Crooked Tree Wildlife Sanctuary, Guanacaste National Park, St Herman's Blue Hole National Park, Cockscomb Basin Wildlife Sanctuary, Blue Hole Natural Monument, and Victoria Peak National Monument. The society engages with communities bordering on the protected zones, offering training in tourism-oriented services, such as scuba-diving and tour guiding, and providing vital environmental education. Looking to do your part for the environment? The BAS offers volunteer opportunities throughout the country. Volunteers will need to cover their own expenses, and commit to a minimum of three weeks. You can sign up via the website.

With the help of a guide, trail systems can be explored throughout Belize on horseback, mountain bike, or on foot.

Unesco has awarded World Heritage status to the Belize Barrier Reef, and miles of these delicate ecosystems have been designated as marine reserves.

Sea kayaking, Tobacco Caye.

Great egrets.

A BIRD-WATCHER'S PARADISE

Belize's tropical location and wide range of pristine habitats attract a remarkable number of bird species.

The great appeal of birdwatching in Belize isn't just the astonishing variety – at last count, over 590 different species – but the fact that these winged creatures are readily visible throughout the country. Belize has plenty of highly elusive wildlife, like the jaguar, but its resident birds? They're not elusive at all: you'll see them everywhere, from your breezy wooden deck in a jungle lodge to strolling on the beach in the cayes to trekking through the rainforest.

Bring a pair of binoculars and some good walking shoes, and start your quest. In fact, even Belize City is a good starting point: There are nearly one hundred species of birds in and around the city alone. Favored locations are the Fort Point area by the Baron Bliss Lighthouse, the marshy lands around St. John's College, wetlands by the Port Authority and Customs, or the grounds of the House of Culture (former Government House). It's even more fun when you learn the local creole names like 'georgie bull,' 'pyam-pyam,' 'banana bird,' or 'shaky batty' (a little bird that bobs its rear end up and down).

With relative ease, you may see everything from ordinary blackbirds (or grackles) to the vibrant banana birds (known elsewhere as orioles). These beautiful little birds are hard to find in the trees; you're more likely to spot one as it swoops down to catch an insect.

You'll probably hear the pyam-pyam (brown jay) before you see it because this bird is a real busybody, chattering or 'talking' whenever someone passes by. In Belize, anyone who talks a lot, or makes comments about others is said to be 'going on like a pyam-pyam.' The tropical mockingbird is also very

The colorful keel-billed toucan.

noisy and is very protective of its young. During the nesting season, they have been known to dive-bomb small children and people with light-colored hair, so watch out.

Like the mocking-bird, the georgie bull (jacana) can be very aggressive, but only with males of his own species. These birds have spurs on their wings, rather than on their legs, so that when two males fight they look like they are boxing. But these macho creatures also have a softer side, for it is the male that hatches the eggs, not the female.

Also common within the city limits are several species of humming-birds, giant flycatchers (kiskadee), royal and sandwich terns, brown boobies, little blue herons, gaulins (egrets), scissor-tails (magnificent frigates), laughing gulls (sea gulls), and kites.

INTO THE COUNTRYSIDE

If you want to join a tour, or take a drive out of town, you can find hundreds of birds along the Northern Highway en route to the Maya ruins at Altun Ha and the Community Baboon Sanctuary in Bermudian Landing.

From the road and down by the Belize River, you're sure to see gaulins (egrets), with their long white necks, and several species of hawks and kites circling above, looking for live prey.

The John Crow (king vulture) is also common in this area. Four species may be spotted along the highway alone. Because they live on garbage heaps and hover near rotting animal carcasses, these ugly birds are so scorned by Belizeans they are even the subject of several piquant creole proverbs (for example: *Ebrey John Crow tink 'e picney white* – Every black bird thinks his children are white, meaning, no one sees the flaws in his own child). Any chicken or game bird

Ocellated turkey.

Ornate hawk eagle.

⊘ BIG BIRD

Belize's largest bird, the jabiru stork, stands about 4ft (1.2 meters) tall and, with its wide wing-span, looks like a small airplane when it is taking off. Jabiru adults are efficient providers, and have been seen carrying snakes, rats and lizards up to their young nesting in the ceiba trees. They also transport water (siphoning it into their beaks), which they spray on their chicks, or give them to drink. Unlike the adults, which are mostly white, jabiru young have matted gray feathers that resemble those of a sick or dying bird, perhaps intended to discourage predators or in order to blend in more completely with their background.

that tastes tough is also ridiculed as being 'John Crow.' Nevertheless, the unsightly vultures are essential in maintaining the web of life, just as much as the most flamboyant bird species.

The **Crooked Tree Wildlife Sanctuary** (also off the Northern Highway, see page 138) is a truly great place to find birds since the nearby lagoon attracts hundreds of migratory and resident species. This sanctuary is a special treat in the springtime, when waterways begin to shrink, serving to concentrate large numbers of birds. The brightly colored jacana can walk upon the softest mud with its extraordinarily long toes. Migrant white pelicans mingle with tiger herons, limpkins and hordes of great egrets.

Guanacaste National Park near Belmopan is another favorite stop for naturalists and birdwatchers (see page 159). Just off the Western Highway and easily accessible by car or bus, Guanacaste has many varieties of hardwood trees and hundreds of birds including flycatchers, tanagers, yellow bill cacique, and bamboo clappers (motmots).

Motmots can also be found at just about any archeological site because they dig their nest burrows in the limestone 'hillsides' formed by unexcavated Maya temples. A nesting motmot burrows a tunnel, then turns 90 degrees and makes a cavity in which to lay her eggs. (If you're lucky, you may see one of these little birds poking its head around the corner.)

GLORIES OF THE TOUCAN

Keel-billed toucans and their smaller cousins, the toucanets, are also common near archeological sites and wooded areas. Belizeans love this colorful creature so much they have made it the national bird.

The placid nature of the pelican has inspired the creole proverb: Sea breeze always blow pelikin wey 'e wan go (The pelican goes wherever the breeze takes him.)

The toucan's image is everywhere, from billboards to T-shirts. There's even a brand of matches bearing the name. Although images of majestic red and blue macaws are also plentiful in the commercial art of Belize, seeing the real thing is a little more difficult. These long-tailed birds reside mainly in the forested areas of the Maya Mountains, accessible via the Mountain Pine Ridge Road, or the back country of the Cockscomb Basin Wildlife Sanctuary; however the best place to see them is in the area of the Maya village of Red Bank in the southern Stann Creek District. It is best to rely on a guide to help you find them between late December to late March, while they feed on the copious fruits of the area. There are reportedly less than 100 pairs of these brilliant-plumaged yet raucous- voiced members of the parrot family remaining in

Belize. If you want to stay in Red Bank, you could contact Programme for Belize (www.pfbelize.org), the wildlife association, which has a tourist facility here, with lodging and good local food.

The other eight species of parrot, including the tiny Aztec parakeets (actually conures, to be correct), are generally more common, with the exception of the endemic Yucatán parrot, which may only be seen in the far north of Belize. In the wild, parrots are active from dawn until dusk so Belizeans describe a job

Yellow-headed parrot.

requiring long hours as 'working from polly to polly.' These smart birds take advantage of nests or holes created by other animals such as termites: often they simply enlarge an existing nest in a dead tree to suit their own purposes.

While it is not illegal in Belize to take parrots from trees to keep in the home, it is against the law to take a polly out of the country. But because they are so popular in the United States, there have been horror stories of smugglers drugging the birds and trying to pass them through American customs in everything from suitcases to plastic piping. Although there are very stiff jail sentences in the US for wildlife smugglers, the practice has proven difficult to stamp out. The sad fact is that this activity results in considerable mortality to the smuggled birds, while increasing the likelihood of spreading avian diseases such as psittacosis. If you must buy a pet parrot, be sure to buy it from a recognized breeder.

In contrast to the clever parrot, the 'who you?' (the common pauraque, also known as the whip-or-will) appears to be rather stupid: these birds like to sit in the middle of the road and are occasionally hit by cars. You can eas-

Frigate birds.

ily spot them during night walks by holding your flashlight up next to your eyes, thereby catching reflected eyeshine from the birds. Owls and potoos may also be spotted in this fashion.

Wetland birds such as rail species ('top knot chick' or 'gallinola') are usually a challenge to see due to their secretive habits; however, the large gray-necked woodrail may be observed along riverbanks during canoe trips on various rivers. Other species to look for in the bush are the owl (barn and spectacled), hawk eagles (which are very rare), and the colorful trogons (which are related to the quetzal of Guatemala), which may sit motionless in a tree and make its distinctively repetitive

call. Game birds include the ocellated turkey, the crested guan, and the great curassow. All these birds, save six species, including the latter two, are protected from hunting in Belize.

Curassows and guans are common only in protected areas, where hunting is prohibited; hunters say that the male and female curassow mate for life and are so devoted that when one is shot, the other expires soon after.

BIRDS OF THE SEA

Along the coast or out at the cayes, you can't miss the brown pelican perched on piers or flying in formation, often riding the wind low and close to the waves.

Laughing gulls (the only gull species common in Belize) are also everywhere, especially in populated areas; piratical magnificent frigate birds – notorious kleptoparasites – occasionally swoop down upon an unlucky tern or cormorant and divest it of its food. The fish-hawk, or osprey, is particularly exciting to watch as he skims the surface of the water to pluck up a fish with his outstretched talons.

The best places to search for sea birds is on Caye Caulker, San Pedro (many migrants stay north of the village) and at Half Moon Caye Natural Monument. Caye bush or littoral forest, and mangroves, are essential habitat for many species of birds, both residents and migrant. Some of these species include the black catbird, Yucatán vireo, white-crowned pigeon, and rufous-necked woodrail. There is even a thriving population of the Cozumel variety of the nectar-feeding bananaquit. Because of the distance and expense involved, the reserve at Half Moon is mostly frequented by divers, but excursions are occasionally available for birdwatchers who want to see the island's huge colony of red-footed boobies.

There are also several small mangrove cayes that have been declared bird sanctuaries due to the fact that they support nesting populations of wood storks, three species of egrets and two kinds of herons, as well as white ibis, magnificent frigate birds, and anhingas, known as devil or snake birds.

BELIZE AUDUBON SOCIETY

Belize's remarkable legacy of environmental conservation is thanks in large part to the tireless efforts of The Audubon Society, which continues to lead the way for a sustainable future.

Bringing educational programs into schools, advocating on important development issues, working with communities, promoting bird-watching in Belize – these may sound like a full plate for any conservation NGO. However, for the Belize Audubon Society (BAS; www.belizeaudubon.org) it is just the beginning. The major mandate for this highly influential organization is actually protected area management.

Founded in 1969 by a group of Belizean families interested in birds and other wildlife issues, BAS at first provided people with similar interests an opportunity to meet and formulate field trips. However, its mandate grew with the advent of natural history-based tourism, then known as 'ecocultural' tourism. In the early 1980s, BAS received a mandate from the government to manage several protected areas in the country.

In the early years, funding was slow to arrive; as the number of protected areas grew, so did their needs – Belize did not want to be home to 'paper parks' (sanctuaries that exist in laws but have no on-site management). In the late 1980s funding for the expanding role of the society came from international donors and the Belizean Government awarded a house on North Front Street, in Belize City, to serve as headquarters for the organization.

One of the most important attributes of BAS policy is its commitment to local recruitment and involvement in sanctuary management in an effort to learn from mistakes made by early conservation attempts that tended to disregard local people, who thereby had little incentive to abide by management strategies.

CHRISTMAS BIRD COUNT

A notable tradition maintained by BAS from its inception is participation in a Christmas Bird Count. These counts are accomplished by Audubon Society members far and wide, from Nome, Alaska, to Panama, and can provide interesting data on general bird population trends over the long term in addition to providing members and interested guests with an excuse to spend an entire day in search of birds. Count areas are circles of 15 miles (24km) diameter, broken up into sections to be covered by counting parties. Coverage is affected by such factors as number of participants, accessibility of areas and transportation.

The first area to be set in Belize begins roughly 12 miles (19km) up the northern highway and includes diverse habitat such as farms, forest, creeks, and coastal mangroves and forest. The second includes portions of the Western and Hummingbird

Bird-watchers at Laguna Seca, near Chan Chich Lodge.

Highways, with both forested and farmed territory. Another area is centered at Gallon Jug, within the Río Bravo Conservation Area, comprising high forest and some open agricultural land. Another area is Punta Gorda, which frequently boasts the highest number of species recorded.

Since its inception, BAS has vastly improved its management presence and techniques, assisted by finance from the European Union. A growing number of national parks and other protected areas in Belize are managed by BAS; contact the society before your trip to learn about these outstanding examples of Belizean habitat. BAS also welcomes foreign membership and participation in Birdathons, held during spring and autumn migrations.

Arriving at Tobacco Caye.

Scuba diving excursion, Half
Moon Caye.

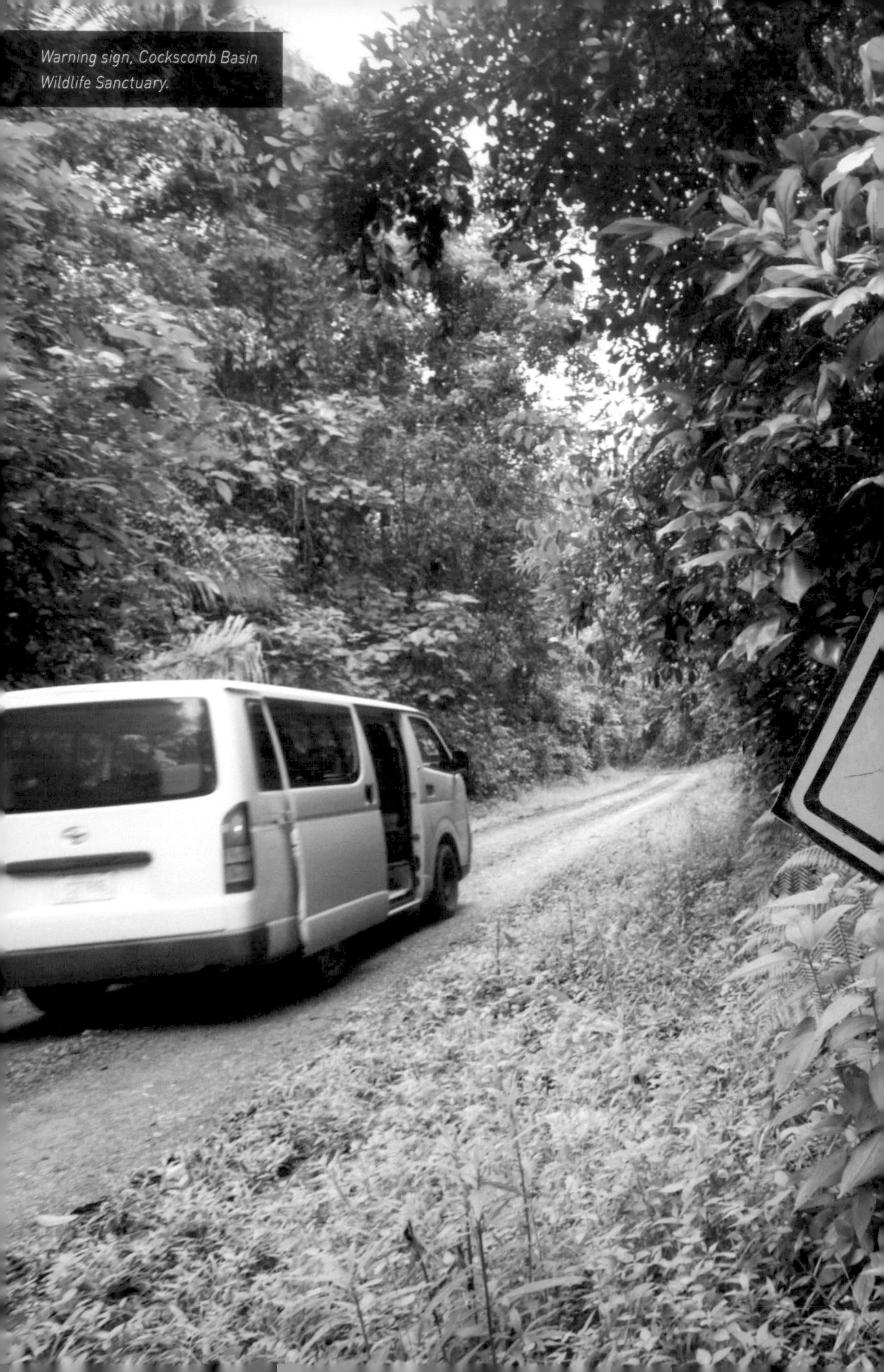

Warning sign, Cockscomb Basin Wildlife Sanctuary.

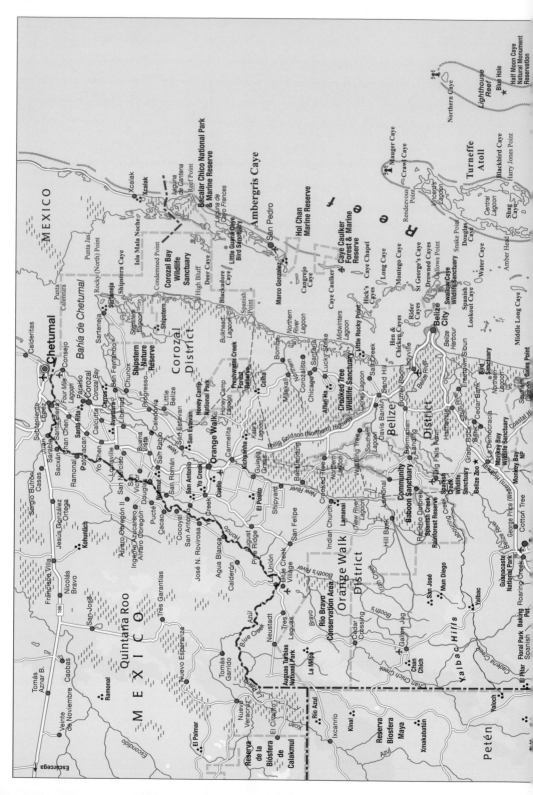

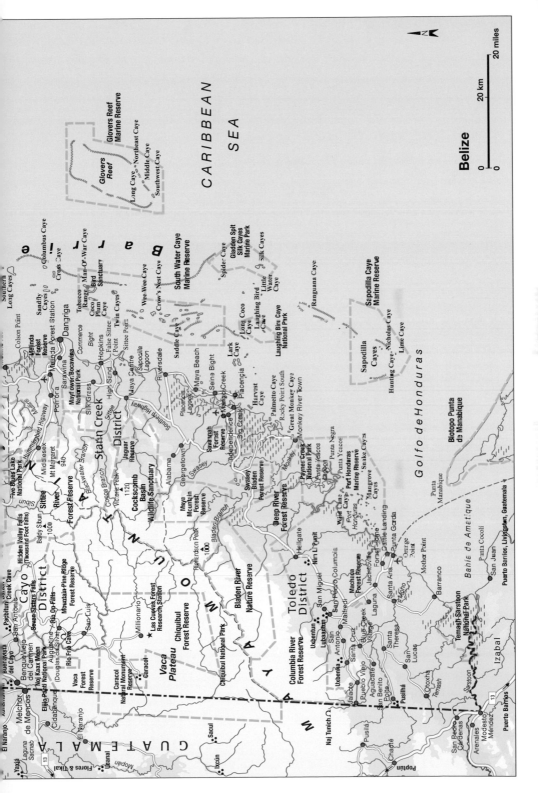

Belize

CARIBBEAN SEA

Golfo de Honduras

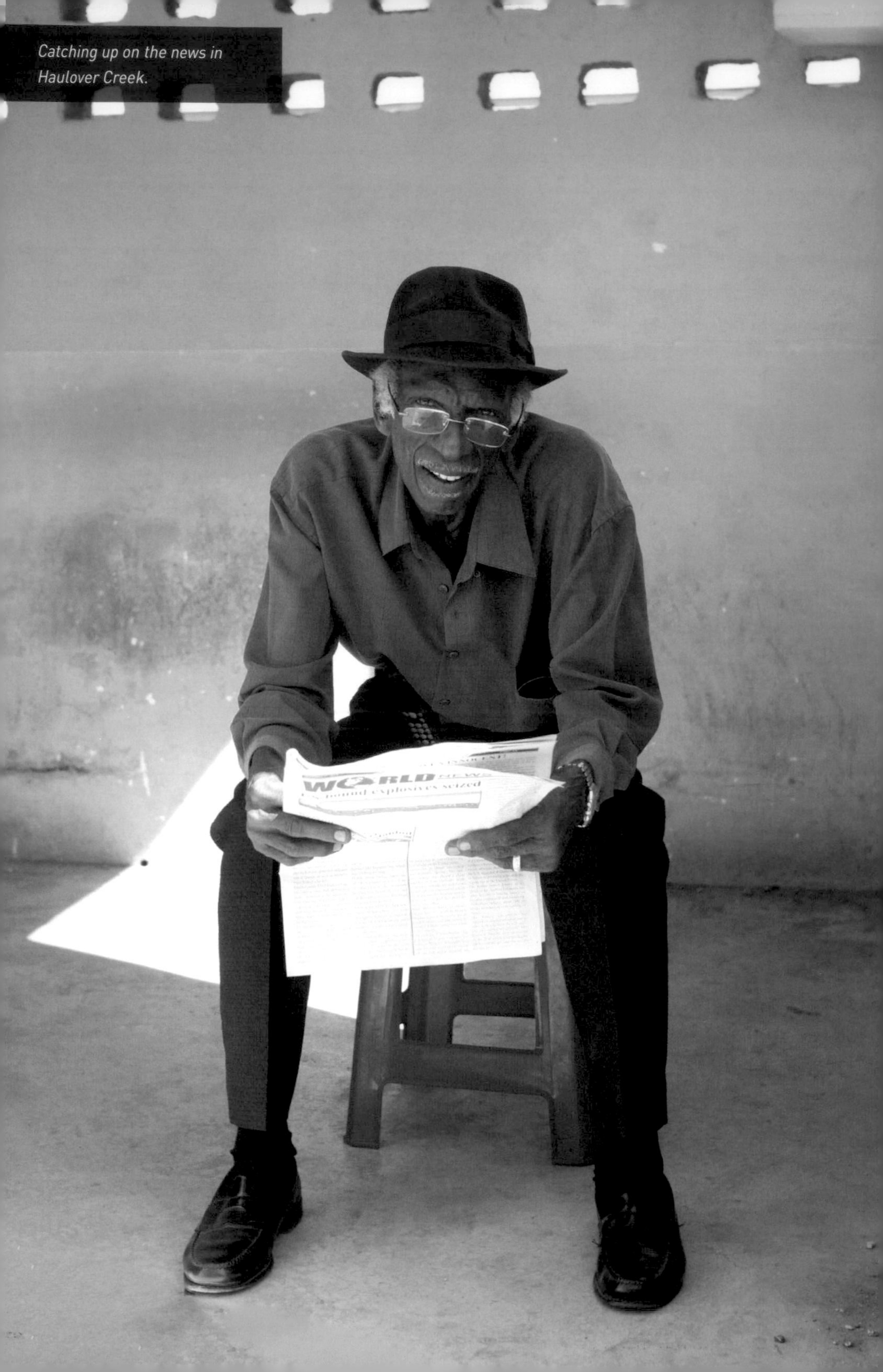

Catching up on the news in Haulover Creek.

INTRODUCTION

A detailed guide to the entire country, with principal sites clearly cross-referenced by number to the maps.

Tobacco Caye.

Belize may be tiny, but it can claim plenty of superlatives, from the longest barrier reef in the Western Hemisphere to among the most important Maya sites in the world. Add to that a tangled rainforest crisscrossed with ancient caves, roaring rivers, and crystal pools, as well as the lively sun-warmed cayes, where you can sip rum cocktails with your toes planted in the sand, and it s easy to see why this is a country that enjoys many repeat visitors: one taste is rarely enough.

Belize City is the vibrant hub, the whole nation under one roof, distilled down into this bustling, ramshackle port town by the Caribbean Sea.

North of the city, riverside creole communities left slumbering since the end of the logging industry in the 1960s are waking up and breathing new life into Belize's environmental treasure chest. Here amid the vast wetlands and pristine rainforest, you'll spy more wildlife in one day than in most other parts of the world in a year.

In the forested northwest, Maya cities hidden for centuries by the jungle are being further unearthed, their mysteries painstakingly studied by teams of archeologists from around the world.

Ceiba tree.

Heading west into the hills around San Ignacio, a welcome drop in temperature is accompanied by a booming network of comfortable jungle lodges. Pump up the adrenalin by tubing down wild rivers, followed by horseback rides up to mountain summits for sweeping views of the jungle canopy. Capped by the Mountain Pine Ridge, home of the great Maya city of Caracol, the region has become Belize's main inland eco-tourism center.

Placencia is blessed with the country's finest beaches, but even with the recent tourist influx, the locals retain a defiantly laid-back lifestyle. More adventurous souls can head for the interior of the far south and Belize's only true tropical rainforest, where Maya villages coexist with nature in a way that has not changed in thousands of years.

Finally, and the undisputed highlight for most visitors to Belize, are the cayes (pronounced 'keys'), a necklace of islands strung the length of the coral reef. Unforgettable islands, the cayes range from upbeat tourist spots to stranded desert isles offering the best diving, snorkeling, and fishing.

Boats in the harbor, Belize City.

BELIZE CITY

Belize City's rough and tumble exterior belies its treasures, which include the country's top museums, beautifully restored historical buildings, and a premiere performing arts center.

Most travelers see just one small corner of Belize City: the airport. The majority of visitors fly in to Belize, and promptly fly back out – to the cayes or elsewhere in the country. But, if you're here to experience all sides of the country, then it's worth lingering for a day or two. In addition to the city's vibrant, albeit ramshackle streets, Belize City is the cultural heart of the country, with several excellent museums covering archeology and the country's history. Note, too, that the city's relaxed attitude blends with an entrepreneurial flair – Belize City is the country's commerce capital, with banks, offices, and shops lining the main streets, while fruit and fast-food vendors elbow each other for pavement space.

The city center is chaotic but laid-back, and unmistakably Caribbean. Unlike the debauched pirate town of Port Royal in Jamaica, which fell into the sea following an earthquake, Belize City, which was equally uninhibited in its buccaneer heyday, was literally raised from the sea on top of empty rum bottles. Built on a swamp, divided in two by the Haulover Creek, and lapped on three sides by the Caribbean Sea, Belize City often seems to be more water than land and is fighting an ongoing battle against submerging – fortunes are spent every year keeping it out of the mud. Yet its almost 62,000-strong population, drawn from just about every ethnic group

Hitching a ride.

under the sun, manages to keep the city afloat, combining to create a metropolis all of its own.

The city was founded in the early 18th century by British 'Baymen' – former pirates who had settled in the Bay of Honduras in the 17th century (see page 41). The Baymen made their first Belizean settlement on St George's Caye, a few miles off the coast of Belize, succeeded by a settlement at the mouth of the Belize River, which developed into Belize City, the country's commercial capital. The city

Main attractions
Swing Bridge
Memorial Park and Marine Parade
Bliss Center for the Performing Arts
Belize Museum
St. John's Cathedral
Belize Zoo

Map on page 112

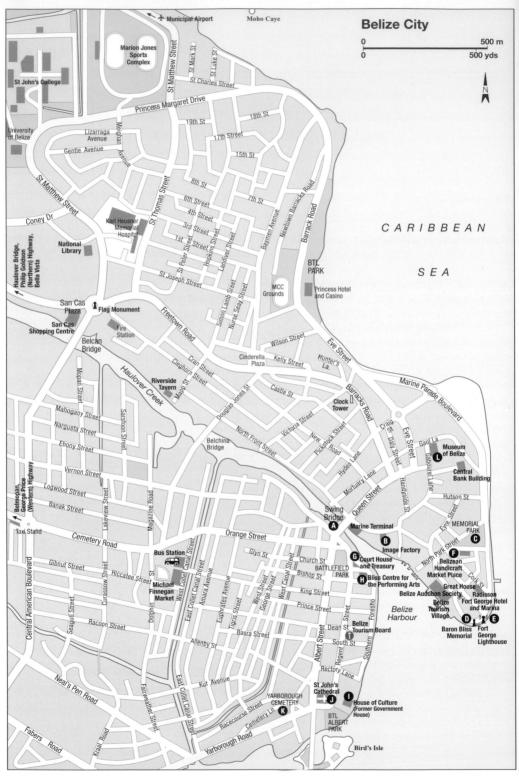

Belize City

0   500 m
0   500 yds

grew with the development of the lumber trade – first logwood, which grew nearer the coast, and then mahogany, found farther inland.

Belize City was the country's capital until a devastating hurricane in 1961 killed hundreds of people and flattened many of its buildings. The seat of government was subsequently moved inland to a purpose-built site at Belmopan.

The city center's busiest hub – and best-known landmark – is the **Swing Bridge** , one of three bridges connecting the city's south and north sides. Constructed in 1922 for what was then primarily pedestrian traffic, the bridge has the distinction of being the only manually operated swing bridge still in existence in the Americas. Using long poles inserted into a capstan, four men lever the bridge to face the harbor mouth so that boats can sail through. The bridge used to open twice daily, but now only operates when large boats are passing through or during special events. Whether it's in use or not, it's worth stopping by for picturesque views of Belize City and the colorful fishing boats bobbing on Haulover Creek.

THE NORTHSIDE

Across the Swing Bridge is what the district residents call, logically enough, 'the northside,' where many of the city's hotels and nicest mansions can be found.

Near the Swing Bridge is the **Marine Terminal**, where boats depart regularly for Caye Caulker and San Pedro. Visitors can browse the surrounding stalls for T-shirts, hats, beach towels, and other souvenirs. Just up the street from the Marine Terminal, heading away from the Swing Bridge is the **Image Factory**  (www.imagefactorybelize.com; Mon–Fri 9am–5pm; free). This is one of Belize's first comprehensive art galleries and it's still one of the few that features local artists and visiting talents, as well as educational exhibits on natural and cultural history.

Continuing up North Front Street is The Fort. This area was formerly Fort George Island; it did have a fort until 1803 and was separated from the rest of the city by a creek.

MEMORIAL PARK AND MARINE PARADE

In 1924 an American construction company reclaimed the land and built some lovely homes – many of which still stand – on Cork Street and facing **Memorial Park** , which commemorates the Battle of St George's Caye in 1798 (see page 46) and Belizean servicemen who served in World Wars I and II. The park is used for open-air concerts and is a favorite gathering spot during the September Celebrations. The **Marine Parade**, which runs along the waterfront edge of Memorial Park, has been renovated over the last decade and is now a breezy boulevard and pedestrian promenade.

LUXURY HOTEL ZONE

With several guesthouses and one of the city's largest hotels, **Radisson**

⊙ Fact

Popular legend has it that thousands of broken rum bottles were used as a foundation to raise Belize City above its natural swamp bed.

Fort George lighthouse, Belize City.

Boat services to Caye Caulker and Ambergris Caye depart from the Belize City's Marine Terminal or from Courthouse Wharf.

Belize City Court House.

Fort George Hotel and Marina, the tip of the northside – known as the Fort – may have more tourist accommodations than anywhere else in town. Nearby rises the aptly named Great House, a welcoming hotel set in a white clapboard four-story building that dates from 1927, with airy rooms and hardwood floors, as well as an excellent garden restaurant, the Smoky Mermaid.

Locals also enjoy the view from the Fort, particularly on Sunday afternoons when families and lovers take a walk out to the lighthouse, past the **Baron Bliss Memorial** Ⓓ. The Baron, a wealthy British invalid who fished Belizean waters for several weeks and then died aboard his yacht in 1927, left the bulk of his estate to the Belizean people in gratitude for their hospitality during his final days.

The **Fort George Lighthouse** Ⓔ is one of the last things visitors see when leaving the city by water taxi and it is still a welcome site to boaters when they approach the mouth of the Haulover Creek. The Baron Bliss Day harbor regatta (generally held in early March) takes place in the sea near the Fort and spectators crowd the area for a wreath-laying ceremony and to watch the sailboats.

The lighthouse and children's park across the street were built for public enjoyment with funds from the Baron's Trust, as was the Bliss Institute, on the Southern Foreshore, which contains a library, an art gallery, and an auditorium.

HANDICRAFTS MARKET

On your way back from the Fort, in the old customs area on the waterfront, is the **Belize Tourism Village**, a large shopping mall and entertainment complex that caters to the vast number of cruise ship visitors. This is the first place that the thousands of cruise ship passengers see as they pass through from the dock. Most head straight out to the waiting tour buses ready to take them to the Maya ruins, the zoo, or perhaps on a tour of Belize City. A few blocks over, near Memorial Park, is the **Belizean Handicraft Market Place** Ⓕ, which is

Ⓞ ELEGANT ORIGINS

Hot and humid Belize City was never supposed to be located on the seafront at all. The original 18th-century settlers preferred the cool, mosquito-free life on St. George's Caye, a few miles offshore, but the expanding logwood trade required a camp closer to the river. Belize was established at the mouth of Haulover Creek only as a temporary solution. But as the years passed, permanent wooden structures became more common, while swampland north and south of the river was reclaimed and connected by a bridge.

It may be hard to imagine today, but journal accounts from the early 19th century describe the settlement as positively charming, the streets lined with gracious colonial homes and lush gardens. Only the privileged few were part of such a genteel picture; the African slaves who made possible the white and upper-class creoles' pampered lifestyle lived in places like Eboe Town, where Yarborough now is. This was composed largely of 'negro houses', long rows of separate rooms sharing a single roof. Indentured servants from India and Garinagu (Garífuna) settlers also occupied less than idyllic quarters in an area known as Queen Charlotte Town, or Frenchmen Town, which was located east of today's Caesar Ridge Road.

filled with Belizean hardwood crafts, such as bowls and picture frames, along with Maya basketry and hot sauces and spices. Hours vary, but it's generally open during the day on weekdays.

LEGAL EAGLES AND POLITICS

On Regent Street is the **Court House G**, where lawyers and judges still wear British-style robes while working in the building constructed in 1926. It replaced the one destroyed by fire in 1918. The clock tower was erected in memory of the colonial governor, Hart Bennett, who was fatally wounded by a falling flagpole during the disaster. January visitors may be lucky enough to watch the ceremonial opening of the first Supreme Court session of the year. The Belize Defense Force Band provides the marching music and the justices, in full British judicial regalia (including white wigs) stand on a platform surrounded by all of the attorneys-at-law. The proceedings on the front steps last only a few minutes, then the entire group retires to one of the courts for a speech by the Chief Justice, which is closed to the public. **The Public Building**, on the same compound, used to be the seat of the Legislative Assembly until it moved to Belmopan in 1971; it is used by several government offices, including the Treasury and Office of the Prime Minister.

Facing the Court House, **Battlefield Park** seems quiet now; it got its name in the 1930s and 1940s for the heated political arguments that took place there. A labor organizer, Antonio Soberanis – whose likeness has been erected in the park – and political activists like George Price and Philip Goldson attracted crowds with their emotional speeches on social justice and self-government.

CULTURE AND THE ARTS

Just around the corner from the Court House, facing the sea on the foreshore is the **Bliss Institute**. Built with funds from the Baron Bliss trust, the building now houses the **Bliss Centre for the Performing Arts H**, a state-of-the-art venue, with a 600-seat theater that features local shows, dance, and music. The center is operated by the

☉ Tip

Beware of petty theft in Belize City. Keep your valuables out of sight and avoid the back-street areas especially at night. Tourist Police patrol the busy areas, which helps keep crime under control.

Crossing the world's oldest operational swing bridge.

Institute of Creative Arts (ICA), which works closely with the Ministry of Education to foster artistic training and education.

The **House of Culture** , formerly the Government House, completed in 1812, rises over the end of Regent Street. This spacious colonial mansion was home to British governors appointed to Belize. In colonial times Belizeans could only enter the mansion and the grounds through special invitation, but today they are open to the public. The House of Culture offers art and music classes, and hosts art exhibitions, concerts, plays, and even fashion shows. The beautiful grounds (daily 9am–4pm) are available for weddings and other special events. Local plants along the nature trail are clearly labeled and a variety of birds either make the garden their home or stay for the winter months. Also here is the restored *Sea King*, the tender of Baron Bliss's yacht of the same name, which stands as testimony to the skill of Belizean boat-builders.

Fort Street flea market.

ST JOHN'S CATHEDRAL

Just across the street from the House of Culture and the BTL park is the oldest Anglican church in Central America, **St John's Cathedral** . Built by slaves using bricks brought to Belize as ship's ballast, the building was completed in 1820 and became the coronation site of four Mosquito Kings, whose people (Native Americans who once inhabited the Mosquito Coast, in what is now Nicaragua) maintained good relations with the British government in Belize, even though they eventually came under Spanish rule. The interior of the church contains wall plaques commissioned by the families of some of the earliest parishioners, and a more recent wooden sculpture depicting the dove of peace by one of Belize's most revered artists, George Gabb. The original roof was replaced after it was damaged by fire in 2002. Fortunately the interior was virtually unscathed.

Lying opposite the cathedral is **Yarborough Cemetery** , named for the land's owner, the magistrate James Yarborough. It was used from 1781 to 1882, first as a burial ground for the colony's more prominent citizens and later opened to the masses. There are no mourners these days, but you may find groups of schoolchildren scampering over the graves deciphering the intriguing tombstones or playing ball. Not too far from the graveyard is a statue of the first self-made Belizean millionaire, Emmanuel Isaiah Morter, a devotee of Marcus Garvey, who owned a great deal of property along Barracks Road and donated much of his fortune to the United Negro Improvement Association (UNIA). The monument also marks the entrance to what was Eboe Town in the 19th century.

REGENT STREET

Heading back down Regent Street, leaving St. John's Cathedral and the House of Culture, are many of the city's best-preserved examples of

19th- and early 20th-century architecture. Regent Street is generally quiet, with doctors, lawyers, and accountants renting many of the old homes for offices. But some families still live on what used to be known as 'Front Street' because it faced the sea at one time, before the southern foreshore was developed. Several structures survived the hurricanes because they were made of bricks. The bricks date these buildings to the early 19th century; iron slave shackles can still be found embedded in some of their interior walls (including the building at the corner of Prince Street), a startling reminder of the darker side of Belizean history.

While Belize City has no organized building preservation effort, most historically significant structures are maintained simply because they are still in use. Parallel to Regent Street is Albert Street, the commercial hub of downtown. There are no skyscrapers but there is cement, plenty of it. If there were old brick buildings, they have long burned down or been knocked down to make way for East Indian, Lebanese, and Chinese shops that sell everything from shampoo to mattresses. The major commercial banks are also located here as well as a large supermarket and department store, Brodies. Central American fruit vendors are also out in full force on Albert Street. The street is at its most active on weekdays after work and on Fridays.

GABOUREL LANE

Queen Street, back over the Swing Bridge, is similar to Albert Street, both in terms of economic activity and hustle and bustle. The main police station, Eastern Division headquarters, is on Queen Street, which ends on Gabourel Lane.

At the end of the street is Her Majesty's Prison, which was in use until the early 1990s, and has been transformed into the excellent **Museum of**

Belize ❶ (Tue–Thu 9am–5pm, Fri–Sat 9am–4pm). It showcases a variety of exhibits that explore the history of Belize City and stunning ceramics and jade jewelry from Belize's Maya culture, including a replica of the famous jade head from Altun Ha.

Behind the museum, on the same grounds, is the Central Bank of Belize, built in a style reminiscent of Maya temples.

INTO THE SUBURBS

The modern areas of Belize City are more spread out, and while you can walk, a taxi may make the heat more bearable. A taxi ride can be quite an adventure in Belize City as cabs speed through traffic, brushing past pedestrians, and sail over bridges that seem to defy the laws of gravity.

If you decide to catch a cab tell the driver to head for the Newtown Barrack and Princess Margaret Drive. You'll pass Sandlighter's Promenade, a tiled walkway that runs along the sea wall up to the Princess Hotel and Casino. The area is dedicated to

⊘ Fact

Belize City's Haulover Creek was so named because cattle had to be 'hauled over' to the other side before a ferry service was introduced.

Museum of Belize.

⊘ Tip

A good spot to spend a few hours, cooled by welcome sea breezes is the **Belize Telecommunications (BTL) Park**, which has picnic tables and a playground. It is also where Charles Lindbergh landed the *Spirit of St Louis* in 1927, the first plane to touch down in Belize.

the sandlighters, or small sailboats, that used to pull up and unload the sand their crews had dug up at the various coastal sandbars and then brought to town for use as landfill or for construction.

Around Princess Margaret Drive is the area of Belize City the more prosperous call home – named, appropriately enough, King's Park. Here, and in the adjacent West Landivar, are also many of the city's schools, the oldest of which is St John's College, established by Jesuits in 1887. Nearby are the University College of Belize and the Belize Teachers' College.

It's obvious to anyone who spends any time in Belize City that there is no room for expansion in the city itself. But as it is reclaimed swamp, and bordered by swamp to the north and west, and sea on the east and south, there is also a shortage of usable land on the outskirts. Housing developments such as Bella Vista and Belama have sprung up immediately outside the entrance to town by the Northern Highway (now called the Philip Goldson Highway),

but the area is subject to flooding, as many proud new homeowners found out during the weeks following Hurricane Mitch in 1998. The highway, which occupied a thin strip of land all the way to mile ten is bounded by the river on one side and the sea on the other, and came dangerously close to being cut off entirely during the Mitch evacuation. The town of Ladyville continues to be developed, along with the sister village of Lord's Bank and land near the international airport. The distance from town is more psychological than actual – its only ten minutes by car – but city folk tease Ladyvillians about moving 'up the road' or 'living in the bush.' All agree the suburbs have their advantages, the greatest of which is the escape from the noise and confusion of the city. And these neighborhoods are generally less prone to crime.

OLD BELIZE CULTURAL AND HISTORICAL CENTER

Five miles (8km) outside the city is the **Old Belize Cultural and Historical Center** (Cucumber Beach Marina, Mile 5 Western Highway [George Price Highway]; tel: 222-4129; www.oldbelize.com), which is a reconstruction of Belize's history. Although primarily aimed at cruise ship visitors, the exhibit is worth the trip out of town. Enter through a mahogany tree, the national tree of Belize and vitally important to the early development of the settlement. In turn you visit a rainforest, a Maya village, a logging camp (complete with a steam engine used for hauling logs), a *chiclero* camp, and a sugar mill. One of the highlights of the display is a reconstruction of an early 20th-century street in Belize City. On cruise-ship days the center hosts Belizean music and dance performances. Cucumber Beach has a huge waterslide, rising 50ft (15 meters) from the beach, as well as a zipline that traverses the lagoon. The on-site restaurant also has good-value Belizean and international dishes.

Aerial view of Belize City.

BELIZE ZOO

There is one place in Belize where you can be sure of seeing scarlet macaws, jaguars, or Baird's tapirs in a natural setting.

What many people fail to realize when they come to Belize is that their chances of seeing the larger land animals are limited. The tangle of vines and thick foliage makes it difficult to see even a few feet off a forest path or road. Also, many tropical creatures are nocturnal, finding safety under the cloak of night. Except for a flash of fur dissolving into the bush, or the snap of branches and rustle of leaves, most visitors will end up experiencing the habitat where wildlife live instead of viewing the creatures themselves.

But there is one place where you are assured of seeing a jaguar or a tapir in a natural setting. Belize Zoo (www.belizezoo.org; daily 8.30am–5pm) is an oasis of ponds, forests, and flowers among the sprawling savannas 29 miles (47km) west of Belize City. More than 60 indigenous Belizean animals live here in large, natural enclosures.

If you can, try to visit the zoo first thing in the morning or late in the afternoon, when the animals are more active. You will often feel that you are in the forest, peering through a tangle of vines and shrubs to catch a glimpse of a puma, jaguarundi, or ocelot. Patience and persistence are necessary to view the creatures here, but your patience will be rewarded: a glimpse of a jaguar staking out his dominion, time in the company of curious and lively kinkajous, or eye-to-eye contact with the towering jabirú stork. Other star attractions include a pair of harpy eagles, the largest eagles in the world, which are nearly extinct in Central America. They are an awesome sight, and of great conservation importance: Panama, the male, is father to several fledglings reintroduced to Belize.

There's also a reptile area where you can see Belizeans snakes including the very venomous fer-de-lance and the boa constrictor. The Belize Zoo education programs concentrate on informing visitors about snakes and their beneficial role in the ecosystem, helping to control rats and other rodents.

The animals and grounds are meticulously cared for, and fun signs spell out the natural habits of each animal and its endangered status, reminding visitors that 'Belize is my home too!' Raised gravel paths lead from exhibit to exhibit through natural savanna and pine ridge vegetation, as well as transplanted rainforest. Belize Zoo is as much a botanical garden as it is a zoo, and it is a focal point for environmental awareness in Belize. It operates on strict environmentally friendly principles, with composting and lots of recycling.

Sharon Matola, the North American founder and driving force behind the zoo, arrived in Belize after a colorful career that included time as a lion-tamer in Romania and on a circus tour in Mexico. She started the zoo to provide a home for animals that were used in a wildlife documentary she worked on. Today the focus of the zoo is on research and conservation – with projects that range from educating schoolchildren about harpy eagles to organizing a national day for the tapir.

Belize Zoo covers 30 acres (12 hectares), and is part of a larger complex that includes a Tropical Education and Research Center; you can stay here, too, in the Belize Zoo Jungle Lodge (www.belizezoo.org), which includes an unmissable night tour of the zoo. As many animals are nocturnal, including wild cats and most mammals, you have a good chance of observing them at their most active. Also nearby is the Belize Savannah Guest House (www.belizesavannaguesthouse.com), a comfortable guesthouse that's run by local naturalists and documentary filmmakers.

Harpy eagle, Belize Zoo.

Sunset on Caye Caulker.

NORTHERN CAYES

From the spectacular Blue Hole to the lively resorts of Ambergris Caye, the cayes of Belize are the country's leading tourist attraction.

Ambergris Caye may get all the glory (and the majority of visitors to Belize), but there's a lot more to the cayes than just this sun-dappled island. Each of the cayes and atolls, from Caye Caulker to Turneffe Atoll, offer a wholly unique experience. In short: to fully experience the cayes is to travel liberally among them. Regular flights from the International Airport in **Belize City ❶** serve both Ambergris Caye and Caye Caulker, and water taxis and boat charters can get you everywhere else.

Keep in mind, too, that not all cayes in Belize are the beautiful coral islands featured in travel brochures. Some are little more than a muddy tangle of mangrove trees. Yet even the most homely cluster of roots plays a vital role in the coastal eco-system.

FOUNDED BY PIRATES

Many of the cayes' names date back to the days of pirates and bucca-neers. Near Belize City, for exam-ple, the **Drowned Cayes ❷** contain such evocative titles as Frenchman's Caye and Spanish Lookout; Bannis-ter Bogue is a channel named after a pirate who later became a logwood cutter in the late 17th century, while Gallows Point was where criminals and freebooters were hanged. The pirate John Colson anchored his ship at **Colson Caye ❸** farther south, but

today lobster fishermen use these mangroves to collect booty of a dif-ferent sort. **Robinson's Point** was once the center of Belize's boat-building industry with a shipyard run by the Hunter and Young families; all that remains is an old lighthouse.

However, if you want to get the feel of why pirates used to love the Belizean – at that time the Bay of Honduras – coastline and secluded cayes, you hardly have to leave Belize City. **Moho Caye ❹**, a short hop off the coast to the north of Belize City

Main attractions
Ambergris Caye
Caye Caulker
Barrier Reef
Turneffe Islands
Blue Hole
Marco Gonzalez

**Maps on pages
122 and 127**

El Pescador Resort, Ambergris Caye.

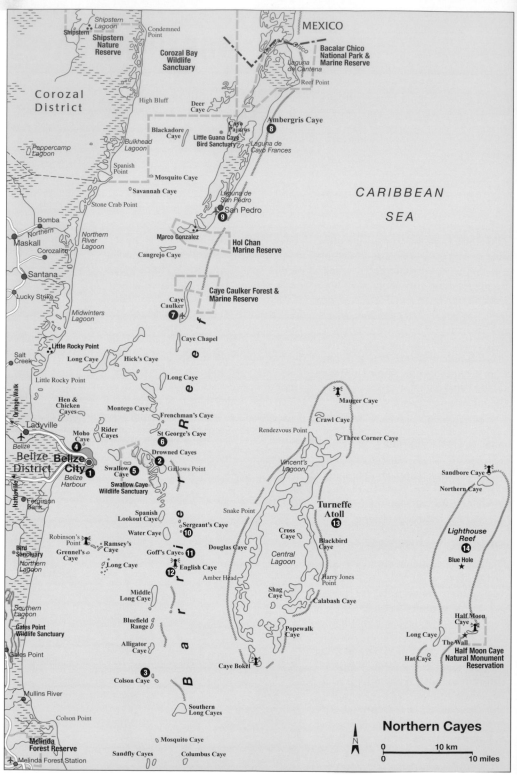

Northern Cayes

N

0   10 km

0   10 miles

(behind St. John's College) is a little C-shaped caye that is now used as a boat marina. The caye has changed owners several times in recent years, but the lodge is still open and the restaurant and bar provide an intriguing little hideaway spot to cool off in the evening and on weekends. (Bring insect repellant though.)

A skiff ferries passengers to and from Belize City every half hour and in the meantime you can wait on an interesting little dock built right on top of mangrove roots along the shore.

There's another little watering hole not too far from Belize City, but the 'regulars' are not people, they're manatees. Although **Swallow Caye ❺** sounds like it is a haven for birds – and you'll see plenty of these too – it's the manatees that enjoy the warm-water sinkhole that draw the crowds. For years, the spot was a secret enjoyed only by those lucky enough to have in-the-know guides leading the way. Now, though, the word is out and many manatee watchers come to the sinkhole. For this reason, locals rallied to designate it a protected reserve and signs have been posted to warn boats to slow down and keep their distance. Although it is tempting to hop overboard and swim with these gentle creatures when you see their snouts peek above the water, it's not allowed or appreciated by those who are trying to protect this endangered species.

Don't expect to see much more than their nostrils blowing air, and some days they can't be seen at all, although they are probably feeding on plants on the sea bed. Or maybe they have just grown tired of visitors. But when you do see their large shadowy form, it's something you won't easily forget. (see page 203 for more information on manatee watching).

SITE OF THE FIRST SETTLEMENT

Just 9 miles (14km) from Belize City, crescent-shaped **St George's Caye ❻** is the most historic of all the offshore islands. It was here that

Playing on the pier, Caye Caulker.

the British buccaneers established the territory's first real settlement around 1650; a century and a half later, they defeated Spanish invaders in the famous Battle of St George's Caye in 1798 (see page 46).

One account, written by a traveling Spanish cleric, reveals that in the mid-17th century, the British pirate Bartholomew Sharpe used St George's Caye as a command center for an impressive fleet of 23 vessels manned by several hundred buccaneers. The priest reports that he was captured by Sharpe's men and taken to the caye, but since he didn't speak any English and Sharpe didn't speak any Spanish, the two communicated in Latin. (Sharpe is reported to have acquired the language in Britain while he himself was training to enter religious orders.) Fortunately for the Spaniard, the gentleman pirate spared his life but put him to good use conducting Mass and hearing confessions, until he was released a few months later.

A quiet road on Caye Caulker.

Today the only reminder of these colorful times at St George's Caye are a mounted cannon on the beach and a small **graveyard** near **St George's Lodge**. A white picket fence encloses what little is left of the cemetery; the elaborate tombstones and many graves of the caye's early settlers were carried away during the 1961 hurricane. The rest of the island is occupied by the vacation homes of Belize's more affluent families, two small hotels and several fishermen's homes.

The caye is very quiet during the week, but on the weekends many Belize City residents come out for fishing and water-skiing, or sunbathing on the kraals (an old colonial system of enclosing an area of sea water, supposedly to protect swimmers from sharks). A mile (1.6km) offshore is an area of shallow water called **The Spit**, a great place to anchor a boat and hop over the side for a swim. The water is only about 1–3ft (0.3–1 meter) deep and the sand is completely free of sea grass and other vegetation.

The only hotel operating on the island, the luxury **St. George's Caye Resort** (www.st-georgesresort.

⊘ THE MARCO GONZALEZ MAYA SITE

The Maya site of Marco Gonzalez offers the unique chance to observe an archeological excavation in progress. The site (open daily during daylight hours) lies in thick forest near Laguna de Boca Ciega, on the southern tip of Ambergris Caye. This intriguing site dates back to the Preclassic period, and archeological studies have shown that it was once an important trade center with close links to Lamanai.

Excavations began in 1984, by two Canadian archeologists, Dr Elizabeth Graham and Dr David Pendergast, who subsequently named the site after their young guide. In 2011, Marco Gonzalez became the first Maya Site National Park on Ambergris Caye. The site itself is still fairly rudimentary – this is a working dig after all – but that's a big part of the draw. In many ways, it offers the opportunity to discover it alongside the archeologists: Walk around dirt mounds surrounded by ink-black earth – and keep your eyes trained on the ground, as you may spot the occasional Maya pottery shard or flint. A great way to explore the site is by going on a guided tour, which is regularly offered by expert guide (and chairman of the Marco Gonzalez board) Jan Brown (email: janbrownbz@hotmail.com).

com), caters mainly to scuba divers. Beyond that, the island isn't set up for casual visitors; some fishing and snorkeling trips may call in for a brief look-around, but that usually has to be requested beforehand.

FISHING VILLAGE CUM TOURIST MECCA

One of the most popular destinations in the cayes is **Caye Caulker** ➐. This working fishing village was originally settled by mestizos (of mixed Spanish and indigenous blood) fleeing the Caste War in Mexico's Yucatán in the mid-19th century; today it has about 1,500 year-round residents, mostly of mestizo descent. The population swells considerably on weekends and holidays, when hundreds of Belize City residents descend on the island's small guesthouses and hotels. The winter holidays and Easter are the busiest seasons, so it's well worth booking in advance, though you can usually still find a few basic spots with rooms available even at the last minute.

Caulker exudes a wonderfully laid-back Belizean atmosphere, with breezy restaurants and sidewalk stands, friendly bars, and plenty of spots where you can sip a chilled beer with your toes in the warm sand.

Sand dredged from the back of the island and pumped to the front creates a lovely – but artificial – beach several meters wide along the seaward shore. **The Split**, at the north end of the village, is a channel through the island made by Hurricane Hattie in 1961. It's one of the most popular gathering places on the island, with a nice swimming area (be careful of the strong current and speedboats, however) and an open-air bar. Children like the Split because the water is shallow for a good stretch in front of the sea wall and the sandy bottom is free of rocks. Little fish, crabs, and starfish along the wall also provide plenty of entertainment.

Caye Caulker's big draw is, as with elsewhere on the Cayes, the accessibility to the longest Barrier Reef in the Western Hemisphere. Numerous tour operators offer diving, snorkeling, boating, and kayaking trips to the reef, where you can explore the colorful underwater world.

Because of its relaxed, bohemian lifestyle, some visitors like Caye Caulker so much they never go home. As a result, the caye now has a number of expatriate artists, and several restaurants and gift shops are run by gringos determined to claim their own piece of paradise. Pleasant as it is, though, the island has its share of problems – including a rising crime rate. Residents who were frustrated by police inactivity organized an extremely successful citizens' patrol program, similar to one pioneered at San Pedro. At the other end of the social scale, residents also want to ensure that tourism growth is controlled and the island does not become over-commercialized.

Growing tourism has also meant growing pressure on the nearby reef.

Tip

As in all Belizean waters, divers and snorkelers are warned not to touch the delicate coral or remove any marine life from anywhere on the reef, particularly now that it has protected status as a marine reserve.

Friendly coconut seller, Caye Caulker.

After a decade of requests from local fishermen and environmentalists, in 1999 the government gave reserve status to most of the reef in front of the caye. The Belize Fisheries Department is continuing to develop the proper regulations in consultation with local fishermen and conservation agencies. Additionally, national fishing regulations apply to everyone, including open and closed seasons for lobster and conch.

At the island's northern tip is the **Caye Caulker Forest and Marine Reserve**, home to mangroves, gumbo limbo, and poisonwood. Other native inhabitants of the reserve's littoral forest include scaly-tailed iguanas (here called 'wish willies'), geckos, and multiple species of land crab. Local tour companies will offer day trips here upon request.

HISPANIC AMBERGRIS

As your boat pulls up to the palm tree-shaded shoreline – or as you catch a bird's-eye view of the verdant island from the plane, ringed by sandy beaches and crystal waters – it comes as no surprise that Madonna's famous song 'La Isla Bonita' was inspired by **Ambergris Caye** ⑧. The hugely popular island commands more than 50 percent of all visitors to Belize – with all the attendant tourist services, from lavish resorts to hostels catering to budget backpackers to all manner of restaurants and bars.

The main settlement on the island is **San Pedro** ⑨, whose name has effectively become synonymous with the caye. Ambergris Caye is separated from Mexico by the narrow **Boca Bacalar Chico channel**, so technically it's not an island at all, but a 25-mile (40km) peninsula extending from the Yucatán.

In the early 1980s, fishing was still the major industry at San Pedro – which is why the town and church were named after St Peter. Now many of the fishermen use their locally made mahogany boats to take tourists to the **Barrier Reef** that parallels the island. But although this is the most touristy part of Belize, the population is still

A beach bar on the The Spit.

only around 5,000. If you like your tourism slick and well-orchestrated, with happening nightclubs and elegant dining, this may not be the place for you. San Pedro and the Caye have lots of charm, but sometimes the eyes and the heart need to make the distinction between run down and quaint.

The population of San Pedro is determined that it should not become another high-rise Caribbean resort: laws have been passed prohibiting any building more than three stories high. The idea is to maintain the small scale of Ambergris and give owners of small hotels a chance to stay in business. That said, on the breezy beachfront several miles north and south of San Pedro, numerous luxury resorts have been built over the last decade – with new resorts regularly popping up.

Even so, life on Ambergris is still pretty mellow, and going barefoot is appropriate just about anywhere. The streets of San Pedro are of soft, foot-friendly dirt, as are many of the small shops. This chill atmosphere has attracted more than a few resident North Americans, who now run hotels, gift shops, and restaurants. Some older San Pedranos resent what they see as the Americanization of San Pedro, but the younger folks don't seem to mind. The local high school students are just as inclined to speak with an American accent as they are to switch back and forth into creole or Spanish.

BELIZE'S LARGEST CAYE

Ambergris, 35 miles (56km) from Belize City, can be reached by water taxi in two hours or small propeller plane in about 20 minutes. San Pedro's airport has a rugged appeal to it, far removed from the crowded world of international terminals. The airport has a barebones terminal with benches outside that serve as 'waiting rooms.' Sometimes, you'll even see dogs snoozing beneath the parked planes.

Located near the southern edge of San Pedro, the airport is a good orientation point. Facing the road that parallels the landing strip, the town proper is to the immediate left; to the right, the road leads through the quiet resorts of the south. Straight ahead, beyond a few buildings, is the Caribbean; behind is the lagoon.

Three streets run north–south through **San Pedro**: shoreside Barrier Reef Drive; Pescador Drive, in the middle; and, lastly, Angel Coral Street. The heart of town is midway along Barrier Reef Drive. On one block, there is the **Town Hall** and **police station**. On the next block is **San Pedro Church**, an airy building whose large windows have jalousies so that the congregation can be cooled by the ocean breeze.

Opposite the church is **Plaza Park**, an open-air, concrete space, with a painted bust of a Maya chief, not too far from the churchyard's painted statue of St Peter. The park also has a basketball court, which is played on every night. People gather to watch the games, if for no other reason than to take advantage

Golf carts are a common sight in the cayes.

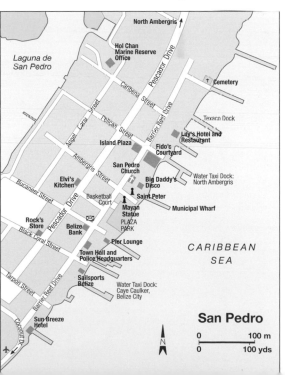

San Pedro

of the sea breeze: games are subject to being interrupted during the rainy season by sudden storms.

EVENING VIBRATIONS

Directly down on the beach from here is the center of the caye's nightlife. The **Wahoo's Lounge** is known for its 'chicken drop' contest on Wednesday night, where you can place a bet on which numbered square a chicken will defecate on. On Sunday night, lively karaoke fills the bar. Also popular is the amiable **Señor Marlins**, with drink specials and theme nights.

While strolling along Barrier Reef and Pescador drives, step back and look at the buildings themselves; many are classic versions of Caribbean architecture. The **Barrier Reef Hotel** is perhaps one of the most splendid examples – it's one of the oldest houses in San Pedro – but even some of the apparently decrepit wooden houses are still architecturally interesting. Some visitors to San Pedro have been looking down instead of up: teams of archeologists regularly visit the streets around

Sunrise off Ambergris Caye.

town, sifting and digging, gradually finding relics from the island's remote past as a Maya settlement.

THE RUGGED NORTH

North of town is the Boca del Rio, known locally as The River: a bridge joins the town to the northern part of the island, where a rugged dirt road leads to the tiny village of Tres Cocos and the northern resorts that lie on beautiful, though largely deserted, beaches. This is the area for those who find even the subdued village life of San Pedro too much and who really want to get away from it all. The dirt road can be traversed by foot, bike, and golf cart, but the preferred way to head north of San Pedro is by boat. There are no towns here, so activity centers around several resorts, including **El Secreto** and **Matachica**, and some good restaurants such as **Capricorn**.

THE LAGOON SIDE OF THE ISLAND

The lagoon side of Ambergris Caye has long been overlooked, with just

a few restaurants and untamed swathes of land that hold pockets of residential homes. With the completion of the ambitious San Pedro Sunset Boardwalk and Water Taxi Terminal in 2014, that's beginning to change. But with the terminal currently only used by international water taxis (local water taxis still pull up on the reef side) this change is reassuringly slow.

SOUTH OF SAN PEDRO

Ambergris Caye owes much of its physical existence to the mangrove, which can be most easily seen to the south, following the sand road from the airport. Untouched except for the occasional plastic wrapping or old shoe washed in by the gentle waves, the mangrove swamp is like a trip into the womb that gave birth to the island.

Before the mangroves is a clearing developed as a park by the local Lions' Club. The area was used as a set for some of the scenes in the movie, *The Mosquito Coast*, which starred Harrison Ford. There's no shortage of the devilish insects here, and having repellent on hand is a good idea, especially at night. Mosquitoes are seldom a problem on the beaches, however, from which they are pushed back by the steady trade winds.

South of San Pedro, the beachfront is dotted with a number of rustic-chic resorts, such as the eco friendly **Xanadu Island Resort** as well as the luxurious colonial-style **Victoria House**. Plenty of outdoor bars liven up the evenings, including **Crazy Canucks**, with 'Sunday Funday' jam sessions fueled by tropical cocktails.

INTO THE CARIBBEAN

Like any other self-respecting tropical island, Ambergris Caye looks to the sea. The island is set in the Barrier Reef, and it is offshore that one heads for swimming, fishing, diving, and snorkeling.

There are no real beaches or even waves along Ambergris' shoreline. Most of the water between the coast and the reef is shallow and grassy – a shoreline for lounging, not surfing.

It was the Maya who discovered a natural cut in the reef, which attracted a wide range of marine life. They called it 'Hol Chan,' Little Channel. In 1987, the area around the cut was declared the **Hol Chan Marine Reserve** – only 10 minutes away by boat, it is Ambergris' principal local site for snorkeling and scuba diving.

Snorkelers look for the beautiful coral formations along the reef and for fish, many of which like to congregate beneath the anchored boats, while scuba divers are attracted to a sinkhole and an underlying cave.

Fishing is not permitted in the reserve, but there's plenty of sea left for that. Most fishing consists of either trawling in the open sea or dropping anchor in one of the larger lagoons, where the water is calm.

Snapper and grouper are plentiful, and the occasional barracuda

⊙ Tip

There are no ferry services to the cayes south of Belize City, such as Goff's and English Cayes, but boats can be hired for the trip from several companies.

Mennonite men selling produce at the dockside.

can appear. The sea also provides a lobster industry. Over the years, however, the lobsters have been over-fished, and between mid-March and mid-July the crustaceans are off-limits.

While San Pedro is the ideal base if you're planning to visit Hol Chan, many dive and snorkel operators from Caye Caulker will also take you there. Snorkeling along the reef is fun, but the truly adventurous will want to take the plunge at Shark Ray Alley. This is only 1 mile (2km) south of Hol Chan and offers the unique experience of diving or snorkeling with stingrays and sharks – well, nurse sharks. They are generally harmless (although they don't look that way at feeding time), but this is not a swim for the fainthearted. You may jump into the water fairly confident but suddenly start feeling a little nervous when the wings of a ray brush against you. You can only visit Shark Ray Alley with an experienced guide. Responsible guides do not pick the rays up out of the water

or try to get the nurse sharks excited by feeding them before you get into the water.

Ambergris Caye exists in a fragile ecology, both socially and biologically speaking. Its future faces the same challenge as most of the world's tourist areas: to be able to develop its resources, while – in the ways that are fundamentally important – remaining the same.

BACK SOUTH

In the waters south of Belize City, there are some lesser-known cayes, where you can find a little piece of tropical paradise all to yourself. Tiny **Sergeant's Caye** ⑩, named for an 18th-century merchant, is almost always deserted except for several coconut trees. **Goff's Caye** ⑪, just to the south has more shade, but also more people, especially on weekends. To protect visitors from too much sun or a sudden downpour, a large thatched roof has been erected over a cement slab, but there are no picnic tables or benches, so it's a good idea to bring a folding stool or a hammock if you need creature comforts.

Goff's Caye may be small, but it is ever-changing. The sands shift around, constantly altering the shape of the island. Sometimes your boat can dock right off the pier for easy unloading of passengers; at other times the pier is marooned offshore and you have to wade in holding your picnic basket over your head. The sand may move but the coconut trees stay put and so does the reef. The snorkeling around Goff's Caye is consistently good and the tide pools where the reef meets the sand are always full of the same shy little fish and crabs that have amused generations of children. Although the water taxis have so far not added this caye to their normally scheduled runs, a number of charter boat agencies will

Halfmoon Caye.

do it and some include lunch in the package. Rates are better if you can get a group together.

English Caye ⑫, farther down the line, sits alongside the main shipping channel. Its steel frame lighthouse, built in 1935, marks the entrance to the channel for deep draft vessels coming into the port of Belize City. There are also several homes here.

BEYOND THE BARRIER REEF

Diving and fishing enthusiasts may venture further into the Caribbean to Belize's three coral atolls. Although most watersport activities take place from charter boats, a surge of interest has fueled the development of a few island-based resorts. Two of these atolls, the Turneffe Islands and Lighthouse Reef, can be reached from Belize City; the third, Glover's Reef, is off the coast from Dangriga (see page 179).

The Turneffe Islands ⑬ are the surface elements of Belize's largest atoll running some 30 miles (48km) from north to south; it has several shallow lagoons, a couple of upscale resorts and two lighthouses. The northernmost beacon, built in 1885, is on Mauger Caye ('Skinny' in creole) while a second lighthouse can be found on Caye Bokel ('Elbow' in Dutch) at the southern tip of the atoll.

Almost all the major charter boat and dive services arrange trips to Turneffe, but guests at the various fishing and vacation lodges are usually picked up by the lodge's own transportation from Belize City.

Lighthouse Reef ⑭ is another atoll with a treacherous boundary of coral. Like Turneffe, there are also two lighthouses here, one on Sandbore Caye; the other, first built in 1828 and replaced in 1848, is on Half Moon Caye, a crescent-shaped island that is easily one of the most beautiful places in Belize. The abundance of nesting sea birds and marine life

made Half Moon Caye and its surrounding waters a natural choice for the Belize's first Natural Monument in 1982. Around 4,000 red-footed booby birds nest on the island; the population is unusual for being white instead of the usual dull brown (the only other similar booby colony is near the island of Tobago in the eastern Caribbean). An observation platform allows unrestricted viewing of the boobies, along with some of the 98 other species of birds that have been recorded on the island,

Forests of black coral sprout like weeds from **The Wall** near Half Moon Caye. This vertical drop-off is sliced by canyons and narrow passages, many of which have overhangs that often coalesce into short caves wide enough for divers to swim through. Closer to shore lies a wide sand bank covered with thousands of garden eels swaying in the current, where they feed off passing plankton. These creatures are extremely shy, quickly pulling back, tail first, into their holes in the sand, at the approach of a diver.

⊘ THE BLUE HOLE

Lying just 7 miles (11km) north of Half Moon Caye is one of the world's most famous dive sites, and one of the most beautiful natural wonders in Belize: the Blue Hole.

Looking from the air like a dark blue pool in a field of turquoise, the site gained fame in 1972 when Jacques Cousteau maneuvered his ship *Calypso* through narrow coral channels to moor and film inside. The Blue Hole is actually a sink hole created by a collapsed underground cavern; over 980ft (300 meters) across and 445ft (135 meters) deep, with huge stalactites hanging from offshoot caves at depths of 100–150ft (30–45 meters).

While there is not much marine life in this vivid blue shaft of water, the geological formations and encircling coral are spectacular. Sharks and turtles abound in the waters around the Blue Hole, though their presence is rarely predictable. This dive is usually reserved for the more adventurous and experienced, under the strict supervision of a dive master. It is definitely not a plunge to be attempted by the novice.

The Belize Audubon Society and the Forestry Department manage the Blue Hole Natural Monument at Lighthouse Reef, which covers an area of 1,023 acres (414 hectares), with the Blue Hole at the center.

NORTH TO ALTUN HA

Besides the impressive Maya ruins of Altun Ha, within a few hours' drive north of Belize City there are pioneering nature reserves and luxurious jungle resorts.

Whether or not they know the archeologists' name for it, everyone in Belize recognizes the Temple of Masonry Altars at Altun Ha. The image is on the paper money, school textbooks, and perhaps even most importantly for some, it was chosen for the logo of the national beer, Belikin.

The ancient Maya site is the centerpiece of northern Belize District, a classically Caribbean landscape of rich, humid, rain-soaked lowlands. The villages here are tiny, usually no more than a few brightly painted wooden houses on stilts clustered along a small roadway, perhaps with a tin-roofed church from which the sound of hymns will drift on a Sunday morning. But although the atmosphere is languid, even soporific, this site is a popular excursion for visitors, because it is easily reached by car from Belize City.

This is also the first part of Belize that many travelers see. **Phillip S.W. Goldson International Airport ❶**, near the village of Ladyville, lies 10 miles (16km) north of Belize City on the Philip Goldson (Northern) Highway, which is well paved and runs more or less unbroken up to the Mexican border.

Only 5 miles (9km) north of the international airport is a rougher dirt road turning off to the left; it continues to tiny **Burrell Boom ❷**, which was a key community during Belize's logging days.

Young visitors at Altun Ha.

A boom was a heavy metal chain that was stretched across the river to catch logs as they were floating downstream. Burrel Boom makes a pleasant base for exploring the area, thanks mainly to the riverfront **Black Orchid Resort** (www.blackorchidresort.com), with spacious rooms with native hardwood floors, a welcoming restaurant with traditional cuisine, and a rooftop jacuzzi.

BABOON SANCTUARY

After driving 13 miles (20km) from the turn-off, you come to the impressive

Main attractions
Burrell Boom
Community Baboon
  Sanctuary
Bermudian Landing
Altun Ha
Crooked Tree Wildlife
  Sanctuary

Maps on pages 134 and 136

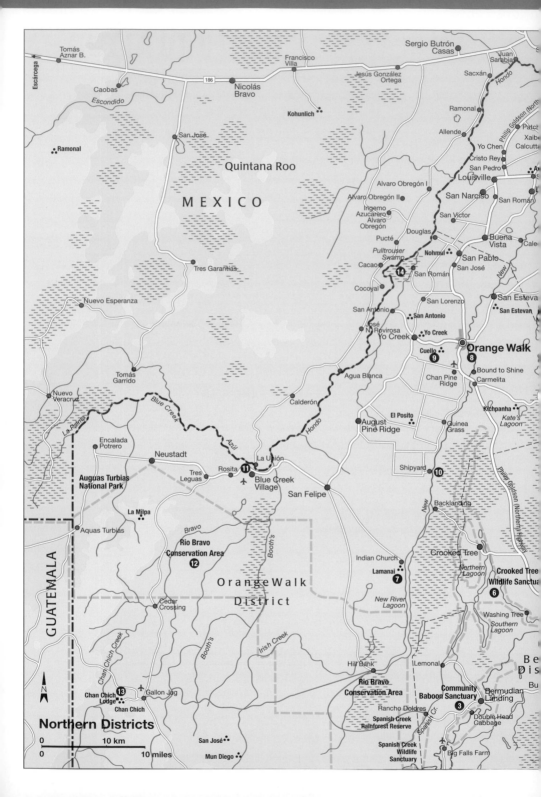

Community Baboon Sanctuary ③ – one of the most popular and successful conservation projects in Belize. Founded in 1985, the Baboon Sanctuary is a co-operative effort between environmentalists (aided by the World Wildlife Fund under the auspices of the Belize Audubon Society) and local creole landowners to save Central America's declining population of black howler monkeys, known as baboons in Belize (see page 86). Apart from Belize, this sub-species is only found in the river lowlands of Guatemala and southern Mexico, where the rainforest has been shrinking at such a rate that extinction was becoming probable.

A zoologist from the University of Wisconsin, Dr Robert Horwich, initially signed an agreement with 16 local farmers along the Belize River: while still working their agricultural lands, the farmers pledged to follow a management plan that would help protect the howler monkeys.

The agreement covered topics as diverse as a coordination plan for cutting and burning local plantations, to the building of 'baboon bridges' – rope and wood ladders hung across roadways to allow monkeys safe crossings. The program was an instant success and has been the basis for other community-based reserves around the world. Since 1985, the number of participating farmers has gone up to nearly 100, allowing the sanctuary to expand; it now covers 20 miles (32km) along the Belize River.

Villagers have profited from the rise in tourism, and have taken up the creole slogan *Baboon ya de fu we* (literally translated as 'the baboons here are our responsibility.') The program has also had an impact elsewhere in the country with howler monkeys being successfully relocated to the **Cockscomb Basin Wildlife Sanctuary** by a team of American scientists aided by Belizean volunteers.

The sanctuary's service village is **Bermudian Landing**, a British logging camp in the 17th century and today a relaxed creole outpost. Check in at the visitors' center here – there are some places to stay, some flat ground for tents, or the station manager can arrange for accommodations with local families. A small museum, opened in 1989, was Belize's first devoted to natural history, and an interpretative trail can be followed. Canoe trips, horseback riding and crocodile-watching tours are also available. All visitors are asked to register at the Community Baboon Sanctuary Museum (daily 8am–5pm). Guided walks along a nature trail are available for a charge.

The Sanctuary is 26 miles (40km) from Belize City and most taxi drivers will take you there for around Bz$100. The bus service is cheaper, but a little trickier. The smaller companies that service the route leave Belize City early in the afternoon or evening, and don't return until the next day. There is no service at all on Sunday, so be prepared to spend the night, or maybe the entire weekend, at a local family bed-and-breakfast. Advance arrangements are recommended; contact the Belizean Audubon Society (see page 236).

VIEWING THE WILDLIFE

Local guides can be hired at the visitors' venter for walks through the sanctuary. As with any animal-watching in Belize, the best time to visit is around dawn or dusk, when the cacophonous shrieks of the howler monkeys echo along the Belize River. The sanctuary is also home to more than 200 species of bird and the usual menagerie of Belizean wildlife, including deer, iguanas, jaguars, anteaters, coatis, turtles, and peccaries. Although classified as riverine rainforest and cohune palm forest, the landscape can be surprisingly dusty and scrubby, especially at the end of the dry season. Having been logged steadily for some 300 years, the forest in the sanctuary is mostly secondary growth dating back no farther than the turn of the 20th century.

A rough dirt road leads south from the sanctuary to the Western Highway, past villages like **Willows Bank** and **Double Head Cabbage** (whose names are the most interesting thing about them). These areas have been depressed economically for years, with many of the younger folk leaving to seek work in Belize City or in the United States, but many community leaders have banded together to try and create jobs, such as small-scale fish farming using native river species, subsistence farming, and preserve processing.

A black howler monkey at the Community Baboon Sanctuary.

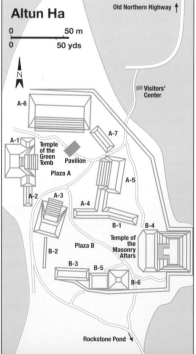

Altun Ha

MASKALL AND AROUND

Heading north again on the new Northern Highway, via Burrell Boom, the turn off to the right after passing through Sand Hill (6 miles/10km) is the rather rougher Old Northern Highway. The tiny villages of Cowhead Creek, Lucky Strike, and Santana pass by in a colorful blur – the houses all seem to be painted baby blue or frou-frou pink, framed by the lush green of surrounding palm trees.

Maskall ❹, although it is no more impressive than the other villages on the highway, functions as the region's local administrative center. Maskall is strategically located – everyone who wants to get to Altun Ha has to pass through here. Even boat operators from San Pedro have to come down the Northern River that runs through the town to bring visitors arriving from the caye on day-trips.

ALTUN HA

The Maya ruins of **Altun Ha** ❺ (daily 8am–5pm), a Classic Period ceremonial center with two large plazas and 13 ancient structures, were probably occupied from 1100 BC to AD 900. Some

3,000 Mayas are believed to have lived here, mostly supporting themselves by farming and trading. Excavation of the site began only in the mid-1960s. The dominant pyramid of Plaza A, known as the Temple of the Green Tomb, is actually several temples built on top of one another. Around 300 artifacts have been found inside it, from skins to jewelry, and stingray spines to parts of an ancient Maya book.

The tallest structure at Altun Ha, the **Temple of the Masonry Altars** (also known as the Temple of the Sun God) looms over Plaza B at a height of 60ft (18 meters). Five of the seven tombs found in the pyramid had already been ransacked, but in 1968 archeologist Dr David Pendergast discovered the untouched remains of an elderly priest.

Other digging at this temple showed that local priests indulged in an unusual form of sacrifice, whereby beautifully carved jade objects were smashed and flung into fires. And one of its seven tombs showed signs of desecration during the end of the Maya period, which has led archeologists to speculate that

The tall jabiru stork, a distinctive sight at the Crooked Tree Wildlife Sanctuary.

Local children in Crooked Tree village.

☉ SACRED MAYA JADE

Buried alongside the remains of a priest found at Altun Ha in 1968 by Dr David Pendergast was the jade head of the Maya Sun God, Kinich Ahau. At 5.8ins (14.9cm) in height, and weighing 9.75lbs (4.42kg), this is Belize's most important ancient relic and the largest jade carving found anywhere in the Maya world. It is now kept in a vault in the Belize Bank. A replica of the carving is on display in the Museum of Belize in Belize City.

Jade was the most precious substance to the Maya, as it had been to other pre-Columbian cultures, such as the Olmecs of Mexico. It occurs in various shades, but the Maya prized the green jade most highly, considering it sacred for its glowing green hues that reminded them of the green leaves of maize, their symbol of life itself. For this reason, only kings and deities were allowed to wear jade, as a mark of their status and power.

Jade was traded throughout Mesoamerica; large quantities were extracted from the Motagua River Valley in the southern Guatemalan Highlands. The raw product was exported to the lowlands, where expert artisans fashioned it into delicate and beautiful items of jewelry and ornaments. These artifacts were then re-exported to the highlands in exchange for other local commodities.

Altun Ha was abandoned after a violent encounter, possibly a peasant revolt – one more clue in understanding the abandonment of the great Maya cities.

Altun Ha is an easy half-day trip for Belize City taxi drivers and tour operators (see page 235) and it is a hugely popular stop on the cruise ship circuit. Bring plenty of water and wear long sleeves and long pants – the insects, and the sun, can be brutal.

PARADISE FOR BIRD-WATCHERS

Due west of Altun Ha on the Philip Goldson (Northern) Highway is a dirt road to the left, leading, after 12 miles (19km) to the **Crooked Tree Wildlife Sanctuary** ❻ (www.belizeaudubon.org; daily 8am–4.30pm). This string of four lagoons, connected by swamps and rivers, is one of Belize's richest bird habitats – nesting here are migratory flocks of egrets, tiger-herons, roseate spoonbills, and hundreds of other species. Perhaps the most impressive, although elusive, is the jabiru stork, the largest bird in the Western hemisphere, with a wingspan of up to 8ft (2.4 meters). The wildlife sanctuary was set up by the Belize Audubon Society in 1984 and is now managed by wardens from the village. Before entering, sign in at the tidy visitors' center, just outside the village of **Crooked Tree**, one of the first 'Banks', or logging camps, founded by British logwood cutters in the 17th century. Before the causeway was built in the 1980s, the only way to get to Crooked Tree was by boat. The lagoon is a natural reservoir in the Belize River Valley and regularly floods in the rainy season.

The origin of the village's name is the source of local humor, with some swearing it was the site of a huge old crooked tree while others claim it was the hideout for three nefarious buccaneers or bandits. Either version seems plausible since twisted trees still abound and almost all villagers seem to have Tillett, Rhaburn or Wade as a surname.

The managers of the sanctuary can provide information on nature trails and birdlife. The ideal way to visit is by taking a boat trip into the swamps and lagoons (call the visitors' center or any of the resorts in Crooked Tree). Peak birdwatching season is between April and May, when hatching begins (most migratory birds arrive in November, and many leave before the rainy season starts in July). As usual, start at dusk. Check in at the Sanctuary Information Center (the visitors' center), when you arrive. There are three daily buses from Belize City, in the morning and afternoon.

Aside from bird life, the waterways of Crooked Tree have thriving communities of turtle and Morelet's crocodiles; it is also one of the last places in Belize where logwood can still be found. Crooked Tree is not only famous for its birds; to Belizeans the name has long been synonymous with cashews. To celebrate this nifty nut, every May the village holds the **Cashew Festival**. It features nut roasting and every imaginable cashew-based product, as well as local cuisine and music.

Paddleboarding on Crooked Tree Lagoon.

Ascending the High Temple
at Lamanai.

FROM LAMANAI TO COROZAL

Northern Belize's economy is based on sugar cane, but its jungle-shaded ruins and pioneering wildlife preserves are the draw for visitors.

While the rest of Belize, from Cayo to the Cayes, is solidly on the tourist trail, Northern Belize remains largely undiscovered. And that's a big part of its appeal. This rural, quiet region nudges up against Mexico and is the territory of Hispanics or mestizos – Spanish is as common as Creole and there's a distinctive Latin flair to the villages and towns. The Latin influence is also noticeable in the cuisine, which is a delicious blend of Mexican and Belizean. As for commerce: sugar cane continues to be king and just about every family is either growing it, trucking it, or processing it.

Tourism is a sideline, so you won't find the eco-lodges of San Ignacio or the lively bars of San Pedro. But if you like your Maya ruins remote and mysterious and your towns and villages untouched and genuine, then you'll enjoy what sleepy Orange Walk, and even sleepier Corozal, have to offer.

LAMANAI

In the case of Lamanai, it's about the journey *and* the destination. The trip to **Lamanai** ❼ (daily 8am–5pm) is often as memorable as the impressive ruins themselves, thanks to the adventurous journey required to get there, via a rugged dirt road or a dreamy river trip through the sinuous waterways of a remote jungle river. Located on

the banks of the **New River Lagoon**, it can be reached by easy day trips from Orange Walk Town. In addition, numerous tour companies offers trips to Lamanai from Belize City and the Cayes.

A rough but easily passable road runs through the finely named villages of **Dubloon Bank Savannah**, **Bound To Shine** and **Guinea Grass**, into the sugar cane country of the New River. Trucks weighed down with cane lumber by, operated privately by local farmers who are paid by the ton. From the small docks at **Shipyard**, motorboats

⊙ Main attractions
Lamanai
Orange Walk
Banquitas House of
  Culture
Corozal
Corozal House of Culture
Río Bravo Conservation
  Area
Chan Chich Lodge
Shipstern Nature Reserve

Map on page 134

Snail kite in flight over the New River Lagoon.

leave for the hour-long journey along the New River's inky black waters.

The river and surrounding swamp is teeming with wildlife, including a healthy population of Morelet's crocodiles. These gave Lamanai its name – Maya for 'submerged crocodile' – and make the prospect of swimming, while safe, rather nerve-racking. Apart from pointing out birdlife, most boat drivers will bump up against gutted tree trunks on the shoreline, waking up a mass of tiny, sleeping bats, and sending them in a cloud over passengers' heads.

THE LAST SURVIVING MAYA CITY

By the time you reach the ruins, you feel like Indiana Jones, and since you may well have the place to yourself, there's nobody to destroy the illusion. A few thatched-roofed houses have been built at the dockside for the ruin's guards, along with an open-air picnic hut and a small museum piled high with Maya artifacts. Several paths run through into the dense jungle, which is inhabited by families of black howler monkeys. The ancient city is continually being unearthed, and workers are constantly having to keep the encroaching vegetation at bay.

Lamanai was first settled some 3,000 years ago and its most impressive temples were built in the Preclassic period around 100 BC. Several centuries later, in the Classic period, the population had increased from 20,000 to 50,000.

What makes Lamanai unique is that it was still inhabited when the first Spanish conquistadors arrived in search of gold here in the 16th century. The population was about a quarter its Classic number, and its most spectacular temples were untended. How Lamanai survived the cataclysm that devastated the other Maya cities is unknown. In any case, Spanish missionaries quickly set about building a church to convert the heathens. The Maya rebelled and burned it in the 1640s, but European-imported diseases soon decimated the community. Even so, there were a few Maya inhabitants here when British settlers arrived in the 19th century;

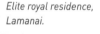

Elite royal residence, Lamanai.

the new colonialists drove them out to Guatemala so the land could be cleared for sugar.

Thomas Gann, a British medical officer and amateur archeologist made the first modern excavations at Lamanai in 1917, but it wasn't until 1974 that large-scale digging was begun by Canadian Dr David Pendergast of the Royal Ontario Museum. His wife, archeologist Dr Elizabeth Graham, worked with him there until the mid-1980s. If you'd like to stay near the ruins, one of the best spots is the Lamanai Outpost Lodge (www.lamanai.com), which has thatched cabanas with private decks and a lagoon-facing restaurant which serves excellent local cuisine.

EXPLORING THE RUINS

The Lamanai pyramids are still known by their dry archeological labels. The first on the path is **P9-56**. While its exterior dates from the 6th century AD, this pyramid was found to have been built over a finely preserved temple from five centuries earlier. The most famous feature is a 13ft (4-meter) high limestone face carved into its side, now protected from the elements by a makeshift roof: its combination of thick lips, bared teeth, dreamy eyes, and elongated forehead (created by the Maya custom of flattening their children's skulls) make the image half terrifying, half serene.

A second statue is known to be on the left side of the temple stairs, but archeologists left it buried to protect it from torrential rains and possible looters.

The giant mask of Lamanai.

Lamanai's best-known and most impressive pyramid is **N10-43**, a steep, 112ft (34-meter) high edifice. It reached its present height by around 100 BC, making it the largest Preclassic structure in the whole of Mesoamerica (although not as tall as the Classic pyramids at Xunantinich and Caracol, it is still considerably higher than any modern Belizean building). Like most Maya structures, it was modified heavily.

The temple's steps are in good condition following restoration and can be climbed for breathtaking views across the jungle canopy and New River, with

View from the high temple at Lamanai.

the cries of birds and occasionally howler monkeys echoing upward. This makes the perfect vantage point for picturing ancient Maya rituals (priests would take positions on the temple, with the rest of the population gathered below in the plaza); or imagining Maya astronomers gathering by night to contemplate the heavens.

Below pyramid N10-43 is the **ball court**, where the violent *pok-ta-pok* was played; Pendergast found pottery containing mercury here, the only time the substance has been found at a Maya site. In the makeshift hut nearby is a **stela** carved with hieroglyphics; underneath it was found the bones of six children, assumed to have been sacrificed.

Aside from the Maya structures, at the nearby village of **Indian Church** are the remains of two 16th-century Spanish missions and a ruined sugar mill built by former Confederate soldiers in the 1870s. Despite an influx of squatters escaping from bloody civil wars in neighboring Guatemala and El Salvador during the 1980s, this once-thriving area remains all but uninhabited – and the more mysterious for it.

ORANGE WALK

Sprawling across to the Guatemalan and Mexican borders, the vast Orange Walk District can be thought of as having two largely unrelated regions. To the east are the urban centers (such as they are), surrounded by seemingly endless fields of sugar cane; as in neighboring Corozal District, the agriculture was largely begun by refugees from the Mexican Caste Wars in the 1850s, and today the small villages have a curious mix of laid-back Caribbean and Hispanic flavors.

Meanwhile, lying to the west of Orange Walk District are great swathes of Belize's most remote savannah and rainforests. Until the mid-1980s, these uninhabited lands were entirely owned by a single logging operation, the Belize Estates Company – a million-acre (400,000-hectare) holding that made up one-fifth of Belize's total area. Today the rainforests have been set aside for one of Central America's

Coat of arms mural, Orange Walk Town.

largest and most ambitious conservation reserves, and include such oddities as the luxurious Chan Chich Lodge (see page 147) set in the main plaza of a lost Maya temple.

Forming the hub of northern Belize's main roads, **Orange Walk Town ❽** is still the most convenient, if not the most interesting or comfortable, base for exploring the north. Although this is the largest town in the north, it's a dusty, quiet place, with just a handful of sights. The **Banquitas House of Culture** (www.nichbelize.org/houses-of-culture; Mon–Thu 8.30am–5pm, Fri 8.30am–4.30pm), a small museum and cultural center just north of the town, has exhibits on the history of Orange Walk and the logwood industry, and some Maya artifacts on display.

Orange Walk Town is fondly called 'Sugar City' by residents because it is smack in the center of the northern sugar industry. Folks from the rest of Belize generally whip through Orange Walk on their way to Chetumal across the border in Mexico. But when they do stop in Orange Walk Town it's for the country's best corn *dukunu*, *tamales*, or tacos sold by vendors in Central Park.

While it may not have the mass appeal of Lamanai, the **Cuello ❾** archeological site on the property of the Cuello rum distillery, some 3 miles (5km) to the west of Orange Walk Town, is believed to be the oldest Maya ceremonial site in the area, dating back some 2,600 years. Permission must be obtained from the distillery to go onto the property. Today, there is not much to see at the site, with one small pyramid and a few earth-covered mounds. Probably because these modest offerings cannot compete with the likes of Lamanai, Cuello is mainly frequented by serious archeology students.

WAVES OF MIGRATION

Just outside the town is the still-active Tower Hill Sugar Refinery. It was built in 1974, and with the closing of Corozal District's Libertad refinery in the mid-1980s, it now handles much of Belize's cane. In the cutting season, all roads leading to Tower Hill are choked with lines of cane-laden trucks and trailers.

Mennonite boys, Indian Creek Village.

The still-unpaved road from Orange Walk to Blue Creek was settled by mestizos and Yucatec Maya fleeing the Mexican Caste Wars, and many villages still bear Maya names like **Yo Creek** and **Chan Pine Ridge**. In the 1950s they were joined by a new immigrant group: the Mennonites.

The Mennonites in Orange Walk District have ended up in two settlements, each representing opposite ends of their philosophical spectrum. The most conservative sect lives in **Shipyard** . Known as the Old Colony, this is where the Mennonite women wear long, dark dresses and large beribboned straw hats in a style brought from Europe, while taciturn men wear suspenders or overalls rather than belts.

Along the Río Bravo escarpment in northwestern Orange Walk District, the more progressive Mennonite community of **Blue Creek Village** has sweeping views and a prosperous mien. The Mennonites who came here in 1958 split the community when they decided to use heavy machinery, forbidden by conservatives, to clear the jungle. The

A northern jacana crosses lily pads, New River.

Blue Creek settlement has a distinctively North American feel, since many of the settlers came from Canada.

UNIQUE WILDERNESS EXPERIMENT

Until the mid-1980s, a million acres (400,000 hectares) of rainforest in Orange Walk District was owned by the venerable, 150-year-old Belize Estates Company. Lumber, mainly mahogany, cedar, and Santa María, was logged from this remote area. The logs were then transported via a railroad, no longer in existence, to the New River Lagoon at Hill Bank. From there they floated by a circuitous route past Orange Walk Town to Chetumal Bay and finally down to Belize City. The logging was always carried out selectively, leaving these forests roughly 75 percent intact, while most of the rest of Central America's rainforests have been devastated.

Then, in the mid-1980s, Belize Estates Company was bought by the late Belizean businessman Barry Bowen and subsequently divided into four parcels, one of which was purchased by a consortium of conservation organizations that joined together to form the Programme for Belize (PFB). In 1988, this land became the **Río Bravo Conservation Area** , which now covers over 300,000 acres (121,000 hectares).

In a formal agreement with the government, PFB is holding these lands in perpetual trust for the people of Belize. The aim is to generate income from eco-tourism which will provide funds for conservation efforts throughout the country and training for Belizeans. The range and depth of flora and fauna is as impressive as anywhere in the country: the region contains some 200 species of trees, and 400 species of birds; all five species of wild cats found in Belize also flourish here.

Within the area's boundaries are also several Maya sites that are now being studied. **La Milpa** is one of the largest in Belize, with at least 18 pla-zas, two large reservoirs and 60 major structures, stelae, and courtyard groups. It is continually being exca-vated by groups from Boston University in conjunction with Belize's Depart-ment of Archeology. The other parcels of land are also being preserved, in different ways. Coca-Cola Foods came under attack from foreign conservation groups for its alleged plans to clear rainforest to grow citrus trees. In fact, the property under consideration was largely savannah, but being sensitive to public pressure, Coca-Cola donated 42,000 acres (17,000 hectares) of its land to the Programme for Belize (PFB) and to date no citrus development has taken place on its remaining property. In addition, PFB, has purchased pri-vate land through funds provided by supporters in the USA, UK, and else-where. The Río Bravo field station is used for university wildlife, sustainable forest management, and archeological study programs, but it also encourages ecotourism. Accommodations include *cabañas* and 'green dormitories' near La Milpa (3 miles/5km from the ruins) and Hill Bank field stations. Prior booking is required from the Pro-gramme for Belize Office (www.pfbelize. org) and applications for field studies and research must be submitted in advance. The Río Bravo management area is 31 miles (50km) from Orange Walk with the main access from Blue Creek Village.

HOTEL IN A MAYA RUIN

Just south of the Río Bravo Area lies the **Gallon Jug** parcel, some 130,000 acres (52,000 hectares) of tropical forest retained by Barry Bowen as a private preserve. Intensive farming is carried out in a small area, with corn, soybeans, coffee, cacao, and cardamom being grown. Also, an unu-sual cattle project is experimenting with English Hereford bloodlines to improve local stock.

But the best known hotel for travel-ers here is **Chan Chich Lodge** 🔞 (www. chanchich.com), situated – with the Archeology Department's blessing – in the lower plaza of an ancient Maya

Harvesting sugar cane.

⊙ THE SUGAR CANE INDUSTRY

Sugar cane has shaped the social history of northern Belize since the middle of the 19th century. Local British settlers were delighted to discover that refugees from the Mexican Caste Wars were competent farmers (a trade that creoles have traditionally disdained).

With mahogany and logwood exports declining, the settlers turned to exporting sugar back to England. By the mid-1860s, sugar produc-tion had risen to 1 million lbs (450,000kg) a year and was being turned into 50,000 gallons (230,000 liters) of rum. By the 1930s the enormous Libertad factory was built here; in the 1960s it was purchased by the British firm Tate & Lyle, which set about increasing sugar production to the maximum.

Even small landowners, formerly subsistence farmers, began to grow the undemanding cane, known as 'the lazy man's crop.' Sadly, US demand for sugar collapsed in the 1970s; although 75 percent of local land was devoted to sugar cane, the Libertad refinery closed in 1986. Having abandoned maize growing and other milpa crops, many small farmers began relying upon relatives abroad or turned to growing the more lucrative marijuana.

While raw sugar cane is still grown everywhere, it is now processed in Orange Walk District.

The colorful heliconia plant is also known as the lobster claw or false bird of paradise.

Fishing on the New River.

site. Chan Chich Lodge was carefully planned to have a minimum impact on the surrounding tropical forest and the Maya plaza (it also protects the site from robbers). It features luxurious thatched *cabañas* and a cozy dining room and bar, paneled in a variety of local hardwoods. There is also a screened swimming pool and Jacuzzi.

As a private preserve protected from hunting, Chan Chich enjoys some of the most abundant concentrations of tropical forest wildlife in Central America. Various tame animals wander around the site, including deer and foxes; there is a wealth of birdlife and jaguar sightings are not uncommon.

With more than 9 miles (14.5km) of hiking trails and a small cadre of natural history guides, the tropical forests surrounding Chan Chich are unusually accessible. Transportation is available to the resort by air to a private airstrip, or by road via Orange Walk.

PULLTROUSER SWAMP

Finally, in the remote region north of the Río Bravo area, in the northeast corner of Orange Walk District, the picturesquely named **Pulltrouser Swamp** ⓮ offers an unusual perspective on Maya agricultural habits. Tropical soils are notoriously poor, but the Maya built an extensive canal system here. Raised cultivation fields were built, with waterlilies used as mulch, hints that the Maya were certainly more sophisticated than simple slash-and-burn farmers. Visible signs of the original canals have been identified on satellite images, but nothing can be seen now from the ground.

COROZAL

Tucked up in the northern limit of Belize, Corozal District looks like it has changed little since colonial days – or, by a further stretch of the imagination, the days of the Maya. The district is still only sparsely populated and scattered with small, sleepy villages. Its entire eastern half is swampy savannah, accessible only by an uneven road that roughly traces the New River and Freshwater Creek; the western coast is dominated by sugar cane, and is one of

the most intensely cultivated agricultural areas in the country.

Corozal District's population has been largely Spanish-speaking for many generations, due to violence across the Mexican border. In the mid-19th century, Mexico's Yucatán Peninsula was wracked by the murderous Caste Wars, waged between enslaved Maya Indians, mestizos, and whites. After the battle of Bacalar in 1849, thousands of refugees, both Indian and mestizo, fled south to the relative safety of British Honduras. While Corozal District shares the mixed ethnicity that so characterizes Belize, many of its people still bear Maya surnames such as Ek, Uck, and Tzul.

Only 20 minutes' drive from the Mexican border is the district's urban hub, **Corozal Town** ⑮. The town overlooks Chetumal Bay and most recreational activity centers around the sea wall that winds its way around the edge of the town – the locals splash around in the waters here, which is especially popular with families.

For an overview on Corozal and the region, head to the **Corozal House of Culture** (www.nichbelize.org/houses-of-culture; Mon–Fri 8am–5pm), housed in a renovated market dating back to 1886. The well-curated museum features a wide range of exhibits, including local art and Maya artifacts. It also hosts special events throughout the year, like Garífuna drumming performances.

Corozal has a number of comfortable resorts, like the airy Almond Tree Resort (www.almondtreeresort.com), which has elegant rooms and a pool, as well as the lively Tony's Inn and Beach Resort (www.tonysinn.com), with landscaped gardens, and Cielo Restaurant, which serves excellent international and Belizean fare.

Because of its proximity to the border, Corozal seems more like a suburb of Chetumal (Mexico) than a Belizean town. Especially since Corozalenos regularly cross over to shop, go to movies or bars, even to buy their groceries. But make no mistake, even northerners with close family ties in Chetumal consider themselves Belizeans through and through and

○ **Fact**

The name Corozal comes from the cohune, a large palm that likes fertile soil and was a symbol of fecundity to the Maya (its name is thought to come from the Spanish *cojones*, meaning testicles, after the tree's round nuts).

A horse trek from Chan Chich Lodge.

would balk at any insinuation that they share dual nationality.

VILLAGE LIFE

Those who live in the many surrounding villages are equally, if not more, attached to their home district. Many young people commute two hours each way on a daily basis to attend school or work in Belize City. Even those professionals who later find employment in the larger commercial center or the nation's capital, Belmopan, prefer to make the pilgrimage home almost every weekend.

And they always return home to vote. Politics is a serious business in Corozal, and the entire north for that matter, with certain party leaders sustaining their reign for decades. Loyalty to color (red or blue) borders on fanatical and campaigning is fierce around the national or local town council elections.

Crime has also taken a foothold in some areas, with residents of beautiful little villages with ancient names such as Xaibe and Patchacan living

in fear of night-time robberies or drug-related activity. But for the most part, traditional family-oriented life continues in the Corozal district on a relaxed, steady and reliable tempo. Villages with Spanish saints' names like San Román, San Narciso, San Esteban, and San Joaquín hold annual fiestas. Everyone turns out to attend Mass, followed by a communal feast, Latino music, and carnival rides.

A BRIEF HISTORY

Founded in 1849 by refugees from the massacre at Bacalar, Corozal Town today is neat and clean, designed on a classically Hispanic grid pattern with three parks and friendly, mostly Spanish-speaking people. Until 1955, its homes and buildings were thatch and adobe. But that year, Hurricane Janet tore the town to shreds; rebuilding took the form of the concrete and wood structures that characterize the town today.

There are the remains of a small fort near the main plaza, from the days of the Caste Wars when Mexican bandits

A cable ferry crossing near Copper Bank.

regularly crossed into Belize; the town hall has a mural depicting local history, by painter Manuel Villamor Reyes (which includes a scene of the Indian massacre at Bacalar, Mexico).

With 13,000 people, Corozal Town is one of Belize's largest settlements, but it retains the sleepy look of an undiscovered outpost. However, research indicates that the place has been more or less continuously occupied from 1200 BC.

Occasionally protruding from the ground in the northern parts of the city are a series of line-of-stone foundations, the remnants of a Maya settlement called Santa Rita. While most Maya structures were elevated, those of Santa Rita were only slightly raised, so subsequent building was made on top of ancient tombs and residential structures. When excavation began in the 1980s, it was found that more than 50 percent of Santa Rita's structures had been paved over by present-day Corozal Town. Some had even been ground up for road fill. Today only one modest structure can readily be seen, near Corozal's bottled drinks distribution center. Interesting finds at Santa Rita included a few gold objects – which suggest possible trade with Mexican civilizations like the Aztecs, since Belize is not a gold producer and gold is not normally associated with other Maya sites in the country. A skeleton inlaid with jade and mica was another unique find at the site.

CERROS

Not far from Corozal Town is the region's best-known Maya ruin, **Cerros** 16 (daily 8am–5pm), which means 'hills.' It is pleasantly situated on the peninsula between Corozal Bay and **Lowry's Bight**, the gateway at the river mouth into the interior of Belize and northeastern Petén. Evidence of intensive Pre-Hispanic agriculture has been identified along these rivers. Cerros was occupied primarily during the late Preclassic period, roughly from 300 BC to the beginning of the Christian era, with a peak population of about 2,000.

Cerros can be reached by boat from Corozal Town or by land along a rough dirt road. Three acropolises and plazas can be seen, although they are covered by vegetation and the tall masks, depicting people and animals, were plastered over by archeologists to protect them from the elements. Cerros' largest structure, Number Four, is 70ft (21 meters) tall with a massive base, roughly 175 by 200ft (53 by 60 meters) and offers a panoramic vista of the coast from its peak. It was possibly abandoned when the Maya started relying on overland trading routes instead of the waterways for which Cerros was strategically located.

SUGAR AND SWAMPS

The paved **Philip Goldson (Northern) Highway** runs south of Corozal Town, through the western half of the district towards Orange Walk Town. The route passes through lands devoted to sugar

Weighing the potato crop.

⊙ Tip

The small fishing village of Consejo is the northernmost coastal settlement of Belize, with a few holiday homes and a couple of hotels.

cane. Five miles (8km) south is the ruin of the **Aventura Sugar Mill**, one of the oldest in the district. Only one chimney remains standing. Local villages are still geared to producing cane, although its value is much reduced and it has to be sent south to Orange Walk for processing.

This is one of the least developed parts of Belize, and until very recently was difficult to reach by car (a better road has been put through, although still dodgy in the wet season – four-wheel drive is advised). Small villages like Little Belize and Chunox dot the way, and at the end of the road is the fishing village of **Sarteneja**. The name means 'hole in a flat rock,' referring to a *cenote* or well. This certainly must have been an attraction to the ancient Maya in this low rainfall district, with levels of precipitation well below the rest of Belize.

Sarteneja is a pleasant enough place to pass an afternoon. The buildings' pastel colors are drained by the fierce sun, and you can go swimming right off the main pier in waters that range from milky to clear. Often local builders can be seen repairing or building boats in dry dock while fishermen cruise in with their catch of lobster, conch, or fish. With only one bus service a day, many Sartenejans find crossing the bay by boat to shop in Chetumal in Mexico cheaper and more convenient than traveling to Belize City.

Just outside Sarteneja – and the main reason for coming to this remote corner – is the **Shipstern Nature Reserve** ⑰ (www.visitshipstern.com), founded in 1988. It was originally a self-sustaining business devoted to exporting butterflies to Europe and the US; the profits were used to finance the nature reserve and preserve 27,000 acres (11,000 hectares) of coastal savannah.

The reserve features an extensive, shallow, brackish water lagoon system, home to breeding colonies of many varieties of birds like the reddish egret and the wood stork. The latter is rapidly disappearing in both North America and Belize – near Shipstern, one of the last remaining breeding

Boat trip along the New River.

colonies of wood storks was almost destroyed by Mexican poachers, who like to barbecue the fledgling young. Today a watchman is stationed in a remote camp in Shipstern to guard a nesting colony of these stately birds, and numbers of successfully fledged young are rapidly increasing.

Shipstern Nature Reserve's headquarters features a few neat stuccoed buildings. Although butterflies are no longer exported, flight cages filled with colorful species are still on view; visitors are treated to a pleasant tour and a visit to the botanical collection. The Reserve's Chiclero Botanical Trail offers a pleasant stroll through dense forest with labeled trees common to this coastal forest type.

The reserve produces a newsletter, *Paces*, which discusses local environmental concerns and is distributed throughout Sarteneja village. Sunny days are the best time to visit the reserve as the butterflies are most active then, whilst on overcast days they tend to hide amidst the foliage. The reserve is managed by the Swiss-based International Tropical Conservation Foundation.

ONWARD TO MEXICO

The border crossing into Mexico is just north of Corozal Town, at **Santa Elena** on the Río Hondo. Regular buses run to the Mexican town of **Chetumal** (passengers disembark for border formalities and walk across the small bridge, where the bus is waiting for them on the other side). Many Belizeans make the trip in a day for a taste of the distinctly different atmosphere of Mexico and to take advantage of the prices in Chetumal's many duty-free stores. In an ironic twist to Belize-Mexico relations, the recently established Corozal Free Zone in Belize is starting to create some resentment among the Chetumal business owners. While they welcome Belizean consumers, they are now seeing thousands of Mexicans lining up, bumper to bumper crossing over into Belize (taking their pesos with them) to purchase duty-free gasoline, name-brand clothing, and other luxury goods.

The coastal ruin of Cerros.

The Mopan River.

WEST TO SAN IGNACIO

From the underwhelming capital Belmopan, to the heartland of Belize's eco-tourism around San Ignacio, the west of the country has vast tracts of wilderness, tamed only by luxurious jungle lodges.

When travelers talk about visiting the interior of Belize, they are usually referring to the lush, mountainous rainforests around the town of San Ignacio, long the heart of the country's ecotourism trade. The region is a nature-lover's fantasy come true. Spread out across a remote subtropical wilderness are dozens of *cabana*-style lodges, many of them quite luxurious. Within striking distance – by car, horseback, canoe, or foot – are secluded, jungle-rimmed swimming holes, enormous limestone caverns, Belize's most significant Maya ruins and Central America's highest waterfalls. The background music is the shriek of tropical birds, while iguanas, gibnuts, and skunks habitually stroll across the well-marked nature trails.

Meanwhile, the rainforests are surprisingly free of Belize's least popular life form, the mosquito – the higher altitude makes days around San Ignacio hot without being overwhelming, while evenings can almost be described as cool.

On the frontier with Guatemala, this is also one of the more Hispanic parts of Belize, populated largely by Spanish-speaking mestizos, and Maya farmers; second in numbers come creoles, followed by a classically Belizean smattering of East Indians, Chinese, and Lebanese. Several large communities

of Mennonites farm the rich land and can be seen clattering along the highways in horse-drawn carriages.

From Belize City, the journey west is itself an interesting one, with Belize Zoo (see page 119) just 30 minutes before you reach Belmopan on the George Price (Western) Highway, Guanacaste Park literally on the doorstep of the capital and St Herman's Cave and the inland version of the Blue Hole just a few miles past Belmopan. All are popular, and worthwhile, detours. For curiosity's sake, you can, of course,

⚙ Main attractions
Guanacaste National Park
Blue Hole National Park
San Ignacio
Cahal Pech
Belize Botanic Gardens
Green Hills Butterfly Ranch
Mountain Pine Ridge Forest Reserve
Hidden Valley Falls
Río Frío Cave
Chiquibul Forest Reserve
Xunantunich

Maps on pages 156 and 168

Hand-winched ferry en route to Xunantunich.

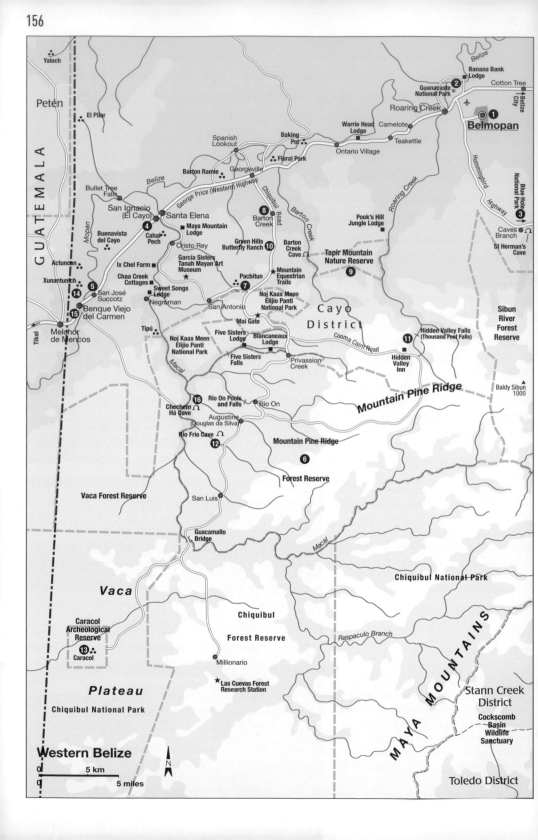

Yaloch

Petén

El Pilar

GUATEMALA

Bullet Tree
Falls

San Ignacio
(El Cayo)
Santa Elena

Buenavista
del Cayo

Actuncan

Xunantunich

Mopan

San José
Succotz

Benque Viejo
del Carmen

Melchor
de Mencos

Tikal

Banana Bank
Lodge

Guanacaste
National Park

Roaring Creek

Cotton Tree

Belize
City

Belmopan

Warrie Head
Lodge

Camelote

Teakettle

Spanish
Lookout

Baking
Pot

Ontario Village

Floral Park

Barton Ramie

Georgeville

Cahal
Pech

Maya Mountain
Lodge

Cristo Rey

Green Hills
Butterfly Ranch

Barton
Creek

Barton Creek
Cave

Pook's Hill
Jungle Lodge

Roaring Creek

Hummingbird Highway

Blue Hole National Park

Caves
Branch

St Herman's
Cave

George Price (Western Highway)

Chiquibul Road

Barton Creek

Tapir Mountain
Nature Reserve

Ix Chel Farm

Garcia Sisters
Tanah Mayan Art
Museum

Pacbitun

Mountain
Equestrian
Trails

Chaa Creek
Cottages

Sweet Songs
Lodge

Negroman

San Antonio

Noj Kaax Meen
Elijio Panti
National Park

Cayo
District

Sibun
River
Forest
Reserve

Tipú

Noj Kaax Meen
Elijio Panti
National Park

Mai Gate

Five Sisters
Lodge

Blancaneaux
Lodge

Five Sisters
Falls

Privassion
Creek

Cooma Cairn Road

Hidden Valley Falls
(Thousand Foot Falls)

Hidden
Valley
Inn

Baldy Sibun
1000

Macal

Chechem
Há Cave

Río On Pools
and Falls

Río On

Mountain Pine Ridge

Augustine
(Douglas da Silva)

Río Frio Cave

Mountain Pine Ridge

Forest Reserve

Vaca Forest Reserve

San Luis

Guacamallo
Bridge

Macal

Chiquibul National Park

Vaca

Chiquibul

Forest Reserve

Raspaculo Branch

MAYA MOUNTAINS

Caracol
Archeological
Reserve

Caracol

Millionario

Plateau

Chiquibul National Park

Las Cuevas Forest
Research Station

Stann Creek
District

Cockscomb
Basin
Wildlife
Sanctuary

Western Belize

0   5 km

0   5 miles

N

Toledo District

stop in the capital, although even more than four decades after its establishment, Belmopan continues to remain largely the domain of government workers – a far cry from the commercial social bustle of Belize City.

BELMOPAN

Founded in 1971, **Belmopan** ❶ is the Brazilia of Belize: an artificial capital that has never quite caught on. Government ministries are based here, but most politicians would rather commute from Belize City than take up permanent residence.

Belmopan was former Prime Minister George Price's vision of 'a modern capital for an emerging nation.' The idea of an inland location had first been fielded after Belize City was devastated by Hurricane Hattie in 1961. Price hoped that a planned city would attract Belizeans from all over the country, and eventually replace Belize City as a commercial and cultural center. He also hoped it would centralize the government by bringing each ministry together on the same compound with new, efficient facilities.

Things didn't go quite so smoothly as on paper, however. The new government offices, designed to resemble a Maya temple and plaza, were much too small, so today many offices are located away from the center of town. Instead of cutting red tape, the move to Belmopan created it. Citizens had to travel all the way to the capital to have documents signed or obtain permits. Before long, government branch offices in Belize City and other towns were given the same power as the head office in the capital.

The biggest problem of all was that Belizeans weren't willing to move to Belmopan – and most still aren't. Belmopan's population hovers around 20,000 inhabitants, many of whom are refugees from neighboring countries in Central America. A large number of Belizeans who work here commute the hour or so each way from Belize City or San Ignacio rather than live here full time. Even after Hurricane Mitch miraculously bypassed Belize in 1998 and forced thousands to bunk in with Belmopan relatives, there was no mass rush to move out of Belize City into the new capital. After considerable pressure from the government, the University College of Belize (now the University of Belize) finally agreed to expand its existing Belmopan Junior College and vacate most of its Belize City classrooms.

It's not that Belizeans don't like Belmopan, it's just that they find the town too quiet. With only a smattering of hotels and a few restaurants, there isn't much for the predominantly young, single, government employees to do for excitement. One of the biggest events of the year is the National Agriculture and Trade Show, held in late April at the fairgrounds, which draws thousands for three days of exhibitions and socializing. Belmopan's searing temperatures don't help lure anyone to settle here either: in the middle of the day, it's rarely below 100°F (40°C) and noticeably devoid of breezes.

Streetside restaurant, Belmopan.

QUALITY OF LIFE

On the other hand, the few who choose to live in Belmopan enjoy well-maintained roads, clean neighborhoods, and a low crime rate. Unlike Belize City, there is ample room for expansion. Belmopan residents also take in their stride the numerous Central American refugees in settlements like **Salvapan**, **Las Flores**, and **Ten Cents Creek** on the outskirts of town. The immigrants here have fitted in more easily than in other parts of Belize, taking jobs as domestic laborers, construction workers, street vendors, or milpa farmers, and sending their children to school. And, Belmopan's merchants and restaurant and bar owners welcome the new business.

EXPLORING THE MINI-CAPITAL

Belmopan has few historical monuments, and most of the buildings are administrative offices – in 10 minutes on the **Ring Road**, you can take in all the sights. But if you have to go to Belmopan on business, or are making a stop en route to somewhere else, there are a few pleasant places to spend a couple of hours.

The best place to start is **Market Square**, which at any given moment is usually the busiest place in town: buses serving destinations all over Belize stop here and there are several banks, the Caladium restaurant, where the menu includes traditional Belizean and international dishes, smaller food stands, and shops nearby. Central American street vendors sell tasty corn and chicken tamales and other local goodies.

Among the city's key national buildings are the **National Archives**, near the ring road and open to the public, which is used mostly for research and contains old government documents, newspapers, and photographs, on everything from Hurricane Hattie to Garífuna history. The Governor General stays at **Belize House**, near the National Assembly.

By following the Ring Road you can find Belmopan's best hotel, the Bull Frog Inn. This is a good place to sample

National Assembly building, Belmopan.

local cuisine or revive yourself with a cool drink. Just behind the inn is Ken-Mar's Bed and Breakfast, a colorful place to stay, with fresh fruit for breakfast. Most of the Ring Road runs past housing developments, with modest homes on streets named for Belize's wildlife and plants. The **Belmopan Hospital** is the only emergency facility between San Ignacio and Belize City.

BACK TO NATURE

After a quick tour of Belmopan, the **Guanacaste National Park** ❷ makes a good place to freshen up, right at the intersection of the George Price (Western) Highway. Not only does Guanacaste have magnificent trees and nature trails, but not too far from the main road there is an incredible swimming spot on the river. The current is very slow here as the water cascades gently over the rocks; locals wade right in with their clothing on, so there's no need to miss the refreshing cold water just because you forgot a bathing suit. A bus from Belize City, Belmopan or points south can drop you right at the entrance to the park making it one of the most accessible natural reserves in Belize.

Heading west from Belmopan, 13 miles (21km) down the Hummingbird Highway is the St Herman's **Blue Hole National Park** ❸. There is one entrance near the Blue Hole itself (at the bottom of a long flight of steps) and another at the visitors' center near St. Herman's Cave. The blue hole is an astonishing sight: it's truly blue, with just a touch of green at the edges of the 30ft (9-meter) diameter pool. The natural wonder is actually a collapsed karst sinkhole, estimated to be about 100ft (31 meters) deep. In the dry season the water is extremely cold because it is cooled by the underground limestone. The Belize Audubon Society manages the park, which also contain more than 250 species of birds and other animals. There are self-guided trails near the cave, which is one of few in Belize that can be entered without a special permit from the archeology department. Camping and caving equipment can be rented at the visitors' center.

> **◉ Tip**
>
> Buses on the George Price (Western) Highway pass right by the entrance to the Guanacaste National Park.

Road to Spanish Lookout.

⊙ **Tip**

A good and easy walk from San Ignacio, taking about half an hour, is due north along the Macal River to its meeting with the Mopan River at Branch Mouth. A pleasant swimming spot here will help you cool off.

CAYO DISTRICT

If you manage to tear yourself away from the Blue Hole or have spent your morning stalking animals with your camera at the zoo, the Maya ruins, and pleasures of the Mountain Pine Ridge still await you farther west. Get back on the George Price (Western) Highway and head for San Ignacio, the base for all eco-tourism activities in the Cayo District.

Historically, the region around San Ignacio has always kept to itself. Maya armies here put up one of the longest struggles against the Spaniards in the Americas. The Spanish conquest of the 1540s never reached this remote region, and later news that the Castilian king expected them to pay taxes, obey Spanish laws and worship the Christian god was poorly received. Newly built churches were burned in rebellion, and, according to the chronicles, several captured soldiers and missionaries were sacrificed.

The inhabitants of Tipu, a city on the **Macal River** (possibly where a farmhouse now stands in the village of Negroman), led the resistance. Two

Franciscan friars thought that they had converted them to Christianity in 1618, only to find a year later that the entire population was secretly practicing idolatry. Twenty years later, the same friars were received by pagan priests who performed a mock Mass with tortillas as the eucharist. The Maya then smashed the crucifix, roughed up the friars, and sent them packing back to the coast.

European diseases like smallpox eventually all but wiped out the Indian population, and by the early 18th century the Spanish were able to assert control and resettle many survivors in Guatemala. British and creole lumbermen arrived, setting up logging camps and bringing with them the power of the British Crown. They quickly sold off Maya land and drove the last dispirited natives into easily manageable towns. San Ignacio started off as the major loading point on the Macal River for mahogany and chicle, growing slowly to its role today as the agricultural center of the region.

Due to its location at the confluence of two rivers, the area around

Paddleboarding on the Belize River.

⊙ LA RUTA MAYA RIVER CHALLENGE

Before Cayo District was linked to the coast by road, the only way to reach Belize City was via epic, 10-day boat journeys down the Macal and Belize rivers.

Recreating those pioneering days, La Ruta Maya Belize River Challenge (https://larutamaya.bz) is an annual canoe race, which starts at the Hawkesworth Bridge in San Ignacio and travels downstream, all the way into the Haulover Creek at Belize City, drawing attention en route to the natural beauty of the area, as well as its cultural history.

The event was first organized in the late 1990s and is held every March, usually around the 9th. In a relatively short time it has become one of Belize's biggest sporting events, with paddlers from Placencia and points south going shoulder to shoulder against teams from the west as well as the UK, US and other countries. If you're in San Ignacio when the three-day race kicks off, it's well worth getting up early to watch from the mist-covered banks of the river.

If you'd like to actually take part in the event, you'll need a three-person team (both women's and men's teams race together), a canoe, and personal supplies. There is a registration fee and some advance training on the river is strongly recommended.

San Ignacio became known as **Cayo**, after the Spanish word for cayes – coral islands off Belize's coast – while San Ignacio itself is also known as **El Cayo**. The name may be a reflection of the isolation early settlers felt from the rest of the world before a roadway was first pushed through in the 1930s. Until then, boat trips to Belize City took about 10 days, horseback journeys anywhere from two weeks to a month.

SAN IGNACIO

Today, however, thanks to the country's best paved road, the George Price (Western) Highway, San Ignacio can now be reached in a mere 90 minutes (for most of the year) by car from Belize City. En route from Belmopan are the tiny villages of **Teakettle** and **Georgeville**. The northern turn off to **Spanish Lookout** leads into the most populous Mennonite area. These Mennonites are by no means traditional, driving around in pick-up trucks, using telephones and machinery. Pancake-flat and rich brown, the country seems indistinguishable from, say, Ohio.

Built in a spectacular valley, on the edge of a ravine above the Macal River, the town of **San Ignacio** ❹ is separated from the neighboring village of **Santa Elena** by the **Hawkesworth Suspension Bridge** – a miniature model of the Brooklyn Bridge. Although it only has one lane, for westbound traffic, it remains one of the more impressive engineering feats in Belize. (Traffic heading in the other direction crosses the river farther downstream over the wooden Low Water Bridge).

San Ignacio was the last frontier in one of the most obscure corners of the British Empire, and several of its buildings retain a faded colonial charm. The police station, for example, perched above the bridge, looks like it belongs in an Indian hill station or a lost provincial outpost in a Somerset Maugham short story. The narrow streets are quiet to the point of somnolence – although the combined population of San Ignacio and Santa Elena is around 21,000, making this the largest metropolis of western Belize. It's worth timing your visit to be here for

Fresh produce at the Saturday market in San Ignacio.

Eva's Restaurant, San Ignacio.

> **Tip**

Horses or mountain bikes can be hired in San Ignacio to visit the village of **Bullet Tree Falls** and the ruins of **El Pilar**, which also have nature trails, with excellent birdwatching opportunities.

Saturday, when local farmers flock to the **market** with their produce.

San Ignacio is dotted with welcoming restaurants and bars, including the **Authentic Flavors Restaurant** on Burns Avenue, serving traditional Belizean fare, and **Serendib**, the only Sri Lankan restaurant in Belize, with tasty and reasonably priced curries. San Ignacio also has a wide range of accommodations, from the friendly budget **Hi-Et Guest House** to the **Midas Resort** on the riverbank.

San Ignacio draws many international travelers and Belizeans from other parts of the country, which translates into a boisterous bar scene, particularly on the weekends. At **Blue Angels** revelers hit the dance floor in between rounds of tropical cocktails, as live reggae and punta music fills the air.

MAYA CULTURE – AND BUTTERFLIES

Just off Buena Vista Road are the ruins of **Cahal Pech**. Although quite important for Belizean archeology, the main temple has been 'restored' for tourists, with crudely plastered carvings in a Disneyland style (and unlikely to impress anyone unless it's their first Maya ruin). Cahal Pech was populated around 1,000 BC until AD 800. The name means 'Place of the Ticks' – given in the 1950s when the area was used as a cow pasture.

Back on the George Price (Western) Highway, some 8 miles (13km) southwest of San Ignacio is the village of **San José Succotz ⑤**, by the rapids of a lush river valley where Maya women wash clothes on the rocks. The village has a strong Mopan Maya history, and many of the locals work at local Maya sites. Just east of San José Succotz is the **Tropical Wings Nature Center** (http://thetrekstop.com/tropical-wings; daily 9am–5pm), a colorful haven for more than 20 species of butterflies.

CHAA CREEK

If you want a taste of Belizean wilderness without having to go too deep into the 'bush', only 5 miles (8km) west of San Ignacio is a turn off that follows a tributary of the Macal River, **Chaa**

Hawksworth Bridge, San Ignacio.

Creek, to the heart of *cabaña* country. The best-known lodge here, the rustic-chic **Lodge at Chaa Creek** (https://www. chaacreek.com), also has one of the best locations, nestled amongst rainforest-covered hills in the Macal River valley. Each room is a separate cottage, decorated with local handicrafts and hardwood furniture made on-site by craftsmen. Cool breezes waft through large open windows facing down on the luscious river valley, and although there are not even mosquito nets, nothing more meddlesome than a flying beetle comes into the room. The all-inclusive resort has its own natural history center and butterfly farm, and offers a wide range of adventure activities in the area; horseback riding, canoeing, hiking, bird-watching, and mountain-biking. There is a fully equipped spa, with massage and other therapeutic treatments, which presumably helps guests to recuperate from all their other activities.

In this same district are a half dozen other places to stay, including the no less comfortable **Sweet Songs Jungle Lodge** (https://sweetsongslodge.com), with their own white-sand beach by the River Macal. The lodge's owners have established the **Belize Botanic Gardens** (http://belizebotanic.org; daily 7am–4pm) in 50 acres (20 hectares) of their property, developed after more than 10 years of reforestation work, planting some 2,500 trees. There is an excellent guided tour of the impressive grounds, which include hundreds of species of native trees, orchids, and a network of nature trails. A wildlife expert offers guided tours of the gardens (which attracts local bird life), or you can explore it on your own. The legacy of the late Ken Duplooy, who founded the garden, continues to inspire: fourteen new species of orchid have been discovered and one, *Pleurothallis duplooyii*, with tiny purple blooms, has been named for Duplooy.

INTO THE WILDERNESS

Cayo is, perhaps more than anywhere else in Belize, the land of eco-friendly luxury lodges. So, while having your own car to explore is an advantage, it

Cahal Pech.

is by no means necessary: Most lodges can organize tours to every corner of the district (or tours can be arranged through operators in San Ignacio).

The most popular excursion in the region is due south of San Ignacio to the **Mountain Pine Ridge Forest Reserve** ⑥. The sudden appearance of the pine forest, looking as if it is straight out of Vermont, is one of Belize's more peculiar geological anomalies. Geologists explain that the unique granite base and nutrient-poor soil content of the area was either thrust up from below Central America countless millennia ago or was a Caribbean island that was effectively pushed on top of the rest of the isthmus during its formation.

Two access roads run into the ridge from the George Price (Western) Highway. The first is the Cristo Rey road from Santa Elena, not far from the San Ignacio bridge. This is the same turnoff signposted to **Maya Mountain Lodge** (www.mayamountain.com), a wonderfully welcoming and well-maintained group of *cabañas*, some with kitchenettes,

Río Frío Cave.

nestled in the forest. They also serve excellent traditional cuisine and can arrange tours throughout the area.

MAYA CRAFTS IN THE PARK

The Cristo Rey road runs through the Yucatec Maya village of **San Antonio**, where Yucatec is still spoken, though much less widely these days. Immediately before the entrance to the village is the **García Sisters Tanah Mayan Art Museum** (daily 7am–7pm), with displays of slate carvings and other artworks by the García sisters; the bus from San Ignacio stops right outside.

Maria García is a charming yet forceful advocate of her Maya culture and plays a leading role in the management of the 12,700-acre (5,100-hectare) **Noj Kaax Meen Elijio Panti National Park**, which stretches from the village to the Macal River and across to the Mountain Pine Ridge.

PACBITUN AND BARTON CREEK

Two miles (3km) to the east of San Antonio, on private land, are the ruins of

Ø MEDICINAL PLANT PROJECT

Connected to the Lodge at Chaa Creek is the Rainforest Medicinal |Plants Trail (daily 8am–5pm), a unique facility devoted to researching the healing powers of tropical plants. Originally Ix Chel Farm (the name comes from the Maya goddess queen, a symbol of healing) it was founded by Chicago-trained herbalist Rosita Arvigo, who convinced a local Maya shaman, Don Eligio Panti, then in his late eighties, to pass on his learning. This ongoing ethnobotany project has collected and classified numerous plants from the neighboring forest that may help in the treatment of a variety of ailments including Aids. In the past, tropical plants have been used in western medicine against malaria (quinine), for anesthesia (curare), treating leukemia (vinblastine), and as ingredients for contraceptive pills (periwinkle flower extract). On the tour, you'll also see and learn about vines that store drinking water, which served a great practical purpose for the Mayans. Come prepared: it's suggested you wear long pants, sturdy footwear and bring a hat, water and insect repellent. The facility gift shop sells numerous remedies, like herbal teas and elixirs that treat everything from bladder disorders to menstrual pains and impotence. A popular item is Traveler's Tonic – an effective preventative and treatment for the ever-present threat of diarrhea.

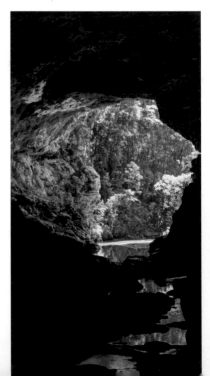

Pacbitun ➐, one of the oldest Preclassical Maya sites (it dates from 1,000 BC and flourished as a trading center into the Late Classic period, around AD 900). Local farmers knew about Pacbitun's existence for generations, but it wasn't until 1971 that the first archeologists made studies here. They found 24 pyramids (the highest is 55ft/16.5 meters), eight stelae, several raised irrigation causeways, and a collection of Maya musical instruments. The name means 'Stones Set in the Earth.'

The second access road heads south from Georgeville through the traditional Mennonite community of **Barton Creek ➑**. This is a breakaway group from the modernized community around Spanish Lookout: you feel as if you've wandered into the 19th century as men walk by with flowing white beards, hats and overalls, while the women wear long black dresses and hats. There is no problem about visiting the Mennonite farms (the elders, who usually speak English, are happy to explain their religion), but remember that they do not like being photographed.

Actun Tunichil Muknal (also known as ATM; 40km/25 miles southeast of San Ignacio) is one of the country's grandest underground sights, consisting of a subterranean river with soaring chambers that are strewn with astonishing Maya archeological finds, including calcified skeletons of human sacrifice victims. ATM is only accessible via guided tour, the majority of which depart from San Ignacio or Belmopan; inquire at your hotel or the tourist office.

TAPIRS AND BUTTERFLIES

East of here, between Barton and Roaring creeks, is the **Tapir Mountain Nature Reserve ➒**, a highly protected area of humid forest in the foothills of the Maya Mountains, run by the Belize Audubon Society. This pristine block of tropical forest, stretching across dramatic limestone karst formations, was given its heritage listing thanks to the efforts of its German former owner, conservationist Svea Dietrich-Ward. The reserve is home to a rich selection of bird species, including the keel-billed toucan, as well as Baird's tapir,

Herd of cattle near Spanish Lookout.

both animals revered as national symbols. However, the reserve is so private that it is not open to the public at all, but only accessible to qualified naturalists and serious researchers with prior permission from the Belize Audubon Society. Farther south is a comfortable ranch, with cozy rooms and a central dining area called the Cantina, run by **Mountain Equestrian Trails**, which offers horseback riding for all abilities.

By contrast to the nature reserve, everyone is welcome at the **Green Hills Butterfly Ranch** (http://green-hills. net; daily 9am–4pm; guided tours available, final tour 3.30pm), where you can walk through a butterfly enclosure and view an impressive botanical collection. Butterfly breeding has become a booming business in Belize in recent years, with numerous such operations throughout the country. Aside from their obvious attractions to tourists, the butterfly farms send pupae in crates to the US and Europe, where they are highly prized – particularly the famed Blue Morpho – by collectors and zoos. Green Hills is at mile 8 on the Mountain Pine Ridge road, near to Pacbitun, and can be reached by traveling through Georgeville or from the Cristo Rey road.

The owners of the ranch have been studying butterflies in Belize since 1989 and are eager to share their passion for these beautiful insects and explain what they have learned about their behavior and communication abilities during a fascinating guided tour. A tour of the colorful botanical garden includes a visit to Belize's National Passionflower Collection.

HEART OF THE RIDGE

After you enter the pine ridge itself, the vegetation changes abruptly to pines, mixed in with bromeliads and wildflowers; the bird life is rich here and the air slowly becomes cooler. A ranger stops traffic at a checkpoint barrier marking the entrance to the Mountain Pine Ridge Forest Reserve, registering names and vehicle license plates to control illegal camping and logging, as well as to keep a record in case of accidents.

Two miles (3km) farther along Baldy Beacon Road you'll come to the turn off to Cooma Cairn Road. After another 4 miles (7km), a short track on the left leads to **Hidden Valley Falls** . These are also known as **Thousand Foot Falls**, although they happen to be 1,600ft (480 meters) high. From the picnic ground you can watch the thin plume of water stream down a cliffside and disappear into the lush forest below. In the vicinity are many smaller but arguably more beautiful falls, including **Big Rock Falls** and perhaps the most charming, **Butterfly Falls**.

Eleven miles (18km) farther southwest (marked on the left) are the **Río On Pools**, natural rock pools and little waterfalls formed by enormous granite boulders, in a serene open setting – also ideal for a swim.

Five miles (8km) south is the turn off to the **Río Frío Cave** , the largest cave in Belize and the most accessible. During the dry season, it is possible to

El Castillo, Xunantunich.

follow the river into the cave's enormous mouth and out the other end (about 870 yds/meters). The rocks are a little slippery, but not unmanageable; inside are unusually colored rock formations, stalactites, and the odd colony of bats. There is also a 45-minute outdoor nature trail for the energetic.

A variety of accommodations have been set up in the area, including **Blancaneaux** (www.thefamilycoppolahideaways.com), a luxury lodge and resort owned by the Hollywood film director Francis Ford Coppola. Relax in suites and *cabañas* with views of the thundering Privassion Creek waterfall, and dine on flavorful Italian cuisine at the resort's Montagna restaurant.

SOUTH TO CARACOL

Passage into **Chiquibul Forest Reserve and National Park**, populated only by a few loggers, tree-tappers, and archeologists, is closely monitored.

The main attraction for most travelers in this remote region is the ruined Maya city of **Caracol** ⑬. Until 1993, Caracol was once only accessible by one of the worst roads in Belize, and archeologists still tell tales of their four-wheel drives becoming mired in mud for three days at a time. A paved road has cut the driving time down to two hours but, despite continual improvements, the going can still be rough, particularly when it rains. The route runs into the **Vaca Plateau**, with a return from pines to the more familiar rainforest foliage and some spectacular views over mountains and river valleys. The only other traffic is likely to be the occasional logging truck.

Beneath the Vaca Plateau are a series of great cave complexes, including the Chiquibul, which may be the largest in the western hemisphere. It was only found by modern spelunkers in the 1970s and remains little explored – although tales of prehistoric fossils being discovered there have sparked interest.

The road becomes progressively more bone-shaking until the ruins suddenly appear – a Maya pyramid, hacked from the jungle, glimpsed through a gap in the vines (see page 171).

The Belize government and the Tourism Board have spent millions of dollars upgrading the road, facilities for visitors, and the site itself. They're aiming to make Caracol the 'centerpiece' of Belize's Maya sites, and hopefully keep in Belize some of the travelers who are presently going on to Tikal in Guatemala, and also attract Guatemalan visitors.

XUNANTUNICH

San José Succotz, a village a few miles/km southwest of San Ignacio is the jumping-off point for the Maya ruins of **Xunantunich** ⑭ (daily 8am–4pm), one of the biggest attractions in the Cayo District, and one of the most impressive Maya sites in all Belize. The ruins are reached by crossing the Mopan River on a hand-winched ferry (there's a boatman paid to work the pulley full time, although he gladly accepts volunteers;

Washing clothes in the Belize River.

the ruins are a couple of miles farther on). In contrast to Cahal Pech, the Maya site of Xunantunich is inspiring, and the view from the top of the highest structure is breathtaking. The view of the Mopan River from the ferry on the way over is itself memorable.

One of the most famous of Belizean ruins, Xunantunich was a major ceremonial site in the Classic Period, collapsing at some point in the 10th century. It was first worked in the late 19th century by a wandering British medical officer; since then, archeological expeditions have worked on the site sporadically, while looters have made their own marks. Digging is still going on, although only a fraction of the site has been unearthed – once work is done, archeologists are hoping to find valuable clues as to why the Maya city-states collapsed.

Xunantunich is best known for the towering pyramid known as **El Castillo**, or **A-6**. At around 130ft (40 meters), this was considered the highest structure in Belize until the pyramid at Caracol was found to top it by a few feet. The ancient Maya name of the site is Kat

Witz, meaning 'Clay Mountain.' Xunantunich's modern name 'Stone Woman,' or Maiden of the Rock was given more recently, but archeologists admit a connection between its phallic structure, the Maya warlords' assertion of power, and the fertility of the earth for producing maize. Two temples have been revealed at its summit, the later built over the first: halfway up on the eastern side of the older temple is the famed **frieze**, restored in the early 1970s. The central mask with ear ornaments represents the sun god, flanked by signs for the moon, Venus and different days. There is also a headless man on the frieze, although why he is decapitated is unknown. Several important **stelae** have been unearthed here and are housed in a building by the guard's house. Paths lead beyond the main plaza to **residential structures** used by upper and middle-class Maya.

Because it is relatively easy to reach – especially compared to Caracol, Xunantunich is a popular destination for school groups and cruise ship visitors, so it can get a little crowded. You

Examining Maya pottery at Actun Tunichil Muknal, near San Ignacio.

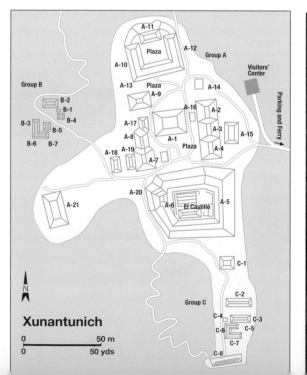

Xunantunich

can walk a mile or so up the hill from the ferry, along a paved road, if you are in fairly good shape, but if not, drive up as far as you can – there is a parking lot just below the entrance at the top.

WEST TOWARD THE BORDER

If you are bound for Guatemala, or just want to get the feel of western border life, the George Price (Western) Highway proceeds on to **Benque Viejo del Carmen ⑮**, a sleepy village founded by Guatemalan refugees in the 1860s. Not much goes on in Benque apart from an annual three-day fiesta in mid-July; and *Los Finados*, the Day of the Dead celebration at the end of October and beginning of November. *Los Finados* includes offerings of food and favorite liquor to the souls of the departed and a candlelit procession through the streets of Benque to the pretty little cemetery at the edge of town.

Unless they have relatives in Benque or it's fiesta time, most people pass straight through en route to the Guatemalan border nearby. Like their counterparts in the northern town of Corozal near the Mexican border, Benquenos travel easily back and forth to the Guatemalan border town of Melchor de Mencos, sometimes too easily. Immigration officials have a hard time controlling the flow of people (and goods) in either direction since many simply bypass the official crossing and wade across the Mopan River.

CHECHEM HA CAVE

A paved road has been driven south of Benque into the Vaca Plateau to service a projected hydro-electric dam. Coincidentally, the road has provided access to one of Belize's more off-beat and exciting archeological visits, **Chechem Ha Cave ⑯**, at **Chemauch farm** (follow the winding dirt road through the mountains for half an hour until a small yellow sign directs you onto a hair-pin turn off). The Morales family set up a few rudimentary *cabañas* on the edge of a ravine

overlooking the Macal River – possibly the most spectacular setting yet in the San Ignacio region (although the lack of running water makes staying there only a notch above camping). Then, while chasing some stray cattle through the rainforest, members of the Morales family came across a cave on their land. Going inside, they found an extensive catacomb with niches full of ancient Maya pots.

Archeologists from Belmopan removed a few of the most important pieces for study, but decided to leave the rest intact. The Morales family now leads small tour groups into the cave, passing by torchlight through the winding caves once used by Maya as a storehouse and refuge. Makeshift ladders and ropes lead into corners crowded with pots (one even contains some decomposed maize); the climax of the visit is a chamber once used as a ceremonial center. However, it's not for the claustrophobic: turning off the flashlights, you're left in total darkness; the only sound is your own thumping heart.

And if that doesn't get your historical imagination going, nothing will.

View of the Plaza, Xunantunich.

One of the immense structures at Caracol.

CARACOL

Belize's most important Maya site is also the most challenging one to access, but it promises a rewarding experience for the adventurous visitor.

Guatemala has Tikal, Honduras has Copán, and Belize has Caracol – the largest Maya site in the country. This ancient Maya city was a massive and sophisticated metropolis that remained hidden from the world under a blanket of rainforest for nearly a millennium. Rediscovered half a century ago, archeologists have realized that Caracol was far more important and powerful than they had guessed: the lost names of Caracol's heroic kings and their legendary battles have triumphantly been returned to their place in history books.

But, Caracol's remote location on the western edge of the Maya Mountains (within the Chiquibul Forest Reserve) means relatively few people have been there. Visitors to Belize are generally far more likely to go to Altun Ha, just minutes from Belize City, Xunantunich, which is just a ferry ride away from San José Succotz in Cayo, or Lamanai in Orange Walk, than to drive several hours to Caracol. The vast majority of visitors explore Caracol by guided tour, which is the easiest and fastest way to do so. If you plan to visit independently, it's a good idea to rent a four-wheel-drive vehicle because the going can be difficult in places, especially during heavy downpours of rain, which can occur at any time of year.

Guiding visitors around the ancient site.

Caracol was in its heyday for more than a century in the Classic Period, when it controlled the rainforest Petén region (in modern-day Guatemala), possibly even lording it over the great – and today much more famous – city of Tikal. Excavations of Caracol's monumental architecture and sculpture continue to confirm proof of the city's past glory.

RE-EMERGING FROM THE RAINFOREST

In 1937 a mahogany logger, Rosa Mai, reported the discovery of the ancient

⊘ Main attractions
South Acropolis
Ball Courts
Temple of the Wooden Lintel
Altar 24
Caana complex

Map on page 172

city to archeology officials in what was then British Honduras. The top archeological official, A.H. Anderson, first visited the site in 1938 and discovered some stelae and the Temple of the Wooden Lintel, the only building then visible.

Anderson named the site "Caracol", which means snail in Spanish, but more recently the hieroglyphic site identification symbol, or emblem glyph, has been translated to mean 'ox witz ha' or 'three hill place.' Thus as the science of hieroglyphic deciphering advances, Caracol is added to the growing number of Maya cities whose ancient name has been identified.

The world's view of Caracol for the next three decades after the archeologist's first visit was formed in three short field seasons in 1950, 1951, and 1953 by the University of Pennsylvania. Several stelae and altar groups were uncovered – and removed. For two seasons Anderson led his own excavation at the site, but in 1961 Hurricane Hattie destroyed most of

There are numerous stelae at Caracol.

Anderson's notes and drawings in Belize City.

Archeologists avoided Caracol, which they considered a medium-size site dominated by Tikal. But in 1983 Paul Healy of Trent University, Ontario, reported that agricultural terracing outside of Caracol's center had supported a much heavier population density than once thought. And, research indicates Caracol may have actually controlled Tikal for a time. The Caracol Project was established in the mid-1980s by Arlen and Diane Chase of the University of Central Florida. There was a continuous series of breakthroughs, including the discovery and translation of an altar that describes a military victory over Tikal in the 6th century, as well as one major and 50 lesser tombs.

The site of Caracol was settled by a well-organized Maya group in around 300 BC in the Preclassic period. The city's epicenter was built on a plateau 1,600ft (490 meters) above sea level, without a natural water source but protected by surrounding hills.

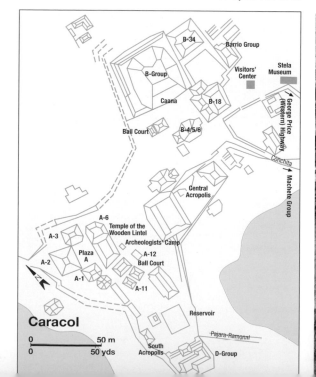

The population depended on human-made *aguadas*, or reservoirs, the remains of which can still be seen (one is used by Caracol Project members for reconsolidation of cement and bathing water).

Stelae show a royal lineage entrenched in Caracol by the 5th century AD, reaching its first peak in the year 562, when the ruler Lord Water defeated Tikal. The city subsequently prospered and grew to its ultimate population of about 180,000 people in AD 650. One of Lord Water's sons, Lord K'an II, continued his father's success with a victory over Naranjo in AD 631. A 9th-century renaissance under Lord Makinahokkawil brought tremendous construction and expansion to the epicenter and particularly Caana.

Surrounding the site is a rainforest environment nearly identical to Tikal. There are grand ceiba trees, cohune nut palms (which provided the ancient Maya with nuts), and escoba trees covered with toothpick-sized spines. Wildlife includes parrots, ocellated turkeys, yellow-billed toucans, red-crowned woodpeckers, a few mot-mots, and the occasional howler monkey. Caracol is a designated National Monument Reserve, so the beauty of the rainforest and its ruins will not fall to developers.

EXPLORING THE SITE

Visitors arrive by road at the epicenter of the ancient city. This is the nexus of Caracol's sacbe, or causeway, a system widely used throughout ancient Mesoamerica, from which at least seven raised roads radiated like the spokes of a bicycle wheel. With names like **Conchita**, **Pajara-Ramonal**, and **Retiro**, the causeways lead to spectacular architectural groups up to 5 miles (8km) away, which possibly defined the geographic borders of Caracol. Along many of these causeways are agricultural terraces that supplied the city with either food or cash crops – such as cacao and cotton – used in trade.

The **South Acropolis**, on the edge of the site, is thought to be an elite

Archeologists looking for Maya artefacts

residential complex, including an amazingly preserved Late Classic tomb with a corbelled vault. Some tombs at Caracol have the closing dates painted in hematite-red still visible on the bottom-side of the central capstone.

Nearby are the **ball courts**, where Caracol's athletes played the traditional ball game. In the center of the main court lies a marker, discovered in 1986, which dates to 9.10.0.0.0. (AD 633). It was dedicated by Lord K'an II in honor of his father, Lord Water, who defeated the rulers of Tikal in AD 556 and again in AD 562. The discovery has helped to explain a century-long hiatus in Tikal, when no stone monuments or new architecture were erected. It was a lucky find: for many years the treasure lay underneath a log trucking road.

Plaza A was the city's cultural focus, containing the largest concentration of stelae and altars. The placement of the **Temple of the Wooden Lintel** and its flanking structures are modeled after the astronomical observatory (**Group E** buildings) at **Uaxactún**, in Guatemala, where two stelae markers on either side of the plaza would line up with the rising sun during the winter and summer equinoxes. The Temple of the Wooden Lintel's original *zapote*, or sapodilla, wood beams in the back room are carbon-dated to around AD 50. Thorough trenching through the center of the building exposed earlier versions of the temple from before 300 BC, the earliest Preclassic days of Caracol. A cache uncovered here yielded a container of mercury, possibly used during a religious ritual.

Structure A2 is 82ft (25 meters) high and supports stela 22, which has the longest glyphic text in Belize. It was also dedicated during the reign of Lord K'an II in the 7th century. Although you can no longer see the bright colors, structure A3 was originally covered in red stucco. A tomb inside dates from AD 696.

The well-preserved palaces of **Barrio** were built in the 9th century above earlier buildings. A major drop to the

Ceiba tree.

south and east of the plaza indicate how much it was artificially raised.

Plaza B, on the north side of the site, is its most massive complex. **Altar 24** in Plaza B has a fascinating relief depicting two stout men facing each other, their hands bound behind their backs and their hair bound in a knot. Save for a loincloth, these royal figures wear no clothing and are stripped of jewelry (papyrus strips have been placed in their ears instead of jade ear flares). The glyphs explain that the man on the right is a hostage from the site of Ucanal, the man on the left from the unidentified site Q.

PINNACLE OF ANCIENT CARACOL

In Plaza B you will find the massive **Caana complex**, or 'sky place,' which is counted among the greatest Maya structures of Mesoamerica. It contains palaces, courtyards, pyramids, and other buildings whose exact purpose is still unknown. There has been speculation that the rooms at the very top were the royal family's residential chambers. The base of Caana is above a natural limestone hill and measures 330 by 395ft (100 by 120 meters). The length of the rooms on the middle level facing the plaza are all similar, each with a wide front entrance and a large, often U-shaped bench. These rooms were designed for a specific purpose – either as a seating area to watch the plaza (like luxury boxes at a baseball stadium) or a place to display prisoners or royalty to the people gathered in the plaza below. To the west archeologists discovered a special staircase to the next level, which could be ascended and descended hidden from the plaza view.

An open room on the eastern side has special entrances to side rooms – Lilliputian 'dwarf' doors that lead to bare rooms with air vents. These rooms might have been used for prisoners, children, animals, storage, or any other practical purpose. Soldiers posted at either end may have guarded access to the second

View from the mighty Caana complex.

level – which contains magnificent architecture that was surely the pinnacle of ancient Caracol. Visitors enter through a special doorway, with a bench on either side (probably a place to catch one's breath). A central plaza is surrounded by three 40ft (12-meter) pyramids (they were much taller when complete) and a long rectangular building.

Directly in front of the northern pyramid, **B19**, lie stairs specially built to give access to a tomb buried in an earlier building (**B19-2nd**). The large chamber once contained the body of a very important woman from the 7th century, but scholars are still determining her identity although some believe she was Lady Batz' Ek who married Lord Water in AD 584. Glyphs in the tomb bear the date AD 634, which may or may not be her date of death; the tomb may have been commissioned some years later as recorded on other monuments by Lord K'an II's artists. Between B19 and the eastern pyramid, **B18**, is the entrance to a palatial courtyard

Carving panels at Altar 21, Plaza B.

surrounded by large rooms. The stucco molding against the south side of B18 represent a weave design used by the royalty.

Looters found three major tombs in the rear of the western pyramid, **B20**, which can be visited via a trail around Caana. In the second tomb, a painted text on the back wall was destroyed.

An earlier version of this pyramid, **B20-2nd**, began more than 13ft (4 meters) below the current plaza. A 10ft (3-meter) earth monster mask stood at the base, with an entrance through the mouth (representing the gateway to the Underworld or *Xibalba*). Inside, excavators found a small room with a burned body and graffiti depicting a procession, with a bound prisoner marching ahead of a ruler carried on a litter. The smoke from this room – either from incense or charred corpses – once billowed out through the eyes of the monster mask, a dramatic device intended to produce fearful awe among the faithful throng.

⊘ HEAVEN AND THE UNDERWORLD

According to Maya beliefs, heaven was composed of 13 different levels. In the topmost layer lived Itzamna, the 'celestial dragon' or serpent, the male figure who was the god of creation, of agriculture, writing, and the all-important calendar. Itzamna was also identified with the sun, with maize and semen, and with blood. His companion was Ixchel (Rainbow Lady) who was also identified with the moon. All the other gods in the Maya pantheon were the offspring of these two.

Each of the 13 layers was identified with a particular god, among whom were the north star god, the maize god, and the young moon goddess. The benevolent rain gods, or Chacs, were also to be found at the four corners of the earth, together with the Bacabs.

The exact number and attributes of these gods is difficult to ascertain. It seems that each of them had four different aspects, corresponding to the colors of each corner of the world. Then, too, they all seem to have had a counterpart of the opposite sex, reflecting the dualism that underlies much of Maya thought. To complicate matters still further, it is thought that the Maya gods had a double in the layers of the dark underworld where, like the sun, all the gods had to pass in order to be reborn.

EXPLORING BELIZE'S VAST UNDERGROUND

Belize's extensive underworld, from echoing caves and roaring river channels to massive sinkholes, rivals the country's above-ground wonders.

Much of the geological structure of Belize is porous karst limestone. This makes it ideal for the formation of caves and underground rivers, and the south of the country is dotted with them. Although many caves have been known of for years, new ones – including some of the most extensive systems in the whole of Central America – are still being explored.

The Maya peoples who first inhabited Belize were particularly in awe of these underground caverns. For them, they were the entrance to the underworld, which they called Xibalba, or the Place of Fear (or 'fright'). The Maya saw the surface of the planet on which they lived as being sandwiched between many other levels in which the souls of the dead, spirits, and their gods lived. There were nine levels beneath the earth, and caves gave a privileged if frightening access to this lower world. At many sites in Belize, you can still see the cave-paintings, the pottery shards, the remains of fires, and even occasionally sacrificial skeletons still wearing their jewelry and other finery.

SINKHOLES AND RIVERS

The caves in Belize are registered archeological sites, which can be entered only with a licensed guide. Among the cave systems you can visit, the most impressive include those at the Caves Branch Jungle Lodge (www.cavesbranch.com), 13 miles (21km) south of the capital Belmopan on the Hummingbird Highway. The lodge, on the bank of the Caves Branch River, is halfway between the immense St Herman's Cave and the Blue Hole National Park, and organises trips into the caves and surrounding areas. Both St Herman's Cave, a sinkhole which continues underground for a quarter of a mile, and the Blue Hole itself, which is another collapsed underground river channel, are worth the visit.

Also hugely popular are the Cayo District caves. These include the Barton Creek Cave, where you can take a mile-long canoe ride along Barton Creek after it dives into the cavern in the midst of luxuriant vegetation. Also, you can search for Maya artifacts at the Chechem Ha Cave (at the turnoff at mile 8 out of Benque Viejo). The many different areas of the cave still house, impressively, intact pottery urns and other vessels.

There are organized tours at Río Frío, in the Mountain Pine Ridge Forest Reserve. A massive opening leads into the caves, with a stream flowing through the middle – and the exit leads to a nature trail that goes on to the equally fascinating Cuevas Gemelas (Twin Caves) and other caves well worth exploring.

AMERICA'S LONGEST CAVE SYSTEM

The latest and perhaps most exciting cave discoveries are still very much for the professional speleologist. Cave divers sponsored by the National Geographic have found Central America's longest cave system, on the Chiquibul River bordering Guatemala in the Maya Mountains. Here there is evidence that the Maya used them for their ceremonies: pots, clay whistles, incense burners, grinding stones, and stone altars have been found, from a time when the rainforest above the caves was home to tens of thousands of people, not almost deserted as it is today.

Exploring the Caves Branch River.

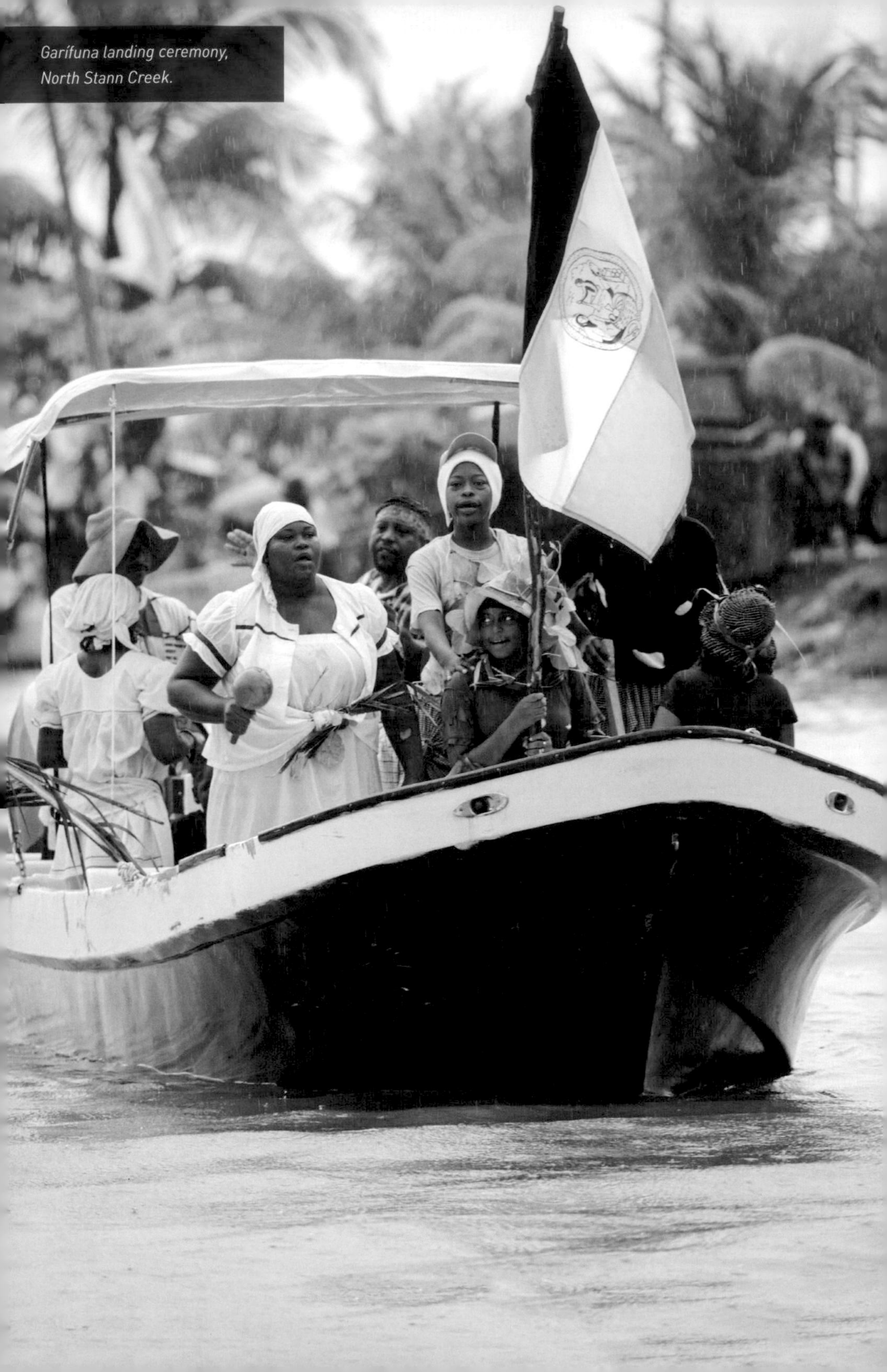

Garífuna landing ceremony, North Stann Creek.

SOUTH TO DANGRIGA

Stann Creek District is the home of Garífuna culture, famous for its arts, dance, and punta rock music. You'll also find some superb caves inland and idyllic cayes out on the reef.

The Hummingbird Highway, running from Belmopan to Dangriga, has a beautiful name, amply justified by the surrounding scenery, which is among the most spectacular and tropical of southern Belize. The road passes through a magnificent forest of cohune palm: Cohune Ridge, as it is known locally. This ridge, which once ran continuously for 30 miles (50km) or more, fringing the base of the misshapen karst limestone hills, on the eastern fringe of the Maya Mountains, has been reduced by road building, hurricane destruction and farming. Large numbers of Central American immigrants have been moving into this area over the years, establishing their own Spanish-speaking communities such as Armenia and Santa Marta, growing vegetables and citrus fruit to sell at the nearby Belmopan market. Throughout the Stann Creek Valley these immigrants form the greater part of the workforce for the citrus growing and processing industry.

TWO NATIONAL PARKS

The first major place of interest you'll come to, some 13 miles (20km) south of Belmopan, is the St Herman's **Blue Hole National Park ❶**, centered around a beautiful, circular swimming hole that is surrounded by dripping forest. The waters come from

an underground river, making them unusually cool (intrepid scuba divers have explored it for several hundred meters). Those unafraid of heights can also dive 25ft (8 meters) from an overhanging cliff. A half-hour walking trail leads from the highway near here (watch out for the sign) to **St. Herman's Cave**, which is one of the largest and most accessible in Belize. There is a visitors' center (where you pay an entrance fee) ten minutes' walk from the cave, as well as a nearby campsite. You can wade through the river into the

Map on page 180

Snorkeling for crabs in Tobacco Caye.

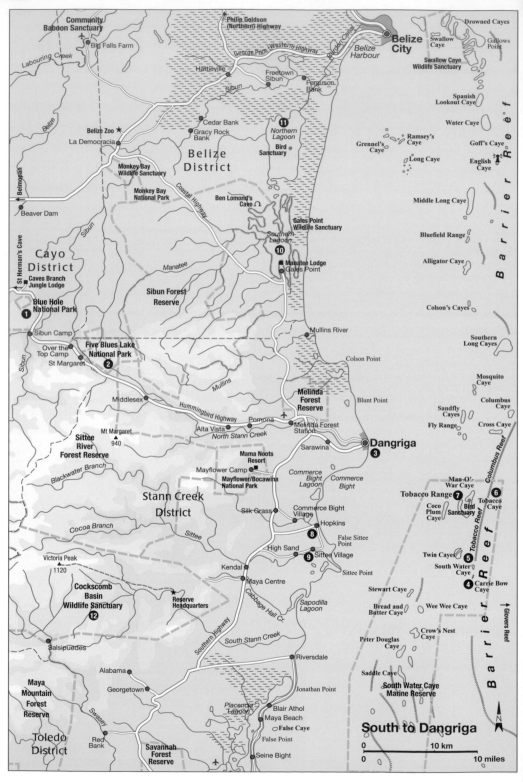

South to Dangriga

cave with a flashlight (carry a spare) for about twenty minutes, but to penetrate further you have to take a guided tour.

Continuing south, the road climbs through mature hardwood forest before passing the citrus groves that dominate the Stann Creek Valley. Ten miles (16km) from the Blue Hole is a track to the **Five Blues Lake National Park ❷**. The lake is so named after the different shades of blue that light conditions produce. The lake is in a beautiful, natural clearing in the jungle and is a *cenote* created by the collapse of a cavern roof. There are forest trails and caves, also containing evidence of Maya occupation, and you can swim and canoe on the lake. Lodging in private houses is available in nearby St. Margaret's village.

South of here, the Hummingbird Highway enters Stann Creek District. Citrus is to Stann Creek what steel once was to Pittsburgh. A few visionaries gave birth to the industry in the mid-1920s by planting 13 trees a few miles west of Dangriga in the rich alluvial soils of the North Stann Creek River.

Today the citrus industry is one of Belize's top foreign exchange earners. Production increased considerably during the 1990s and continued to grow – between 2002 and 2016, revenue from citrus cultivation went from around $30 million to $96.4 million but in 2017 it fell to $78.4 million.

The largest town in Stann Creek District, **Dangriga ❸** takes its name from the local Garífuna language, loosely meaning 'standing waters'. It lies peacefully along the banks of the North Stann Creek River, whose water is legendary: the town's drinking supply is refreshingly cool and arguably the best-tasting water in Belize. A well-known Belizean saying warns that once you drink from *gumaragaru* (the Garífuna name for the North Stann Creek River), you must come back to Dangriga. And a famous Belizean song by Lord Rhaburn, Belize's king of calypso, chants, 'Gumaragaru water, sweet, sweet water.'

Of all the larger settlements in Belize, Dangriga has most obviously resisted the unrelenting pull of the present. It was settled in the early 19th century by the Garífuna (also known as Garinagu or Black Caribs, see page 189), a cultural hybrid of escaped African slaves and Caribbean Indians. The town's dreamy atmosphere still harks back to a past age. The houses are made of weathered wooden planks and raised on stilts (the founding townspeople quickly learned that raised houses caught the evening sea breeze in this otherwise stiflingly hot location, and saved them from the occasional flood in the rainy season). Old-fashioned wooden fishing dories lie tied up along the banks of the 100ft (30-meter) wide river, beside canopied ferries with hustling fishermen unloading their day's catch. A number of high-powered passenger boats are also parked along the river preparing for a charter to carry tourists to the nearby cayes. Vegetable and fruit stands and clothing bazaars

Streetside stall selling Johnny cakes.

crowd the narrow streets near the riverside market; Central American refugees display their wares alongside their Garífuna neighbors.

Of course, the modern world has crept in. Instead of pursuing traditional fishing and farming, many Garífuna have become teachers and civil servants. A steady flow of cash from large expatriate communities in the US has allowed some wooden houses to be replaced with the cold practicality of concrete and satellite television is the norm. Youngsters on flashy mountain bikes now speed past graying Garífuna women carrying firewood or plastic buckets of water on their heads.

At heart, though, Dangriga is a celebration of Garífuna culture, marked by one important landmark – the **Drums of Our Fathers** monument, in the southern part of town, that pays homage to the key role of drumming in Garífuna history. Dangriga is bisected by North Stann Creek, crossed by a bridge; on the north side are the town hall and small market, on the south the post office. There are budget hotels,

Sunrise in Dangriga.

lively restaurants, and raunchy bars in the center of town, if you're up for some local color. Just north of town is the **Pelican Beach Resort** (www.pelican beachbelize.com), which maximizes its beachfront perch with breezy rooms and a restaurant with views out to sea.

AFRO-CARIBBEAN CULTURE

Most people come to Dangriga as a base for exploring the rest of Stann Creek District, including the offshore cayes, or getting to know the unique Garífuna culture. Despite the changes, it is the devotion of the Garífuna to their roots that sets them apart from other ethnic groups in Belize.

A mystical spiritualism is the glue that holds the culture together: although the Garífuna religion shares similar West African roots to voodoo practices found in other parts of the Caribbean, it has developed into something quite distinct. Central is the magical practice of *obeah*, whereby forces of good and evil are directed toward individuals through spells. The assistance of a *buyei*, or shaman, is

necessary to guide the way through a complex series of rituals and use of talismans that can take many hours. Great care and thought is needed, because the spells cannot easily be broken. In fact, if the person placing the spell on someone else dies, it can never be broken.

FAMILY TIES

The basis for the religion is the powerful spiritual bond between past, present, and even future members of any family group. In a ritual called *adugurahani* or *dugu*, people communicate with their deceased relatives. Outsiders rarely observe the ritual, which contributes to misconceptions and conjecture. Though all *dugus* follow certain broad guidelines, no two are exactly alike. Families go to great expense to secure fresh seafood, pork, and fowl, while cassava bread is carefully prepared. Money is collected from family members to pay drummers and the *buyei*, who can commune with the dead.

Where the solemnity and secrecy of the Garífuna religion breeds distrust among outsiders (as recently as the 1960s, some Garífuna were afraid to hold *dugus* in Dangriga for fear of disapproval from local magistrates), this same spiritualism spawns a wealth of creativity among its people in the form of music, dance and art. From clubs and dancehalls throughout Belize blares the energetic rhythm of punta rock, a modern musical interpretation of a cultural dance by the late Dangrigan Pen Cayetano and his turtle shell band. During the punta dance, the man attempts to seduce the woman. While turning down these advances, the woman makes her own overtures. The seductive movement of pumping hips and the rhythmic drumbeat make this one of Belize's most popular dances.

GARIFUNA ARTS AND CRAFTS

The Garífuna are also skilled artists and craftsmen. Primitivism dominates in their painting, with great elaboration of detail, flat colors, and unreal perspective. The lobby at Pelican Beach Resort displays some of the earlier works of Benjamin Nicholas, one of

Brown pelicans are a common sight in Dangriga.

A game of street cricket, Dangriga.

Garífuna musicians.

the better-known painters. Especially impressive is the mural of the 1832 Garífuna landing.

Pen Cayetano of punta rock fame is also an accomplished artist, having displayed at many art exhibitions in the United States and Europe. Pen's work is more realistic than other Garífuna painters, but it still retains the attractive aspects of primitivism. To view Cayetano's works, pay a visit to the **Pen Cayetano Studio Gallery** (www.cayetano. de; hours vary), near Ecumenical Drive, which also features historical exhibits on Garífuna culture, drumming demonstrations, and more.

Dangriga teems with crafts, and throughout the town, you'll find skilled artisans creating everything from drums made with cedar and mahogany, and deer and cow hides; stuffed cotton dolls in traditional Garífuna dress; coconut-leaf baskets and hats; to maracas made of dried calabash gourds. Ask at any of the local restaurants, and they'll point you in the direction of craftspeople who are selling their wares. For an excellent overview

of Garífuna culture, head to the **Gulusi Garífuna Museum** (www.ngcbelize.org; Mon–Fri 8am–5pm, Sat 8am–noon), on Stann Creek Valley Road, which features in-depth exhibits tracing Garífuna history, as well as artworks, traditional dress, and more.

DANGRIGA NIGHTLIFE

Dangriga bars have a markedly local flavor – a dusty dancefloor, rum-based drinks, and a blaring sound system. **Illagulei**, on George Price Drive near the roundabout, draws revelers on the weekends, with a dancefloor that fills up as the hour grows late. Other late-night spots, like the **Kennedy Club**, are also popular, but be aware that they can get a bit rough.

INTO THE CARIBBEAN

Some 12 miles (20km) offshore from Dangriga lie a row of tiny coral cayes perched on top of **Tobacco Reef** like gems on a necklace. All are lined by perfect sands and dotted with coconut palms, and can be easily reached in an hour's boat ride from Dangriga. There are some beautiful clusters of coral in the shallow waters off these cayes, offering great snorkeling opportunities. In addition to the usual kaleidoscopic array of tropical fish, there is also a good chance of spotting moray eels, turtles, and nurse sharks (generally harmless to humans unless provoked, this species is unusual among sharks for its habit of resting motionless on the seabed.)

Of the three inhabited islands, each has a different character that will appeal to different types of visitors. The smallest is **Carrie Bow Caye** ❹, home to the Smithsonian Institution's Marine Laboratory. Since 1972, scientists from all over the world have come here to study the intricacies of coral reef and mangrove biology. Though much of the work is esoteric – such as measuring flow rates from the openings of sponges or listing obscure animal

groups – an invaluable database has been collected.

Since the waters around Carrie Bow Caye are pristine, this database can be used as a measuring device to gauge the health of other sites along the barrier reef. Although drop-in visitors are discouraged, scheduled visits are welcomed (arrangements can be made in Dangriga, through Pelican Beach Resort, which has another resort on neighboring South Water Caye, below.)

Just north of Carrie Bow Caye lies **South Water Caye ❺**, a small and beautifully maintained caye, with a superb array of accommodations, such as **Glover's Atoll Resort** (www.glovers.com.bz), with breezy thatched *cabañas* on the beach, and a welcoming restaurant that serves fresh seafood; and **Pelican's Pouch Resort** (www.pelicanbeachbelize.com), the sister resort to the Pelican Beach Resort in Dangriga, which is set on a gorgeous private beach, where you can swing in a hammock under palm trees, soaking up the sun.

Snorkeling is ideal off the southern point of South Water Caye; pristine coral reef can be reached just by walking off the small, sandy beach, without the need of a boat. Day visitors are welcome here; there are several jetties on the shore side of the caye, and tables and hammocks slung in the shade are ideal for picnicking or unwinding after a rigorous morning's snorkeling. Pelicans bob and dive for fish by the shore, and frigate birds may also be seen wheeling overhead, and will compete with the pelicans when one of the fishermen is cutting up his catch and throwing scraps into the water.

Farther north, **Tobacco Caye ❻** has been used for centuries as a trading post and fishing camp. Several rustic but good value guesthouses and cabañas are dotted around the island. These are run by local fishermen and their spouses who supplement their incomes by offering boat tours, modest meals and accommodations.

Most of the other cayes in Stann Creek District are mangrove covered, and some are home to pelicans and cormorants. One, **Man-O-War Caye ❼**, supports one of the largest colonies of

Boatman in Tobacco Caye.

nesting frigate birds in the entire Caribbean. Some cayes have temporary fishing camps while most are uninhabited. The reefs surrounding many of these remote cayes are spectacular, making this central portion of the long Belize Barrier Reef one of the best-kept secrets in the country.

BEYOND DANGRIGA

While Dangriga is the largest Garífuna settlement in Belize, smaller colonies lie scattered farther down the coast. Eight miles (13km) south of Dangriga lies the village of **Hopkins** . It can be reached by sea from Dangriga across the **Commerce Bight Lagoon**, or from the west along a 4-mile (7km) road linked to the Southern Highway. The entrance road crosses over a wide, marshy area rich with coastal birds such as tiger herons, cormorants, and great egrets.

The seashore at Hopkins is lined by scores of tall coconut trees sprouting from mountains of soft sand. Nets, draped over palmetto poles, lie drying in the sun beside fishing dories

A pair of frigate birds engage in an eye-catching courtship display.

pulled up on the beach. Clumps of Maya-style homes – palmetto walls and palm-frond roofs – sit perched on stilts with magnificent views of the azure Caribbean to the east and jungle covered mountains to the west. This sleepy but famously friendly village relies heavily on harvesting seafood from the reef that lies 5 miles (8km) offshore. Perhaps more than any other of the villages in the south, Hopkins has enthusiastically embraced tourism, with a growing number of guesthouses and *cabañas*, like the cheery Hopkins Inn B&B (www.hopkinsinn.com), along with colorful restaurants, bars, and craft shops. **King Cassava**, by the crossroads at the northern entrance to the village, is an enterprising business, offering gifts, local handicrafts, tourist information, and drumming performances. Fun eateries include the **Driftwood Beach Bar**, which serves everything from crisp pizzas to juicy barbecues, and **Laruni Hati Beyabu**, with top-notch traditional cuisine, including whole grilled fish.

GARIFUNA CUISINE

Most meals in Stann Creek are served with one form or another of the versatile cassava – an integral part of Garífuna heritage (some writers even translate the word Garífuna as 'cassava-eating people'). Cassava, or manioc, is a woody shrub or herb, which, like potatoes, has tuberous roots. But unlike potatoes, the juice in the fibers of the manioc root is poisonous.

The secret of extracting the root, passed down through the Caribbean, involves a two-day process. First, the root is dug out before daybreak. The skin is peeled off, and the root is grated into a mash on stone-studded boards. This mash is placed into a *wowla*, a long, narrow, loosely woven tube made of palm fronds. When stretched, the *wowla* compresses the mash, squeezing out the poisonous fluid. The resulting dehydrated cassava mash is then sun dried and made into flour, which can be sifted and baked into flat round loaves. The coarse 'trash' left from the sifting is baked black and simmered with ginger, sugar, and sweet potatoes into a local favorite drink called Hiu. Like a fevergrass tea called bachati, and citrus juice, all sweetened with heaps of sugar, Hiu is one of the typical Garífuna drinks.

Local Garífuna cuisine is based on coconut milk, garlic, basil, and black pepper. Banana and plantain (a larger, starchier banana that must be cooked) are grated, mashed, boiled, or baked. Fish boiled in coconut milk, called *serre*, served with mashed plantain called *hudut*, is a deliciously rich meal. If you're in Belize to sample some good Garífuna food, you're in the right place here.

RUINS OF THE SUGAR INDUSTRY

A coastal road heading south out of Hopkins leads to the village of **Sittee ❾**, perched on the high but eroding banks of the Sittee River. During the 18th century, the river was a major artery for the flow of sugar and lumber from the interior. The old **Sittee Sugar Mill**, discovered in 1990 as bulldozers cleared land to make way for citrus plantations, lies one mile east of the Southern Highway on the Sittee road. The original mill was opened in 1863, owned by the Serpon Estate and the Regalia Estate, who imported the mills from England and Scotland, transporting them overland by mules. The mills were powered by locomotive engines, one of which has been identified as being made in Richmond, Virginia.

The site now is all but abandoned, aside from a basic shelter and a mural by the roadside, depicting the sugar processing as it was done here in the 19th century. Vines and trees hide towering smokestacks and huge rusted gears. One of the first steam railroad locomotives in Belize sits in a jungle clearing, a tree growing from its boiler. Parts of an old sawmill lie strewn about the banks of the river, often

Garífuna Settlement Day celebrations, Hopkins Village.

found by farmers chopping bush from the citrus groves.

Today, instead of the whine of sawmills and the clank of steam engines, toucans and parrots squawk above the river banks, feeding on the wealth of mangoes, figs and other natural fruit trees that thrive in the rich alluvial soils. Three-ft (1-meter) long iguanas bake in the sun on towering fig trees. Manatee frequent the lower reaches of the river and jaguar have been spotted swimming across the river from bamboo forests on one side to dense mangrove swamps on the other. A boat trip up the river is a perfect introduction to the biological wealth of tropical watersheds, for the Sittee River drains a huge region fringing the north border of the Cockscomb Basin.

North of Dangriga lie the superb wildlife habitats of **Southern Lagoon** ⑩ and **Northern Lagoon** ⑪. Surrounded by limestone hills, mangrove forest, and savanna marshland, they provide breeding and calving grounds for one of the highest concentrations of manatee in the Caribbean. Two islands in Northern

Tropical palms.

Lagoon support tremendous nesting colonies of white ibis, great egrets, and other small herons, while on the coastline opposite Southern Lagoon is found the largest nesting concentration of loggerhead and hawksbill turtles in Belize. The government of Belize has recognized the lagoons' ecological significance by declaring them protected against development as part of a Special Development Area.

A narrow, 2-mile (3km) long spit of land called **Gales Point** juts into the middle of Southern Lagoon, and is a popular spot for day-trips from Dangriga. A small creole settlement of the same name, with a long history as a fishing and farming community, serves as a base in the area, with the **Manatee Lodge** (www.manateelodge.com) offering faded but comfortable rooms, as well as tours to explore the lagoon, which forms part of the Burdon Canal Nature Reserve, the largest manatee breeding ground in the Caribbean basin. The boat tours offer the chance to spy everything from manatees and loggerhead turtles to storks and crocodiles.

⊘ DUGU FESTIVITIES

During Christmas, the popular *wanaragua*, or John Canoe dance, is performed in Dangriga, bringing the town alive with its color and vitality. The dancer wears a mask, which resembles an English face with a pencil-thin moustache, topped by a colorful hand-made hat similar to the English naval hats of the 18th century. The entire body of the dancer is covered with white and black clothing and knee rattles made of shells. The warlike dance was first performed to hone the skills of warrior-slaves.

A carnival atmosphere consumes Dangriga during the celebration of Garífuna Settlement Day on 19 November, which commemorates the landing of Garífuna leader Elijio Beni and his followers at the mouth of the North Stann Creek River. This is the most important local holiday, when the town swells with Garífuna from all over Central America and the United States. Singing and dancing crowds, all in traditional Garífuna costume, follow drummers from house to house until sunrise, when everyone gathers at the riverside for a re-enactment of the Landing. This is followed by a procession to the Sacred Heart Roman Catholic Church, to attend the special Mass performed entirely in Garífuna to the rhythmic beat of the drums. Many restaurants and bars, particularly in Dangriga and Hopkins, also offer special meals and drinks in honor of Garífuna Settlement Day.

THE GARIFUNA

The Garífuna (or Garinagu) are descendants of Carib, Arawak, and Africans, who trace their history back to the island of St Vincent.

The story of the Garífuna begins on the island, where, years before the Europeans arrived, Carib Indians had sailed north from South America to explore the Caribbean territories of the indigenous Arawak tribes. The Caribs raided Arawak territories, killing the men and taking the women for wives, and over time a language evolved with a female Arawak version and a male Carib version, understood by both sexes.

English and French sailors first ventured into the Caribbean in 1625. A treaty between the British and the Caribs guaranteeing the latter perpetual possession of the islands of St Vincent and Dominica was broken by the British a few years later. As the British began to settle the islands, the independent Caribs grew closer to the French military, who saw them as a useful ally in their colonial wars with the British. French words found their way into the Carib language, and the Caribs gradually converted to Roman Catholicism.

AFRICAN ORIGINS

Meanwhile, in 1635, two Spanish ships carrying captured African slaves were shipwrecked just off the St Vincent coast. Some of the captives managed to swim ashore and found shelter in Carib settlements. The relationship between the indigenous Caribs and marooned Africans followed a stormy course over the next century and a half, ranging from reluctant acceptance to intermittent warfare and finally resulting in a wholesale fusion of the two cultures.

By 1773, this hybrid people, the Garinagu (whose culture is 'Garífuna') was the dominant population of St Vincent. Yet more and more British settlers landed on St Vincent, until it was clear the colonial forces would never tolerate a free black community at the very heart of their own slave plantations.

Following repeated raids on the British settlers, in 1795 the Black Caribs attempted one final all-out attack, led by Chief Joseph Chatoyer. His fatal wounding by a British soldier in a sword duel eventually led to the Garinagu surrender in June 1796.

Less than a year later, fearful of a resurgence of the Black Carib power, Britain deported 2,000 Garinagu to the island of Roatán off the northern coast of Honduras. While many died of disease on the journey, and the rest were abandoned with supplies for only three months, this marooned population not only survived but flourished, establishing fishing and farming communities along the coastline of the Honduras mainland.

An abortive takeover by royalists against the republican government of Honduras in 1823 found the Garinagu siding with the losing faction and facing continued persecution. They began to move up the coast to British Honduras (now Belize) and, in 1832, led by Elijio Beni, a large group of Garinagu landed at Stann Creek.

GARÍFUNA SETTLEMENT DAY

Today, they are a thriving community along the southern coast, and Garífuna Settlement Day on November 19 each year commemorates this landing. Nearly all Garinagu are trilingual, speaking English and Spanish along with their own language. Traditional activities such as the *dugu*, a sacred ceremony involving ancestral spirit worship, are reminders of a distinctive heritage, while modern Garífuna culture has created 'punta rock', a lively dance music based on Garífuna drum rhythms.

Garífuna drums and a doll in traditional dress.

A shady creek in Cockscomb Basin Wildlife Sanctuary.

COCKSCOMB BASIN

Its rugged isolation has attracted an impressive wealth of animal species to this sanctuary, in particular the awesome jaguar, while Victoria Peak draws hardy hikers.

Seen from satellite photographs, the Cockscomb Basin looks like a huge meteor crater blasted from the center of the Maya Mountains. From closer to earth, it is a lush mountain basin, full of pristine tropical forest and riddled through with jungle streams. It has one of Central America's densest concentrations of jaguars, and was the site of the world's first jaguar reserve, the **Cockscomb Basin Wildlife Sanctuary ⑫** (www.belizeaudubon.org; daily 8am–4.30pm).

Although it is the jaguar for which the sanctuary is famous, you will be lucky to glimpse one of the big cats, which mostly hunt at night. The chance to experience nature attracts an increasing number of people to visit since the basin has an intense concentration of other wildlife that makes up the jaguar's prey. Ernesto Saqui, the former director of the sanctuary, once said that the healthy jaguar population is direct evidence of the overall quality of the habitat. 'Without plenty of peccary, deer, and other prey species, we wouldn't have so many jaguars.'

REFUGE FOR THE ENDANGERED

The Cockscomb Basin, referred to locally as simply 'the Cockscomb,' is spread over 160 sq miles (415 sq km) of rugged gullies and steep slopes in the middle of Belize, all carpeted by dense rainforest. Hemmed in on all

sides by ridges or the Maya Mountains, the Cockscomb actually consists of two smaller basins, each a complete watershed for two of Belize's major rivers. Annual rainfall averages from 100–120ins (2.5–3cm), with the wettest months from June to October.

Over the past 60 years, selective logging and hurricanes have created dense secondary forest in much of the basin, with an upper canopy of 45–130ft (13.5–40 meters). This tangle of vegetation, while inhospitable to humans, allows animal life to flourish.

Main attractions

Anglican Church, Placencia
Ben's Bluff Trail
Victoria Peak

Map on page 180

Jaguar on the prowl.

The Cockscomb Basin is home to a number of rare species, including the red-eyed tree frog.

This rugged sanctuary supports a profusion of endangered wildlife. The bird list for the sanctuary stands near 300 species, including the brilliant scarlet macaw, the great curassow, the colorful keel-billed toucan, the king vulture, and the secretive agami heron. The sanctuary is predominantly known to be a safe haven for the largest raptors, such as the solitary and white hawk eagles. Besides the jaguar, four other species of wildcat prowl the basin's forests – the puma, ocelot, margay, and small jaguarundi. There is also an abundance of reptiles and amphibians roaming around, including iguanas, various snakes, and the red-eyed tree frog that periodically appears in the thousands at the start of the rainy season.

Special recognition should be given to the Belize Audubon Society and the Wildlife Conservation Society, thanks to whom howler monkeys transplanted from northern Belize again roar at dawn.

But the natural state of the Cockscomb has not always been so pristine. Humans have lived here since the time of the ancient Maya, who left

View over the treetops

a Classic- era ceremonial site called Chucil Baalum, now buried in the forest. In 1888, the Goldsworthy expedition to the Cockscomb Peaks recorded mahogany logging camps hard at work. And from the 1940s, regular logging operations were taking place in the western portion of the basin. Old logging camps with names like 'Go To Hell' and 'Salsipuedes' (Leave If You Can) are dotted about the basin. In support of the fledgling lumber industry, a small Maya community of workers grew around the main logging camp at Quam Bank, site of the present-day headquarters of the Wildlife Sanctuary. The hunting of jaguars and other wildlife flourished. Only the inhospitality of the jungle prevented an all-out onslaught on its natural inhabitants. Meanwhile, Hurricane Hattie wreaked devastation on much of the forest in 1961, knocking down many of the taller, older trees.

FIGHT TO SAVE THE JAGUAR

In 1974, the Belizean government forbade jaguar hunting, but ranchers and

hunters in the 1980s began a campaign to overturn the law. Alleged livestock kills were blamed on the increased jaguar population, with one Belizean businessman claiming that the big cat had run him out of the cattle business. Citing the disappearance of calves, he pronounced: 'I got tired of raising beef to feed the jaguars.' The government requested a study of the cats' distribution, numbers and habitats in Belize.

In October 1982, Dr Alan Rabinowitz, a young wildlife researcher working with the New York Zoological Society, answered the call. He examined forested sites throughout Belize and ranked them according to several criteria, including jaguar density, prey abundance and development potential. The Cockscomb received extraordinarily high marks on all counts. Since the jaguar had been very little studied, the results prompted Rabinowitz to spend two more years within the Cockscomb. He managed to trap and radio-collar six jaguars. Subsequent tracking of the cats led to some of the first data on the ecology and behavior of the cat in Central America.

FOUNDING THE SANCTUARY

In the Cockscomb, Rabinowitz found that jaguars consumed at least 17 different kinds of prey, including snakes and fish – but no cattle. Only injured cats (often with shotgun wounds) or those incapable of catching natural prey, such as the old or very young, turned to the livestock. If Belize could set aside enough territory to protect a 'viable population,' the cats would leave the cattle alone.

Armed with Rabinowitz's hard scientific data, conservation groups within Belize successfully lobbied the government to award full protection status to the Cockscomb. In 1984, the Cockscomb Basin became a forest reserve and no-hunting zone, and in 1986, 3,600 acres (1,460 hectares) around Rabinowitz's research camp were set aside as the world's first jaguar reserve. Finally, in 1990, the entire 100,000 acres (40,000 hectares) of the Cockscomb Basin was declared a Wildlife Sanctuary, managed by the Belize Audubon Society and funded entirely by private contributions and the entrance fee.

> **⊘ Fact**
>
> Altogether, 55 different species of mammals make their home in the Cockscomb Basin, which is 75 percent of the total found in the whole of Belize.

Saddleback caterpillar.

Today, the Cockscomb Basin Wildlife Sanctuary stands as the flagship protected area for Belize and an important refuge for the jaguar. The small Maya village that once existed within the basin was relocated to the entrance road to the sanctuary, allowing the jungle to regrow and animals to roam at will. Most of the staffers of the sanctuary come from this Maya community, called **Maya Center**, while other villagers derive indirect income from the sanctuary as naturalist guides or by selling crafts. There's a craft center by the roadside at the entrance of the reserve, where local handcrafted souvenirs are sold.

The sanctuary is about an hour's drive south of Dangriga on the Southern Highway, with a rough 6-mile (10km) track entrance road beginning at Maya Center leading to the headquarters of the sanctuary. Twelve self-guided hiking trails – all carefully mapped, well maintained and safe – can provide days of rainforest exploration, while a visitors' center explains the geological, anthropological, and natural history.

Jaguar footprint.

BRINGING IN THE BABOONS

The distinctive roar of the black howler monkey (known in Belize as the baboon) once filled the air in the Cockscomb Sanctuary. However, in the early 1960s, they were driven to local extinction by the combined effects of hunting, yellow fever and hurricane destruction of the forest canopy. A few individual monkeys had been seen nearby, but none made it into the sanctuary because of the high ridges surrounding the basin. When the sanctuary was made legally secure in 1990, Dr. Rob Horwich, founder of the Community Baboon Sanctuary in Bermudian Landing (see page 135), formed a team of local and international conservationists to re-establish a viable, self-sustaining population of the baboons in the Cockscomb. In 1992, three complete troops of baboons were relocated without loss, including two pregnant females, and since then, slowly but surely, the baboon population has flourished.

HIKING TRAILS

Cockscomb's network of well-marked and maintained trails offer the chance of spotting some of the sanctuary's wildlife while taking in its scenic beauties, such as delicate waterfalls spraying the pristine jungle. There are short walks of less than an hour, and long hikes of several days. Self-guiding maps are available at the visitors' center, but for the longer walks it's more suitable to hire a local guide. For the best views of the basin, follow the muscle-building **Ben's Bluff Trail** (a 2.5-mile/4km hike to the top of a forested ridge) to get a wholesome view of the entire Cockscomb Basin.

The truly hardy can even hike to **Victoria Peak**, Belize's second-highest mountain and possibly its most spectacular. This demanding three- to four-day hike is rapidly gaining a reputation as one of the best mountain trails in Belize. But it's not for the faint-hearted; it could be done in three days, but more comfortably you should allow one and a half days to reach the base of the peak and another half a day to get to the top. The terrain is up and down some quite steep hills, through hot and humid jungle, and wading through numerous creeks. The final ascent is a steep climb on all fours, hauling yourself up by clutching onto trees. Your reward at the top – of course – is a great view of the whole sanctuary and the surrounding, undisturbed jungle.

Although the trail is well marked, you are advised to take a local guide, who will know what to do if you get into trouble (i.e. they know jungle remedies in case of accident, they can make an arm sling from jungle leaves, and can construct temporary overnight shelters with a sleeping platform off the ground). Hikers must register with the Belize Audubon Society. There are rudimentary camping shelters and pit toilets at two points along the trail. You have to take all your own food for the journey, so the option of hiring a porter (BZ$60 60 per day) from the Maya Center village might appeal. Plentiful creek water en route is drinkable, but it's wiser to filter it (using water bottles with built-in filters, which are commercially available from specialty stockists). Suitable footwear and clothing is also very important; lightweight, fast-drying clothes are best, as you'll get wet a lot: tight-fitting shorts, like those worn by cyclists, have been recommended, as they also prevent chafing.

The best time of year to climb Victoria Peak is in the dry season, from January to May. As well as avoiding the worst of the insects, which are a real nuisance during the wettest season from July to September, it is also much more colorful then, when the flowering plants, including orchids, are in bloom.

Besides this major adventure, taking a night walk along one of the sanctuary's shorter trails is a perfect way to meet some of its nocturnal animal residents, and admire the incredible variety of plant species of the forest (long pants, sturdy footwear, a flashlight and insect repellent are recommended). You'll see ferns and orchids, and trees such as mahogany and ceiba.

SUPPLIES AND ACCOMMODATIONS

Overnight accommodations within the sanctuary are grouped around the visitors' center, comprising comfortable dorms and rooms, and some private cabins. There is also a campground nearby, with tents available to rent. Shops in Maya Center sell basic snacks, supplies, and cold drinks. There is a rainwater cistern for drinking, and fresh water is drawn from nearby streams for bathing. Reservations are recommended if you want to stay overnight in the sanctuary.

You can also make a day-trip to the sanctuary from the nearby villages of Hopkins, Seine Bight, Placencia or even in Dangriga, where you'll find everything from basic *cabañas* to luxurious resorts.

> **⊘ Tip**
>
> To cool down after a morning hike, try tubing down the South Stann Creek River or swimming in crystal-clear pools beneath refreshing mountain waterfalls. Ask at the visitors' center for details.

A Morelet's crocodile floating in the shallows.

Silk Caye.

PLACENCIA

The best beaches in mainland Belize, plus some of the loveliest offshore coral cayes combine to make Placencia one of the country's top holiday destinations.

The roots of Placencia's name vary depending on who you ask: Some say 'pleasant point,' others think it means 'peaceful point,' while still others believe it stands for 'patience.' The exact meaning doesn't really matter, as Placencia is both pleasant and peaceful, which has made it one of the country's top tourist destinations. And, as a gateway to the longest sand beaches in Belize, Placencia is firmly on the itinerary for visitors, who come to enjoy the sun by day, and the lively restaurants and bars by night.

FRENCH HERITAGE

Placencia's name, shared by the village and its peninsula, was given by Huguenots. Members of this strict Protestant sect fled religious persecution in Europe, tried out Nova Scotia in Canada, then immigrated to Belize in 1740. They chose this remote point, which the ancient Maya had once used as a fishing camp (as excavated pottery shards and house mounds indicate).

The Huguenots were eventually beaten by the tropical heat and diseases from the nearby swamps, abandoning the settlement in 1820. But they did have occasional good times: dozens of 17th-century bottles and clay pipes have been dug up at the appropriately named **Rum Point**, a couple of miles (3km) north of town, where it is thought that Huguenot men came to smoke and drink alcohol

out of sight of their womenfolk and away from religious restrictions.

Though little concrete evidence exists, local legend has it that buccaneers often used the excellent protection of the lagoon at the Placencia Peninsula as a harbor.

Placencia was restarted as a fishing camp in the mid-19th century, and with the wealth of marine life and proximity of the Barrier Reef, prospered. Though many of the fishermen have given up their lines and spearguns for binoculars and dive gear, cashing in on their local

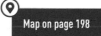

Main attractions
Anglican Church, Placencia
Sidewalk Arts Festival, Placencia
Seine Bight
Laughing Bird Caye National Park
Silk Cayes
Placencia Lagoon

Map on page 198

Relaxing on the beach at Placencia.

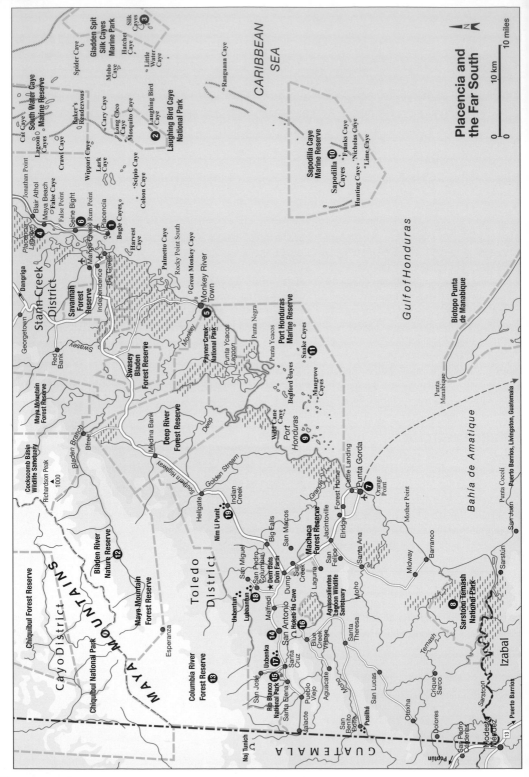

Placencia and the Far South

N

0   10 miles

0   10 km

CARIBBEAN SEA

Gulf of Honduras

Bahía de Amatique

MAYA MOUNTAINS

GUATEMALA

knowledge to guide tourists around, the village still celebrates June 29 as Fishermen's Day. A Catholic Mass, boat parade and the blessing of the fishing fleet precedes a town-wide party where visitors are welcomed.

The dirt road running 26 miles (42km) along the peninsula's spine was built in 1986, and connects Placencia to the **Southern Highway**.

Placencia's airstrip lies 2 miles/3km north of town, and is well serviced by around 10 flights daily on the Belize–Punta Gorda route. On arrival, hop in a taxi (around Bz$10) from the airstrip into Placencia village.

TROPICAL CALM

Placencia ❶ must be one of the most laid-back places in Belize – which is saying a lot. **Main Street** is actually a narrow, raised concrete sidewalk running through the village, first built 30 years ago (and rebuilt after Hurricane Iris struck the peninsula in 2001). It's the main artery of life in town, and is flanked by pastel-colored clapboard houses on stilts.

The north end of the sidewalk starts at the beach designated for campers and tents. To the south, it ribbons its way past numerous local businesses. Along this 100ft (30-meter) section, you can browse around several small gift shops, selling fine wooden carvings and other local crafts. Beware of buying any black coral on display, however; it is strictly protected under international agreement and you are prohibited from bringing it through customs if returning to Europe, the United States, or Canada.

Stroll across the walkway toward the beach and sample local creole dishes or fresh seafood at one of the growing number of beachfront bars and restaurants. Or try some homemade ice cream and pastries for dessert at a snack stand. Then take in the volleyball next to one of Placencia's oldest structures, the octagonal **Anglican Church**, built in 1943 (thanks to termites, not

many of Belize's older wooden buildings last very long, and those that do survive the voracious insects then have to contend with the hurricanes).

A sandy path goes around the peninsula toward the lagoon, with a string of resorts, restaurants, a bank, a rental business, and a gas station. This is also the Placencia Tourism Center (www.placencia.com), which is the best place to find out what's going on locally. A wide selection of seafront bars and resort restaurants offer relaxing places for a sunset drink and meal. Just offshore are many foreign yachts tugging at their anchors and local fishing skiffs bringing in their daily catch.

Placencia is a cool place at any time of year, but there are a couple of annual events that will make a visit even more enjoyable. The **Sidewalk Arts Festival**, held in February around Valentine's Day, is a popular showcase for artists from all over Belize, and during **Lobster Fest** there are enthusiastic celebrations at the opening of the lobster season in late June; there is plenty of eating, drinking, and dancing to local bands.

⊙ Tip

The best way to get around the long, narrow Placencia peninsula is by bicycle; sturdy machines with chunky tires can be rented in town, or are free if you're staying at one of the upscale resorts.

Colorful stilt house, Placencia.

BELIZE'S FINEST COASTLINE

Placencia is one of the few places in Belize where you can walk for miles along a sandy beach. It is possible to stroll 7 miles (11km) north to the village of **Seine Bight** without interruption. Despite the many upscale resorts lining this coast, there are still many secluded beaches to call your own for the afternoon. Belizean law actually prohibits construction within 66ft (20 meters) of the shoreline of beach areas, specifically in order to ensure free access to all, although many resorts have all but taken over their own stretch of sand.

Swimming is best at the points of land where sand builds up. Snorkelers will find meadows of grass beds bordering the coastline, dotted by clusters of small coral patch reefs. Beware of boats while swimming. Tourist and fishing boats continually ply the coastal waters of Belize. In Placencia village, the town council has placed buoys along the shore to mark an idle zone – for all boats – to help protect swimmers.

Belizeans have always known that the diving is also better in the southern half of the country. Today there are some major dive operators, all offering complete dive packages. Several scuba shops offer equipment rental and instruction, while smaller outfits such as Nite Wind Guides do snorkeling trips to nearby cayes and take visitors to **Gladden Spit** to see whale sharks feed on snapper eggs during the spring at full moon.

What makes the diving so interesting off Placencia is that it marks the change in the Barrier Reef's structure from northern Belize to the south. North of **Columbus Caye**, the area behind the reef is mainly flat, with extensive grass beds and patch reefs. As you move south toward Placencia, the reef structure transforms into a region of sink holes, pinnacles, and formations called 'faroes' – atoll-like structures that support a vast array of marine habitats (an example is **Laughing Bird Caye National Park ②**, named after the laughing gulls that used to nest here). South of Columbus Caye, the Barrier Reef drop-off becomes a near-vertical wall beginning in only 35ft (10 meters) of water.

AROUND THE CAYES

A typical diving excursion might include a morning dive outside the Barrier Reef on the drop-off amongst marine life such as spotted eagle rays, hawksbill or loggerhead turtles. Lunch can be taken on one of the picturesque islands inside the reef, such as the **Silk Cayes ③**, followed by snorkeling around the rich waters. The final dive for the day could be at any of the hundreds of possible sites inside the inner reef. On the way home, if you pass by **Long Coco Caye**, chances are that a pod of dolphins will chase your boat's bow wake. If you are lucky, you can slip quietly into the water and observe from a distance the graceful underwater ballet of these marine mammals.

Even if you can't dive, snorkeling can offer more than a glimpse of the wonders of the Belize marine waters. Coral gardens abound in 10–15ft (3–5 meters) of water around the **Scipio** and

Placencia Harbor.

Colson's Caye. Frigate birds, brown boobies, and brown pelicans nest on a trio of small islands around what is known as **Lark Caye**. The rich birdlife above the water is fueled by an explosion of marine life below, including tremendous schools of small herrings and anchovies. The bottom is alternately carpeted by sea grass, colonial anemones, and corals, and sinkholes and drop-offs are accessible even to beginner snorkelers.

Both Laughing Bird Caye and the Silk Cayes group (sometimes called the Queen Cayes) offer spectacular underwater scenery, in deep water as well as snorkeling depth.

The rich variety of marine habitats also makes Placencia an excellent place for sport fishing. Grassy shallows around many of the islands are home to schools of bonefish, tarpon, and permit. Trolling along drop-offs and channels nearly always lands barracuda and jacks, and occasionally the mighty kingfish. Outside the Barrier Reef, the catch includes grouper and snapper. Many of the diving companies can arrange fishing trips. **Trip'n Travel** (www.tripntravel.bz) specializes in fishing trips in the area, and you can pick up fishing equipment at **Fred's Fishing Gear and Rental** (http://fredsfishing.tripod.com).

PLACENCIA LAGOON

The mangrove habitat is one of the most important ecosystems in Belize and the brackish waters of **Placencia Lagoon** ❹ provide the perfect conditions for the taproots of the white mangrove plant, which has formed a tangled fringe all along its shores. Mangrove is a halophytic plant, which has the unique ability to thrive in salty water, by filtering out 80 percent of the salt through its roots.

Kayaking and canoeing around the long thin lagoon is an ideal way of silently viewing the tremendous amount of wildlife living among these ecologically important aquatic plants. Most of the larger resorts dotted along the seashore

a short walk across the peninsula road provide access, guides, and watercraft for a quiet afternoon's paddling. Even when the sea is choppy on the other side of the peninsula it is usually calm on the lagoon and its numerous side channels provide the ideal opportunity for exploring in a small boat.

Though unpredictable, herbivorous manatee feed in the extensive grass beds and calve in the secluded bays and rivers emptying into the lagoon. White ibis, snowy egrets, boobies, and pelicans feed, roost and nest around and on many of the small mangrove islands. Beneath the water level, the mangrove also provides a home to marine species: lobsters protect their young among the underwater roots, whilst other crustaceans and various fish feed and find shelter here.

EXCURSIONS FROM PLACENCIA

Nestled together across the lagoon from Placencia, the small towns of **Big Creek, Independence**, and **Mango Creek** owe their existence to the revived banana industry in Belize.

There are plenty of charming guesthouses to choose from in Placencia.

Diving at North Wall, Silk Cayes.

Tip

Kayaks and canoes are ideal for getting close to the noise-shy manatee, although local regulations prohibit motor boats from running their engines within 25yds/meters of sighted manatee.

Prior to the 1940s blight, bananas were loaded on railroad cars and shipped to the coast at **Monkey River Town** ❺ to be loaded on shallow drafted barges. This creole and Garífuna outpost has never recovered from the industry's crash. The empty shell of the town's former medical center stands as a reminder of its more affluent past. Today, tourism is the main source of employment for young people in the town. Much of the surrounding forest along the Monkey River has been declared a Special Conservation Area and a few small, communal guest houses have appeared. There are a couple of inns and restaurants right by the jetty (where you can order lunch in advance if going up the river in the morning), and a gift shop by the river mouth offers local handicrafts, fishing, and wildlife tours, snacks, and drinks.

Located 10 miles (16km) south of Placencia, the town is accessible only by boat. On the way is **Rocky Point South**, a manatee hangout. A slow ride up the jungle-lined river is a chance to view iguanas, monkeys, crocodiles, and a variety of tropical birds. Most day excursions will also moor on the riverbank and take you into the jungle for an hour or so. Howler monkeys will probably make an appearance here (but beware of standing directly beneath them as they have a habit of urinating when excited!). Mosquitoes are also a hazard, even in the middle of the day in the dry season, so bring plenty of repellent.

About 5 miles (8km) upstream is a clear swimming hole (there are crocodiles, but they are very shy and non-aggressive) and a sandbar where you can eat a picnic lunch before drifting quietly back down the river.

SEINE BIGHT

The Garífuna people of **Seine Bight** ❻, the neighboring town to the north of Placencia on the peninsula, have the cheery reputation of being the friendliest in Belize. It's sometimes referred to as a 'grandmother village' because many younger people have left to find jobs, sending money back to the grandparents who take care of the children.

The town is pure Garífuna – and one of its main challenges is to open up the village to tourism while still maintaining its authentic culture. Thus far, Seine Bight offers a taste of both. Accommodations include the elegant **Inn at Robert's Grove** (www.robertsgrove. com), while shops include **Goss Chocolate**, where you can indulge in truffles and organic dark and milk chocolate. **Lola's Art Gallery**, meanwhile, sells colorful paintings of Garífuna traditions, seascapes, and village life.

On the north end of town, the owner of the **Nautical Inn** also runs a wildlife project in conjunction with Belize Zoo (see page 119), breeding green iguanas in order to return them into the wild. This species has become endangered, mainly due to the loss of its natural habitat. The reptiles are kept in an enclosure in the resort grounds and subsequently released when they are big enough to fend for themselves.

BANANA BOATS

In the late 19th century, plantation owners began growing bananas in the flat fertile land between Placencia and Dangriga for export to Europe. In the early 20th century, however, most of the crops were ruined by diseases, and in the 1940s the banana plants were virtually wiped out by the sigatoka virus.

A slow recovery has been underway since the 1960s, boosted by British importers, and the opening of a port at Big Creek in Belize's Toledo district has allowed container ships to take bulk loads of the tropical fruit.

Environmentalists aren't so enthusiastic, however. While providing employment and foreign exchange for Belize, the heavy use of fertilizers and pesticides on nearby plantations is affecting the delicate offshore ecosystems, while large expanses of tropical forests are being leveled to plant bananas.

In the past, some importers branched out from fruit, and offered a round-trip in private passenger cabins in one of Fyffes' cargo ships on a 14-day cruise from London to Belize. British readers may be interested to note that HP sauce used to stand proud on the dining table and the purser's store even sold Old Spice aftershave. Sadly, these trips no longer operate.

MANATEES

Embark on a tour of Manatee Hole to learn about these endangered placid 'sea cows,' and the impressive efforts being put forth to preserve them.

Viewing manatees in their natural habitat is an unforgettable experience. When skiffs arrive at the mangrove embankment known as Manatee Hole, the powerful outboard engines are shut off. From here, Belizean guides pick up their boat-poles and propel the skiff quietly through the shallow lagoon. A dense carpet of sea grass (essential food for manatees) can be clearly viewed through the clear water. Look for shadows looming beneath the boat, and you'll soon see a round, glistening grey protuberance breaching the still water's surface. The first manatee has arrived.

The West Indian Manatee (Trichechus manatus), popularly known by some as 'sea cow', is an endangered species worldwide. More than 100 countries that have signed CITES (Convention on International Trade of Endangered Species) agree that no part of it should be traded on the international market.

GENTLE GIANTS

Official protection has been important for these large, gentle creatures, up to 12ft 6ins (3.8 meters) in length. Like a cross between a dolphin and a seal in body design, they share this somewhat ungainly appearance with few relatives worldwide, including three manatees and the more widespread dugong – the manatees' counterpart in Australasia. The West Indian Manatee occurs from southern North American coasts and rivers, throughout the Caribbean. The North American manatee population is considered a distinct subspecies from the remainder, which are termed Antillean Manatees. Belize is home to the largest population of Antillean Manatee, which may serve as a source population to neighboring countries.

Manatees are slow to reproduce – a trait that renders them vulnerable to extinction. One calf, occasionally twins, is born after an 11–13 month gestation and cared for extensively by the mother for 1–2 years. New calves are born only once every 2–5 years. As the calf matures it is gradually introduced to its plant diet. In the sea this is turtlegrass and manatee grass; in fresh water it is a variety of aquatic plants. Manatees reach sexual maturity at age 3–4 years.

PROTECT THE MANATEES

While most Belizeans and visitors regard manatees in a positive light, there remain threats; poaching and collisions with boats are two of the main culprits, whilst drowning in fishing nets and poisoning by chemical pollutants are also suspected dangers.

The most important things you can do to protect manatees are:

Speak only quietly while you are on manatee grounds.

Keep garbage inside the boat.

Refrain from buying items made with manatee bones (ivory), which may be offered for sale by some vendors.

Your best chance of seeing a manatee is on an organized tour, led by a skilled and licensed Belizean guide. A variety of trips are available at various sites up and down the coast: at Sarteneja, Caye Caulker, San Pedro, and Belize City (Manatee Hole), as well as Punta Gorda, Monkey River, and Placencia.

The docile manatee.

A road through the jungle.

THE FAR SOUTH

The once-remote south of Belize has opened up to visitors, offering undeveloped cayes, mountain rainforest scenery, and rich Maya culture.

⊙ **Main attractions**
Punta Gorda
Port Honduras
Sapodilla Cayes
Bladen River Nature
  Reserve
Lubaantun
Nim Li Punit

The residents of the **Toledo District**, to the far south of Belize, often refer to their home as 'the forgotten land.' It is the poorest part of the country, with pot-holed dirt roads when you turn off the paved Southern Highway and isolated Maya villages surviving on subsistence farming. In the early 1980s, it was even proposed that the area south of the Monkey River be ceded to Guatemala in exchange for relinquishing its 150-year-old claim on Belizean territory. Fortunately for Toledo and all Belizeans, the proposal was met by widespread riots, and was quickly rejected.

But it's precisely the fact that Toledo is less touristy than elsewhere that makes it an exciting destination for adventurous travelers: This is a land that's rich in primary rainforest, mon-strous caves, and jungle-covered ruins. Outside Punta Gorda, the only town of any size, restaurants are quite basic. Accommodations are also spare, like a simple room under a thatched roof. Travel arrangements can change from day to day, so it is best to be flexible, open minded, and in no rush to get from place to place.

The Toledo District is first and fore-most Maya country: more than half the population belongs to one of two Maya groups: Mopan or Kekchi. Traveling south along the **Southern Highway**,

clusters of thatched huts appear with increasing regularity. Maya women herd their children along the road-sides while balancing washloads on their heads; Maya men return from their milpas or working plantations with machetes in hand.

THE LAY OF THE LAND

The Toledo District can be divided into two main areas. The uplands, located in the interior, include the southern ramparts of the **Maya Mountains**; these are the rugged remains of a hard,

📍 **Map on page 198**

Celebrating Garífuna Settlement Day in Punta Gorda.

Performers from the Maroon Creole Drum School, Punta Gorda.

Punta Gorda waterfront.

white, limestone shelf, now blanketed by some of the most pristine rainforest in Belize. The coastal lowlands consist of softer sediments, formed from the deposits of silt-laden rivers; here, striking groups of steep, jagged, limestone hills stick up like Maya pyramids.

Six major rivers snake past, draining the torrential rains of the uplands. They often flood at the height of the rainy season, in September and October, creating vast flood plains and seasonal swamps, cutting off side roads (but not the main highway) for days at a time.

This complex terrain has influenced human settlement of the far south. For centuries, Maya cities and ceremonial centers dotted the region. Pacified and converted by the Spanish in the 17th century, thousands of the Maya farmers were driven out by the British in the 18th and 19th centuries. Many settled in the vast lowland forests of Petén department in northern Guatemala, home of some of the greatest Maya ceremonial centers, in particular, Tikal and El Mirador.

In the mid-19th century, Garífuna settlements were founded at Punta Gorda, Punta Negro and Barranco, followed by Confederate gun-runners seeking asylum at the end of the American Civil War. Sugar soon became the dominant cash crop and by 1870, twelve sugar mills were in operation, all owned by the North American immigrants. But the price of sugar began to drop; tired of fighting the rains and insects, most of the North Americans returned to their homeland.

MAYA COMING HOME

From the 1880s, two distinct groups of Maya – Mopan and Kekchi – began moving back into the region as laborers. Although related, tradition separates the two cultures, and their languages are as distinct as Italian and Portuguese (with different words for everything from 'sun' to 'tortilla').

Coming back from the Petén, the Mopan Maya have a long tradition as independent small farmers; they settled in the uplands of Toledo around the village of San Antonio. The Kekchi

Maya, on the other hand, came to the lowlands of Toledo, from the high-altitude Alta Verapaz Department of central Guatemala, where they had suffered under exploitative conditions on foreign-owned coffee plantations. Their villages are small and isolated, often requiring long treks over mud-died trails to reach, making them the most self-reliant as well as the poor-est of the many ethnic groups in Belize. Adding to the melange are mestizos, creole (of Afro-Caribbean origin), Chinese, and East Indians who came as loggers and sugar-cane laborers and never left.

URBAN HUB OF THE SOUTH

Known locally as 'PG,' **Punta Gorda** ❼ is the southernmost town in Belize, and is the capital of the Toledo District. In the past, most travelers only passed through Punta Gorda en route to some-where else (it is a departure point for the twice daily skiff service to Puerto Barrios, Guatemala, and Puerto Cortés in Honduras). These days, although the town receives fewer visitors than most other parts of the country, more people are venturing south to seek out the genuine atmosphere of a fron-tier outpost without the hard edge of Belize City. Buses leave the capital six or seven times a day, and the trip takes 6–7 hours on the well-paved South-ern Highway, taking in some stunning scenery on the way.

The air is crystal clear here, possi-bly due to the annual 160ins (400cm) of rain continuously washing the dust from the air. Perched on a limestone escarp-ment, much of Punta Gorda lies only 15–20ft (4.5–6 meters) above sea level.

The long, narrow town only stretches back a few blocks from the coastline, which slopes to pebbly, dark sand beaches where fishing dories lie pulled up on shore. Farther south, the Carib-bean ceaselessly nibbles away at the land, dragging old houses and grave-yards into the sea.

The pace of life is slow in PG, even by Belizean standards. The town is charm-ingly overgrown: huge mango trees tower majestically along the streets, providing welcome midday shade; flowering bushes and potted plants decorate the verandas of lichen-stained clapboard homes; and tall grass flour-ishes in most yards. That said, the town also has a good collection of accom-modations and restaurants, as well as an excellent tour infrastructure in place – you can easily find quality guides to take you out to the Barrier Reef or on inland adventures.

Punta Gorda is an alluring slice of southern Belize. Fishermen leave in their dugout canoes at sunrise, returning around noon with fish for the market. Little blue herons, snowy egrets, and flocks of sandpipers for-age for invertebrates on the beaches north of town, all but ignoring quiet bird-watchers. In the center of town is a stocky clock tower, built by a local politician. On Wednesdays and Sat-urdays, Main Street swells with color as villagers from all over the district

Hitching a ride on the Southern Highway.

converge to sell produce, embroidery, and plastic wares.

The best places to check for the most recent tourist information are at the Belize Tourist Office on Front Street or the **Toledo Visitors' Information Center** on Front Street near the Punta Gorda Wharf. The leading authority on the area's burgeoning eco-tourism industry is the **Toledo Institute for Development and Environment** (www. tidetours.org), who run a wide range of activities, from organizing training courses in sport fishing for local fishermen to providing information for visitors on recommended specialist nature guides and tours to the cayes and the Maya Mountains. Welcoming accommodations include the relaxing **Nature's Way Guesthouse** on Front Street, the all-pink **Beya Suites** (www. beyasuites.com) and the upscale **Copal Tree Lodge** (https://copaltreelodge.com).

EXCURSIONS FROM PUNTA GORDA

About 4 miles (6.5km) outside of town is the small but impressive **Church**

A street in Punta Gorda.

of the Nazareth. Royal palms line the drive to this spacious chapel and nearby novitiate for the Pallotine Sisters. For an all-encompassing view of Punta Gorda, the Caribbean, and a glimpse of Honduras, follow the New Road west for just over a mile (2km) to the city's waterpump station, where an old military trail leads up **Cerro Hill**. Though fairly strenuous, the 30-minute hike follows along a well-marked trail with good footing in the dry season.

Joe Taylor Creek snakes along the northern boundary of town. A two or three-hour ride in a dugout canoe, paddling between limestone outcrops, is a good introduction to the mangrove/ riverine habitat in Belize. The lower reaches of the creek are lined by mangroves, which quickly meld into broadleaf forest; orchids and bromeliads add to the riverbank vegetation.

To experience the largest and oldest mangroves in Belize, hire a boat to travel the 13 miles (20km) south to the **Temash River**. Declared part of the 41,000-acre (16,400-hectare) **Sarstoon-Temash National Park** ❽ in 1992, the Temash River trip is spectacular if only for the tall red mangrove forest towering over both river banks. Amongst the orchids and huge bromeliads that coat the thick stilt roots of the mangroves, the 6in (15cm) wide, iridescent blue wings of the Blue Morpho butterfly can be spotted.

Many of the tributaries draining into the Temash are black from the tannin of the decaying matter in surrounding swamps. Gibnut, peccary, and warrie (a species of peccary), as well as their natural predators the jaguar and crocodile, are abundant here, one of the most remote places in Belize.

The Temash is only one of many rivers along the Toledo coast. The **Sarstoon River**, forming the southern border with Guatemala, nourishes the only comfrey palm forests in Belize at its mouth. Between the Sarstoon and Temash Rivers lies an expanse of sand bars, too shallow even for the use of an outboard motor. Huge schools of minnow and shrimp support a thriving population of sea birds. The coastline is quickly eroding away here as tall, thin white mangroves topple into the sea like a giant game of pick-up sticks. Manatees are common along many of the river mouths, feeding on the rich grass beds and calving in the quiet lagoons and bays of the rivers.

THE CAYES OF TOLEDO

Just north of Punta Gorda is **Port Honduras** ❾, a large bay containing more than 100 small mangrove islands. Four major rivers drain into this bight, turning the water brown during most of the year. This influx of nutrient-laden sediment makes it a prime feeding ground for marine fish, manatee, and dolphin; fishing is also excellent around the many coral shoals, river mouths, and channels. Wooden house poles and a jade axe have been discovered here, but the most astonishing find is an ancient Maya canoe paddle – the only such artifact found to date. The ancient Maya knew of the wealth of marine resources and established an important ceremonial center on **Wild Cane Caye**, as well as fishing camps on many of the islands. In recent years, all this coastal stretch has been rapidly gaining a reputation as a superb site for fly-fishing, particularly for the highly-rated permit. With tightening limitations on net fishing in the protected waters, an increasing number of local fishermen are adapting their skills to become game-fishing guides, and the tourist information offices in Punta Gorda can provide you with details of a number of recommended experts.

The farther south in Belize you travel, the farther the Barrier Reef splits from the mainland. Off Punta Gorda, the reef lies nearly 40 miles (64km) east and makes a great hook as the Caribbean deepens into the Bay of Honduras. On the shank of the hook lie six gems, the **Sapodilla Cayes** ❿, the southernmost islands in Belize and now a marine reserve, protected by TASTE (Toledo Association for Sustainable Tourism

A shallow blue lagoon in the Snake Cayes.

> **⊙ Tip**
>
> If you're paddling in the shallow water around the cayes, drag your feet across the sand rather than step down, as this will alert stingrays, which sometimes lie invisibly under the surface, and which can give you a painful sting.

A bus route through the Maya Mountains.

and Empowerment). The reserve covers an area of about 48 sq miles (125 sq km), and is rich in fish and other marine life, and the crystal clear waters make it ideal for diving and snorkeling. You may well see angelfish and parrotfish as well as larger species such as whale sharks, manta rays and dolphins. A high coral sand beach in the shape of a horseshoe lines the eastern shore of **Hunting Caye**, one of the most beautiful beaches in Belize. Large numbers of turtles come here to nest during the late summer and fall months. A number of tour guides offer snorkeling and diving trips to the cayes.

Closer to the shore and less expensive to visit are the **Snake Cayes** ⑪, a group of four islands 17 miles (27km) northeast of Punta Gorda. Only West Snake Caye has a gorgeous coral sand beach, which makes for fine snorkeling and a picnic. As on all the cayes, be prepared for insects.

INTO THE INTERIOR

The 92,000-acre (37,000-hectare) **Bladen River Nature Reserve** ⑫

lies along the southern slope of the Maya Mountains, encompassing most of the upper watershed of the Bladen Branch of the Monkey River. Protected by the government of Belize in 1990, the Bladen is probably Belize's most pristine protected rainforest. Largely unexplored, the Bladen River valley contains massive limestone outcrops, sinkholes, caves, waterfalls, and such environmentally endangered animals as the jaguar, Baird's tapir, and Southern River otter; there are over 200 species of bird.

Within one of the remote alluvial valleys lies an un-investigated Maya ruin called **Quebrada de Oro** (Spanish for Passageway of Gold). Access is via a 5-mile (8km) dirt road, inaccessible during the rainy season. Since nature reserves receive Belize's highest level of preservation, it is necessary to get permission to enter them. Information concerning permits and access can be found at the Belize Audubon Society (see page 236) in Belize City or BFREE (Belize Foundation for Research and

Environmental Education; www.bfreebz. org) in Bladen.

To the southwest, and adjacent to the Bladen River Nature Reserve lies the 103,000-acre (41,000-hectare) **Columbia River Forest Reserve** ⓭, which a 1993 study found to harbor the most biologically diverse ecosystem in Belize. This is one of the only large, continuous tracts of undisturbed rainforest left in Central America. Rugged limestone hills are pock-marked by caves and sinkholes – one of which, near the village of **Esperanza**, swallows a whole river as if it were a giant drain. This reserve is not a place for weekenders: you must be totally self-sufficient in terms of equipment and food. Guides can be hired at the village of **San José** for the strenuous Maya Divide Trail – a five-day hike to Las Cuevas in the Chiquibal Forest, near Caracol (see page 167).

MAYA VILLAGES

Lying in the heart of Maya country, among the rolling foothills of the Maya Mountains, **San Antonio** ⓮ is at the center of a group of villages in the vicinity, where some enterprising grassroots eco-tourism organizations are bringing more money into the community, including helping to finance local schools.

Lying some 20 miles (32km) northwest of Punta Gorda, San Antonio is the second largest town in Toledo, but is a quiet and simple market outpost. The center of town is dominated by a stone **church** built of limestone salvaged from surrounding ruins. The early morning and late afternoon light pours through the beautiful stained-glass windows, illuminating the well-worn woodwork of the church interior.

A short walk out of San Antonio, along the road below the church, is the tranquil San Antonio waterfall and pool. A few wooden benches make it a perfect place for lunch and a cooling afternoon swim. Watch for multicolored dragonflies feeding among the stream-side vegetation, and hummingbirds, that bathe in the spray coming off the small falls.

⊘ Tip

Every August, the village of San Antonio holds the Deer Dance, a colorful festival of music and costumed dance, as part of the Festival of San Luis.

Río Blanco Waterfall Park.

Eight miles (13km) farther on, between the villages of **Santa Cruz** and Santa Elena, you'll come across the **Río Blanco National Park** . Declared a protected area in 1992, this 500-acre (200-hectare) preserve has been called an Indigenous Peoples' Park – it is controlled by the nearby villages of Santa Cruz and Santa Elena.

Here, the **Río Blanco** flows through wide, shallow pools and gentle cascades formed of smooth slabs of mudstone and sandstone, before pouring over a 12ft (3.5-meter) ledge into a deep pool. It's an ideal swimming spot and a popular stop-off if you're touring the Maya Mountains.

BLUE CREEK

One of the most impressive natural sites in Toledo is the **Hokeb Ha Cave** at Blue Creek. The huge cave entrance is carved from the summit of a hill where the Blue Creek gurgles up from underground. After leaving the cave, the creek cascades over limestone boulders, under the towering shadows of the surrounding rainforest.

Game of dominoes.

Archeologists have found inside many Late Classic ceramics and an altar, leading them to theorize that the Hokeb Ha cave was used specifically for ceremonial purposes. The cave lies within the Blue Creek Preserve, a private sanctuary, with cabins by the riverside and various amenities, including an excellent canopy walkway strung between the trees, 80ft (24 meters) above the river. To get there from San Antonio, follow the road to Punta Gorda 2.5 miles (4km) to Malfredi, at the junction with the road to **Aguacate**. Follow this road 5.5 miles (9km) to **Blue Creek Village**. Park before the bridge, walk along the gravel path to a swimming hole, then follow the muddy river path 15 minutes upstream to the cave.

ARCHEOLOGICAL DISCOVERIES

Toledo is rich in Maya ruins, but the government of Belize lacks funds to maintain them for tourists. Many are overgrown, with little, if any, information available. For example, **Uxbenka** (Ancient Place) is a small

⊘ TOLEDO'S ECOTOURISM PROJECTS

One especially rewarding way of visiting Toledo district is through several village projects offering accommodations and guided visits to local attractions. The projects provide villagers with a livelihood, and an alternative to the lumber industry that is causing deforestation in the region at an alarming rate.

The **Toledo Ecotourism Association** (TEA; tel: 722-2096) is run by a grassroots organization of Mopan, Q'eqchi' Maya, and Garífuna leaders. Guesthouses have been constructed in several villages, where families are chosen on a rotating basis host visitors. Nature trails, planned and constructed by the villagers, lead to local sites of interest. These can be found in the communities of **San Miguel** (bat cave and a river walk), **San Pedro Columbia** (river trip), **Santa Elena** (waterfall and ruins), **Laguna** (wetland and caves), **San José** (forest walk), and **Barranco** (Garífuna village and Temash River).

The villagers have a wealth of knowledge in herbal medicine, flora and fauna, and Maya folklore, which they are proud to share with visitors, enabling you to gain a unique experience of this traditional way of life. The TEA offers a wide range of tours and packages that cover everything from Garífuna drumming to Maya song and dance to cooking and crafts.

ceremonial center built on a hill outside the Maya village of Santa Cruz. Lacking the large-scale architecture of some bigger sites, Uxbenka is now being excavated by Wichita State University, studying the Maya practice of terracing hills. Investigations have revealed that Uxbenka is one of the earliest Maya centers in southern Belize. The numerous terraces here were probably constructed for cacao production in the fertile soil.

A much better-maintained site is **Lubaantun** (Place of Fallen Stones) ⓲ the largest in Toledo, which lies high on a ridge above a valley cut by the Columbia River, 1.5 miles (2.5km) from the village of **San Pedro Columbia** and about 13 miles (21km) west of Punta Gorda. The ruins were first excavated in 1915, and subsequent archeological study suggests that Lubaantun was built completely without the use of mortar; each stone was precisely cut to fit snugly against its neighbor. The slim, square-cut stones are one of the distinctive features of Lubaantun; it is also exceptional among Maya ruins for the complete absence of carved stelae, particularly in contrast with those of nearby Nim Li Punit. The site consists of five main plazas, around which are grouped 14 main structures, including several ball courts. Pottery and other archeological finds discovered at the site are on display in the visitors' center.

Uphill from nearby **Indian Creek** village is the ceremonial center of **Nim Li Punit** (Big Hat) ⓳, with splendid views and 26 stelae, eight of them carved, and among them the tallest ever found in Belize. The ruins were first discovered in 1976, and archeologists think that the center may have had a reciprocal relationship with Lubaantun: Nim Li Punit being a religious and political center, while Lubaantun concentrated on trade and commerce. The site's name comes from a detail of a figure carved on one of the site's stelae (Stela 14), which is the longest such ancient

monument found in Belize. This stela, together with several others, is on display in the attractive visitors' center at the entrance to the site. There is a small, walled ball court in the center of the site, as well as a burial site, named the 'Plaza of the Royal Tombs.'

One example of Belize's positive approach to eco-tourism just outside of San Pedro Columbia is the 20-acre (8-hectare) **Dem Dats Doin Experimental Farm** (http://demdatsdoin.com; e-mail: demdatsdoin@gmail.com), which is trying to replace the Maya's slash-and-burn traditions of milpa farming – only sustainable at low population densities – with a more environmentally sound system of agriculture for the 21st century.

Described as an 'Integrated, Energy Self-Sufficient, Low Input, Organic Mini-Biosphere,' it is run by a couple of transplanted Americans. Between a biogas digester and photovoltaics, they have reached 95 percent energy self-sufficiency. At the time of writing, in 2019, the farm had been put up for sale and is awaiting new owners.

The Lubaantun ruins.

📷 TRADITIONAL LIFE IN TOLEDO'S FORESTS

Many Maya farmers live much as their ancestors did a thousand years ago, and today they are welcoming tourists into their homes.

Nestled in the foothills of the Maya Mountains in the interior of Toledo district are a cluster of small villages, inhabited by Kekchi and Mopan Maya farmers, originally from Guatemala, who have settled here over the last 200 years. Many of the farmers still employ the traditional slash-and-burn land use, but a few use organic methods, producing a wide range of crops, including maize, bananas, citrus fruits, cacao, herbs, and vegetables. Each family transports their own produce by local bus to trade at the weekly market in Punta Gorda.

FAMILY LIFE

A number of Maya families in the Maya Mountains are branching out from farming and opening up their communities in response to a growing influx of tourists. Several innovative projects enable visitors to experience life in the Maya villages first hand, either in simple guesthouses or, in some cases, with the families themselves. In order to fairly share out the workload – and the benefits – from this tourism influx, a rota system is operated. Your visit is guaranteed to give you an insight into a rare way of life, but don't come expecting a lie-in: breakfast starts at 4.30 am, with tortillas toasting over the fire for father's 'pack-lunch,' after which the children are dressed in time to walk through the jungle to catch the bus to school.

Whilst most Maya men have long since taken to jeans and T-shirts, many women still wear colourful, hand-embroidered blouses and skirts.

Local farmers use labor-intensive methods to harvest crops like corn, a mainstay of the Mopan diet. It is used to make tortillas and left to ferment as a massa wrapped in waha leaves.

Maya homes are simply built of wood, with roofs of thatched palm leaves and floors of beaten earth, and an adobe stove and hammock inside.

A cacao seed pod.

Local export success story

One of Belize's most successful agricultural products in recent years has been the humble cacao bean, grown by the Maya since ancient times.

Today, farmers in Toledo District produce a world-leading crop, using strictly organic methods. The harvested and fermented beans are stored by the Toledo Cacao Growers' Association in Punta Gorda and, in a unique move that resurrected the local cacao industry, sold the beans to Green and Black's chocolate manufacturers in the UK. The trade is overseen by Fair Trade Agriculture, a system set up to enable developing countries to sell their produce at prices comparable with those in the developed world. In the case of the Belizean cacao farmers, this means earning considerably more than they were being paid previously, when selling to other chocolate manufacturers. Green and Black's (originally owned by Cadbury and later bought by Mondelēz International – previously Kraft) continues to have a contract with the Toledo farmers, though it's not as steady and lucrative as in the pre-Mondelēz days. That said, the relationship has been a boon for the area, helping to fund such key initiatives as schools and health care.

Maya children are hardworking students, getting free education up to age 14, after which the boys go to work in the fields and the girls may help their mothers sell handicrafts to tourists.

A Mopan woman roasts coffee over a wood-fired stove.

As part of your stay with a Maya family you may be taught how to make baskets from the jipijapa plant, after a process of shredding, washing, bleaching, and drying the fibers.

AN EXCURSION TO TIKAL

Across the Belizean western border in Guatemala lie the remains of one of the most magnificent ancient cities anywhere in Central America.

Certain archeological sites become national symbols, appearing on everything from travel posters to airline ads, guidebook covers, and the local currency. What would Peru be without Machu Picchu, Cambodia without Angkor Wat, Egypt without the Sphinx? The Maya ruins of **Tikal**, one of the wonders of the ancient world, play the same symbolic role for Guatemala.

It's a rare traveler to Central America who hasn't seen a photo of the Temple of the Giant Jaguar (Temple I) at Tikal jutting above the tropical rainforest like a ghostly ship lost in a sea of green. The image is so famous as an emblem of Guatemala that a caption is usually unnecessary. Luckily, this spectacular ancient city is located in the Guatemalan department of Petén, on Belize's western border – making a Tikal pilgrimage an easy option.

ORIENTATION IN GUATEMALA

The Belizean domestic airlines run regular flights from Belize City and San Pedro, landing at the airport at **Santa Elena** outside the town of **Flores**, main jumping-off point for the ruins some 55 miles (90km) away. Alternatively, visits can be organized by land from San Ignacio, crossing the frontier at Benque Viejo and following the 55-mile (90km) route to Flores.

Flores is on an island in Lake Petén Itzá, connected by a causeway to the mainland. Taking travelers to Tikal is the town's major business: buses, taxis, and minivans leave for the site throughout the day. There are hotels and pensions catering to both fat and thin wallets in Flores and Santa Elena, as well as several moderately priced hotels at Tikal itself. In Flores, relax at the lovely **Casazul** (https://hotelesdepeten.com), with comfortable rooms and a terrace overlooking the lake. The ruins are so extensive that at least two days

Main attractions
Flores
Museo Tikal
Great Plaza
Temple of the Giant Jaguar
Temple of the Masks
Temple IV
Temple V
North Acropolis
Central Acropolis
Ball Court

Map on page 218

A Montezuma oropendola.

⊙ **Fact**

Archeologist Michael Coe
of Yale University called
Tikal's Central Acropolis
'an incomparable
architectural achievement
in ancient America.'

are necessary to see them thoroughly, although you could touch on the highlights in a single day.

The distances involved may be relatively short, but traveling from Belize to Guatemala plunges you into an entirely different world. The change is apparent at the frontier, where Spanish supplants English and Belize creole, quetzales replace dollars and kilometers roll by instead of miles. Volcanic applies not only to the geology of the Guatemalan highlands – where there are at least six volcanoes over 11,000ft (3,400 meters) – but also to the country's history and politics. The long-suffering citizens have been embroiled in bloody wars and repression since the time of the Preclassic Maya (see page 220).

Unlike sparsely populated Belize, Guatemala has a population of more than 17 million people packed into 42,042 sq miles (109,306 sq km). Two thirds of the country is mountainous; the narrow Pacific lowlands are divided among large estates growing sugar, maize, bananas and cotton; coffee is cultivated on the western slopes of the

mountain ranges. Guatemala's Caribbean coast can also be reached via Punta Gorda in Belize's south. Once a prime banana-growing region, it's better known now for its surfing beaches.

In northern Guatemala, around Tikal, the mountains drop off to the low grasslands and dense, hardwood rainforests of the Petén, a sparsely populated region that constitutes one-third of the country's territory. The rainforest around Tikal is rich in the flora and fauna already familiar to visitors to Belize – the classic menagerie of deer, fox, jaguar and howler monkeys.

About 55 percent of Guatemalans are *indígenas*, descendants of those remarkable people, the ancient Maya. The other 45 percent are *ladinos*, which is a cultural rather than racial term. A person becomes *ladino* by adopting Euro-American-style dress rather than wearing *traje* (traditional dress), by speaking Spanish rather than one of the more than 20 different Maya languages, and by adopting other non-indigenous cultural traits. Most *indígenas* live in the highlands and in Alta

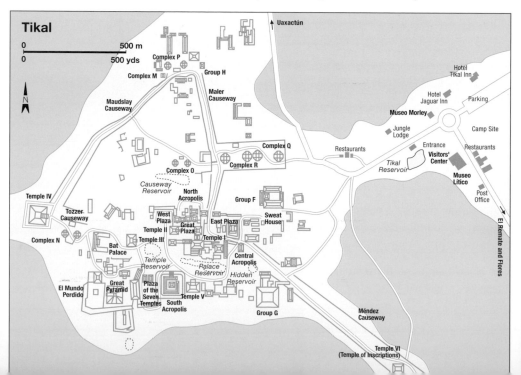

Verapaz, farming small *milpas* (fields) of maize and beans.

TIKAL AT ITS ZENITH

Before starting a walk through the site, imagine the city in its original glory, around AD 705. At its height, Tikal was home to 100,000 people, living within an area of 23 sq miles (60 sq km). The great city's many structures were constructed of limestone rubble; limestone also provided lime for stucco and plaster to cover the temples' surfaces, which gleamed white above the jungle. Flashes of red and touches of other colors glinted off the roof combs. The colors were symbolic: green represented the young maize plant (considered sacred), as well as jade and the quetzal feathers worn by royalty, water, fertility, and the ceiba tree at the center of the world.

THE LIVING SCENE

Picture the city alive with activity. Smoke drifts from thousands of cooking fires in outlying residences and from copal incense lit by priests on the temple steps, mingling with low, scudding clouds. Nobles and other upper-class citizens wager on games in the ball court just south of where laborers are working on the construction of Temple I. This pyramid represents a sacred mountain, considered to be the source of maize.

According to Maya cosmology, in the center of the world stands a giant ceiba tree, whose roots extend through the nine layers of the underworld, ruled by the Nine Lords of the Night, and whose branches reach to the top of the thirteen layers of the upper world, also ruled by deities. These gods were all considered manifestations of the creator god, called Hunab Kun or Itzamna. (If this is confusing compare it to the Christian Trinity.) It is no accident that the ruler of Tikal in AD 705, Hasaw Chan K'awil, constructed the pyramid-tomb with nine levels, each slightly smaller than the one below, like the tiers of a wedding cake, since nine is the number of the Lords of the Night. The top of the temple was capped by a roof comb with a large carving of Hasaw Chan K'awil himself.

Nearby, in the East Plaza, the market activity is at its height. Men and women with babies tied on their backs sit behind piles of maize, squash, breadnuts, chili peppers, beans, tomatoes, yucca, sweet potatoes, cacao (these chocolate beans also functioned as currency throughout Mesoamerica), salt, honey, mats, flowers, dyes, tobacco leaves, cotton textiles and pottery. A few women sell hot tortillas and beans to hungry clients. At one end of the market there might be a boy with a tame parrot or monkey, and a row of vendors with fish, venison and a few tethered rabbits, turkeys, turtles and ducks.

At the other end of the market, specialty trade items might include stingray spines from the Caribbean for ritual self-mutilation; obsidian cores for tools; volcanic rocks from the Guatemalan highlands used for grinding

An intricately carved stela from Tikal.

TIKAL'S PAST

Tikal was one of the great Classic Maya cities abandoned around AD 900. But Maya civilization did not disappear – it continued in an altered form in southeastern parts of Mexico and in areas of Guatemala.

Today, there are still keepers of the 260-day calendar in highland Guatemalan towns, healers use traditional methods, copal incense is burned to old gods, Maya languages are spoken, and women weave and wear their beautiful *trajes*.

This culture survived a second shock, the Spanish conquest in the early 1500s. After Hernán Cortés conquered Mexico, the Spanish turned to the south and Pedro de Alvarado's forces invaded Guatemala in 1523. The Itzá Maya, held out in Tayasal (Flores) for almost two centuries, until 1697, when they were finally defeated.

Maya figure of a deity holding a human head, Museo Tikal.

Guatemala was a Spanish colony from 1524 until 1821, during which time the Maya *indígenas* – at least, those surviving diseases introduced from Europe – became virtual serfs on large Spanish land-holdings. After independence from Spain, Guatemala briefly became part of Mexico, then joined the short-lived United States of Central America (along with El Salvador, Honduras, Nicaragua and Costa Rica). The Central American federation soon splintered and the Republic of Guatemala was founded in 1839.

The 19th and 20th centuries witnessed a dismal procession of dictators supported by the armed forces, large landowners and, at first, the church. Reform-minded presidents came to power in rare free elections in 1944 and 1950 and were instantly seen as a threat. In 1954, as President Jacobo Arbenz was instituting desperately-needed land reform, he was overthrown in a CIA-engineered coup. The country still suffers from the effects of this interference.

In 1977, the Guerrilla Army of the Poor was founded in the Guatemalan countryside, opposing the terrible inequities in land distribution and wealth (as well as governmental incompetence and corruption following a disastrous 1976 earthquake). Guatemala erupted in a bloody internal conflict, resulting in the destruction of at least 400 highland villages and the disappearances and deaths of thousands of civilians (mainly *indígenas*) at the hands of the army and right-wing death squads. More than 200,000 Maya *indígenas* have taken refuge in Mexico; others fled over the border to Belize and El Salvador.

In 1992, a Maya *indígena*, Rigoberta Menchú, won the Nobel Peace Prize for her efforts on behalf of human rights in Guatemala. In 1996, after a decade of fraught negotiations between the armed forces and the Guatemalan National Revolutionary Unity, peace accords were finally signed. General elections in 1999 brought Alfonso Portillo of the right-wing Republican Front to the presidency. The peace has held since then, but the government still faces the challenge of alleviating widespread poverty and lasting stability for ordinary Guatemalans.

Meanwhile, refugees, archeologists, anthropologists and tourists continue to return to Guatemala in increased numbers. And at the center of the country's attractions remains the ruins of Tikal.

stones; and *spondylus* shell beads from Ecuador. Clients pause, bargain and trade, then load their purchases in net bags, slinging their tumplines across their foreheads, and heading home along the paved causeways (*sacbes*), followed by their children carrying tiny bundles.

The divine ruler of Tikal, Hasaw Chan K'awil, is a striking figure sporting a quetzal feather headdress, jade necklace, ear ornaments, wristlets and pectoral jewelry, a jaguar skin over a kilt and underskirt, belt, cotton loincloth, elaborate loin ornaments, anklets, deerskin sandals, and miscellaneous ritual paraphernalia. He reposes on a small hassock in the Great Plaza surrounded by retainers waving away mosquitoes. Like all Maya rulers, he is quite strange-looking by our standards. His forehead slopes back sharply, a mark of beauty to the Maya, who practiced cranial deformation – when Hasaw Chan K'awil was a baby his mother would have tied a board over his forehead to elongate his skull.

Hasaw Chan K'awil interrupts his inspection of the construction of Temple I, which will commemorate his reign and serve as his tomb, to receive a delegation from Kaminaljuyú in the highlands. Their arrival is heralded by six musicians playing trumpets, drums, flutes, and rattles. Related by blood to the rulers of Kaminaljuyú, he is involved in secret talks with them concerning an alliance against other Maya city-states. Like the city-states of ancient Greece the Maya polities are a fractious lot and fight among themselves to try to claim power and assert their dominance over aggressive rivals.

Inside Temple II, constructed earlier by Hasaw Chan K'awil, his mother pierces her tongue and pulls a thorn-embedded cord through it. She collects her blood on bark paper, which she will offer to the gods for the success of her son's venture, along with the blood-soaked cord. Both ritual blood-letting and the sacrifice of prisoners of war are carried out at Tikal to propitiate the gods before important ventures and to commemorate such

Temple I.

events as the end of a time period and the ascension or death of a ruler. Later on, Hasaw Chan K'awil will use a stingray spine to pierce his cheeks, ears and penis, to satisfy the gods' demand for blood.

WALKING TOUR OF THE RUINS

The best place to start a tour of the ruins is the **Museo Tikal** (www. parque-tikal.com; museum daily 8am–6pm, Tikal National Park daily 6am–5pm), located just outside the ruins in Tikal village, at the western end of the airstrip. Among the displays is a reconstruction of Hasaw Chan K'awil's tomb, including ceramics, incised bone artifacts, and jade jewelry – necklaces, ear ornaments, wristlets, and head-dress decorations. (Other artifacts from Tikal are housed at the National Museum of Archeology and Ethnology in Guatemala City.) The museum also sells maps of the ruins and books on archeology and natural history.

The path from the museum to the ruins ends at a three-way junction. The trail to your right leads to **Complexes P, Q**, and **R** and the **North Zone**; the left fork takes you to the **Temple of the Inscriptions (Temple VI)**; and the branch straight ahead leads to the heart of the site: the **Great Plaza, Temples I** through **V**, the **North, Central**, and **South Acropolis**, the **Ball Court**, and other important buildings.

Go straight ahead first to the reconstructed **Great Plaza** area, which is today the center of the Tikal ruins (in the Classic era, however, the heart of the city was the East Plaza, where the main market was located). The Maya frequently built new constructions over old; in the Great Plaza, four different plaster floors were laid one on top of the other between 150 BC and AD 700. Seventy stelae and altars, originally painted red, are located in and around the plaza. The stelae, each of which originally had an altar beside it, commemorate the rulers of Tikal. Many of these rulers are carved in bas relief in profile on one side of the stela, although some are shown full face. The other sides contain

View of the Great Plaza.

glyphs giving dates and genealogies (sometimes including a god and the Tikal emblem glyph).

Hasaw Chan K'awil's tomb, **Temple I**, is also called the **Temple of the Giant Jaguar**, because of the jaguars carved on the lintels inside it. The temples represent one of the main architectural styles at Tikal, a squared-off wedding-cake pyramid topped by a temple with a roof comb in a two-thirds to one-third ratio. The pyramid is about 100ft (30 meters) high, and the roof comb rises another 50ft (15 meters). The three small rooms at the top were probably the preserve of priests and kings, adorned with beautifully carved zapote wooden beams and lintels. The tomb is embedded deep beneath the temple, and a collection of stately goods buried with him is now on display in the Museo Tikal.

What surprises many people is the small interior size of these buildings. The Maya had not developed the true arch in their architecture, but used instead the corbeled vault. Stones on each wall are progressively set inward until they almost meet and are topped by a row of capstones, resulting in long, narrow rooms, usually with carved wooden lintels over the doors. The temples were not designed to hold large numbers of worshippers, however, but to impress the great mass of people standing in the plaza below.

Opposite Temple I, to the west, is **Temple II**, also called the **Temple of the Masks** after two huge masks, now barely visible, that were carved on each side of the stairway just below the temple door. A giant face once adorned the roof comb. This temple was built by Ah Cacau and may have been dedicated to his wife or mother; the portrait of a woman is carved on one of its lintels.

Temple III, the **Temple of the Jaguar Priest**, is located behind Temple II. This building has not been reconstructed and is probably the last pyramid and temple built at Tikal, since the stela in front carries the date AD 810.

Temple IV is located farther to the west and is undergoing a major reconstruction. It stands 212ft (65 meters) high, making it the tallest structure

Temple II.

⊘ **THE ROOTS OF THE RUINS**

Tikal, like Rome, was not built in a day. In fact, the occupation of the site spans 1,650 years, from 750 BC (the Middle Preclassic) to AD 900. The city, consisting of at least 3,000 buildings, was situated near great swamps where raised fields were constructed for agriculture, with higher paved causeways along the canals serving as main roads. Ecologists agree that slash-and-burn agriculture as practiced by modern Maya could not have supported the populations of the ancient large cities in Belize and Petén. A fish nibbling on a water lily is often found on royal Maya dress, symbolizing abundance and wealth, and there is evidence that Classic Maya society was organized on a feudal model, with nobility controlling the land.

Much of what we know about Tikal has resulted from archeological research over the last few decades. The University of Pennsylvania's Museum conducted extensive excavations between 1956 and 1969, when the Guatemalan Institute of Anthropology and History took over the excavation and restoration work. Other scholars have made considerable progress in deciphering the Maya's written language, providing us with an understanding of the meaning of the glyphs on the stelae and buildings throughout the site.

at Tikal and one of the tallest pre-Hispanic buildings still standing. The temple was built during the reign of Hasaw Chan K'awil's son, Yik'in Chon K'awil (Divine Sunset Lord, also known as Ruler B), around AD 741, but there is some debate as to whether he is buried under it. From here there are spectacular views of the other temples rising out of the rainforest.

The best approach to **Temple V** is along the path from the Plaza of the Seven Temples, as you emerge from the forest you see the restored monumental limestone staircase. The structure was thought to be among the last of the great temples to be built, but findings from burials here indicate that it was in fact the earliest, dating from around AD 600 and almost certainly constructed by Tikal's governor at the time, Kinich Wayna. The temple was built early in the Mid-Classic hiatus.

DISMANTLED PYRAMIDS

On the north side of the Great Plaza is the **North Acropolis**, a group of

buildings that were begun around 200 BC as monuments to the ancestors of various rulers. Such early classic kings as Jaguar Paw, Stormy Sky and Curl Nose are buried beneath pyramids in this group. Like the Great Plaza floor, the pyramids have been built over several times by later rulers. How do we know what's inside? A team from the University of Pennsylvania dismantled the pyramid and temple called structure 5D-33, revealing successive onion-like layers. This edifice is in the first row (the third from the left as you face the North Acropolis). What you see now are two earlier cores and part of the last pyramid, which was originally more than 100ft (30 meters) high and which hid the rest of the Acropolis.

To the south is the **Central Acropolis**, also known at the Palace Group. The 42 palace structures span 4 acres (1.6 hectares) and housed rulers, priests and administrators. They represent a second major architectural style at Tikal: elegant, rectangular buildings, one to five stories high, with narrow, windowless, corbel-vaulted rooms, all grouped around a courtyard to form an enclosed area. At the time of their occupation, these palaces were stuccoed and painted inside and out and richly furnished with mats, ceramics, and textiles. Some have built-in platforms that may have served as beds and benches. The buildings were probably used primarily for sleeping and storage, as Tikal's climate allowed most activities, including teaching, to be carried on outside.

Southeast of the Central Acropolis is **Group G**, another palace and administraive complex. Group G is also called the **Palace of Vertical Grooves** because of the unusual vertical stone facings on the exteriors. These structures, too, were built over earlier buildings; the walls of one room covered entirely by the last

The view from Temple IV.

construction were embellished with graffiti.

ANCIENT GAMES

The **Ball Court** is between Temple I and the Central Acropolis. The ball game was a quintessential Maya activity – . We know something of the game because it was portrayed on ceramics and mentioned in the Maya creation epic, the *Popul Vuh* (see page 36).

There are also ball courts in the **East Plaza**, and three courts, side by side in the **Plaza of the Seven Temples** – which, located southwest of the Central Acropolis, received its name from seven temples that line the east side of the complex. Previous excavations indicated that the plaza was plastered over a number of times.

The third main architectural style found at Tikal is the truncated pyramid (a layered pyramid without a temple on top). A good example of this style is the **Lost World Pyramid**, which is southwest of the Central Acropolis. Originally this structure was 100ft (30 meters) high, with four stairways flanked by giant masks. Its core may date to as early as 500 BC; it was rebuilt in its final form some time before AD 300.

The pyramid's main function was calendrical or astronomical. Mayanists insist that the word 'observatory' should not be used to describe these temples because many were not used to follow the movements of the planets and stars, but were used in such ceremonies as those marking the end of a solar year or the beginning of a 52-year cycle.

The trail leading southeast past Group G is actually a causeway. It leads to the **Temple of the Inscriptions** (**Temple VI**), as does the left fork of the trail at the entrance to the ruins. This pyramid and temple were completed around AD 736 to mark the inauguration of Ruler B. Later the roof comb was added; its glyphs give a different date, AD 766.

The east side of the roof comb contains glyphs listing the genealogies of Tikal rulers over a period of nearly 2,000 years. The stela and altar on the west side of the temple commemorate Ruler B, who must have been fearsome: the altar shows a bound, face-down captive, perhaps someone who was sacrificed at Ruler B's accession to the throne or captured by him in warfare and sacrificed on some other occasion.

At the opposite end of the ruins is the **North Zone** and **Complexes P, Q** and **R**, reached by the right-hand trail at the entrance or by a causeway leading north behind Temple I. **Complexes Q** and **R** both have twin pyramids with stairways on all four sides that face each other on the east and west sides of a plaza. The north side was occupied by a stela and altar marking the *katun* ending, while a single-story palace-type building anchored the south. **Complex P** is unexcavated, but also contains twin pyramids and a stela and altar erected by Ruler B.

Dense foliage surrounds the site.

Albert Street, Belize City.

BELIZE

TRAVEL TIPS

TRANSPORTATION

GETTING THERE

By Air from the US and Canada

There are many flights from the US to Belize, as well as several from Canada. All international flights into Belize land at the Philip S.W. Goldson International Airport, which is 10 miles (16km) northwest of Belize City on the George Price (Northern) Highway. American Airlines operates direct flights from Dallas/Fort Worth, Los Angeles and Miami, Delta Airlines from Atlanta, and United Airlines from Chicago and Houston. Air Canada offers direct flights from Toronto and WestJet from Toronto and Calgary.

By Air from Europe

To fly to Belize from the UK or Europe you need to change planes at one of the US gateways. This can sometimes be inconvenient, as flight times may not match up and can result in long stopovers in the States. Tropic Air and Maya Island Air offers flights between Cancún and Belize City and it is also possible to take a bus or drive from Cancún to Belize.

By Road

Several companies run regular buses from Chetumal in Mexico to Orange Walk and Belize City. If you want to bring your own car into Belize you may incur significant customs charges, so it is worth checking before you travel.

GETTING AROUND

The main roads in Belize are paved, and there are frequent, cheap buses to most destinations. There is also an excellent network of internal flights, which is the quickest way to get around. Boat transfers to the cayes are also plentiful and relatively cheap.

From the Airport

At Philip Goldson S.W. International Airport, there is a currency-exchange window near the exit (if this is closed, you can get by on US dollars without a problem), as well as an ATM and a tourist information booth.

Most tour operators put visitors straight on to connecting flights or provide a minibus service to out-of-town hotels or jungle lodges.

There is a taxi rank outside the airport. Rates into Belize City are fixed and are fairly hefty for the 20-minute ride (B$50/US$25). One way to save is to share the taxi with other travelers. Rates to other parts

The bus station at Punta Gorda.

⊘ Flight Information

Aeromexico: www.aeromexico.com
Air Canada: www.aircanada.com
American Airlines: www.aa.com
Delta: www.delta.com
United Airlines: www.united.com
WestJet: www.westjet.com

of Belize can be negotiated (confirm the price before you get in).

By Air

Small propeller plane services cover most of Belize. This is by far the most convenient way to get around. Most of the flights run on time and few take longer than half an hour. The most popular destinations are from the International Airport to San Pedro on Ambergris Caye (which takes 20 minutes, and gives you spectacular views of the coral reef), and to Placencia and Dangriga, both

Island ferry service, Caye Caulker.

in the south. If leaving from Belize City, make sure you know whether the flight you are taking will be departing from the International Airport, or the smaller but more commonly used (and cheaper) Municipal Airport in the northern suburbs of Belize City.

National Operators

Maya Island Air
Tel: 223-1403
www.mayaislandair.com

Tropic Air
Tel: 226-2626
www.tropicair.com

By Boat

The alternative to flying to Caye Caulker or Ambergris Caye is to take a boat service from Belize City's Marine Terminal next to the Swing Bridge, or from Courthouse Wharf on the other side of the creek. Some services will stop off at St George's Caye on request. Transportation to and from other cayes by boat is mostly arranged by hotels. Alternatively, you can book your own boat at the docks.

By Bus

Buses run at least hourly between Belize City and the major towns to the north and the west, and hourly to Punta Gorda in the south. Most are the non-air-conditioned US school bus variety. The main bus station in Belize City is just west of the center, and is used by all companies serving all the towns and main roads in Belize; smaller bus lines serving some villages depart from nearby streets. Most buses will stop whenever requested, but Express buses, which cost a little more, only stop in the main towns.

By Car

One way to start your trip is to pick up a rental car (preferably a 4x4) from the airport. Your own transportation comes in very handy in the interior of Belize. Lodges tend to be in isolated areas, and having your own vehicle allows you to come and go as you please; you are free to visit wildlife reserves and archeological sites at your own pace, and make trips into town whenever you wish.

Driving is on the right-hand side of the road, and speeds and distances are measured in miles. Note that renting a car in Belize is expensive and a large damage deposit, taken by credit card, is required; insurance is about US$15 a day. The other drawback is the bad condition of some roads; in particular, take great care with the deep potholes, which can cause damage to the car (and, potentially, the people inside it) unless negotiated cautiously. Both the companies below have offices at the International Airport and in Belize City.

Budget
2.5 Miles George Price (Northern) Highway, Belize City
Tel: 223-2435, 223-3986
www.budget-belize.com

Crystal Auto Rental
5 Miles George Price (Northern) Highway, Belize City
Tel: 223-1600
www.crystal-belize.com
This is the largest rental fleet in Belize, excellent value, and the only company that allows you to take its vehicles to Tikal.

By Taxi

Downtown Belize City is small enough to handle on foot, and during the heat of the day this is the best way to get around. At night, you should travel by private car or taxi, even for short distances; expect to pay US$3.50–5 for a ride. Hotels and restaurants are used to calling for taxis, which arrive almost immediately; always remember to confirm the price with the driver before setting off.

Transfers between hotels are often pre-arranged for tourists by their tour operator. It is also possible to hire taxis to travel between towns or to explore the countryside.

A

Accommodations

Belize has a wonderfully diverse array of accommodations, from comfortable budget hotels to luxurious beach resorts to jungle lodges. Travelers with special interests are well catered to – there are remote dive resorts on the outer cayes, lodges catering to the eco-tourist and the bird-watcher, and spa resorts for those in need of serious pampering. Styles and atmospheres differ wildly: the environment makes a difference, as does the personality of the owners. Many of these places have American and European owners, who make their mark on the feel of the places.

Accommodations in lodges and on some cayes usually offer deals that include diving or fishing trips, or rainforest treks. The packages are mostly quite expensive, but very convenient and usually worthwhile. There is also a compulsory government hotel tax of 9 percent added to prices, and most hotels add a service charge of 5–10 percent.

Hotel prices vary greatly depending on the season. High-season rates are usually charged between November 15 and May 15, but may vary between hotels. Prices may drop dramatically in the low season. See also Budgeting for Your Trip.

Admission Charges

In Belize, admission fees for museums, attractions, Maya sites, and wildlife sanctuaries range from Bz$10 to Bz$30. Admission fees for snorkeling and diving at protected marine areas are Bz$20–80. Most tour companies include admission prices to sites and attractions in the tour price, but it's worth confirming before booking.

B

Budgeting for Your Trip

Overall, Belize is up to 40 to 50 percent more expensive than its Central American counterparts. That said, you can still find plenty of budget options, including for food, transportation, and accommodations, across the country.

A main course at an upscale restaurant starts at Bz$50; at a moderate restaurant, Bz$35; and at a budget restaurant, you can dine on a hearty meal, particularly at lunchtime, for as little as Bz$12–15.

Accommodation prices also cover the spectrum: Average prices range from $Bz50 at a simple budget guesthouse to $Bz150–250 for a decent mid-range hotel to $Bz400–500 and up for luxe resorts.

A taxi journey from the international airport into Belize City costs Bz$50. If you want to cut the cost, one option is to share with other travelers. Buses are perhaps the best transportation deal in the country. Regular buses start at around Bz$4–10 one-way; tickets for express buses are just a few dollars more. Most of Belize's main towns and destinations are linked by domestic flights; trips are short, from 25 minutes to an hour and prices start at Bz$70–100. The local airlines often offer seasonal deals and discounts.

C

Children

Belize is a very child-friendly destination, and there is plenty to keep kids occupied. In particular, Belize is an excellent place to introduce children to the natural world – and the importance of protecting and sustaining it – with numerous opportunities for jungle treks and wildlife spotting. Top sights and activities that are often popular with the younger set include the Belize Zoo, the Community Baboon Sanctuary, cave-tubing in Cayo, and swimming in the Caribbean waters on the cayes. Few hotels and resorts prohibit children, though it's worth asking before you book. The more upscale resorts and hotels have a number of amenities for children, including cribs, high chairs, childcare amenities, and children's menus. Also, the hotel staff can often help you find recommended local babysitters.

Climate

Belize enjoys a subtropical climate, tempered by brisk prevailing tradewinds from the Caribbean Sea. There are two seasons: the rainy season is from June to January, with a brief dry period in August; the dry season is from February to May. It should be stressed that this is a flexible division, and torrential tropical downpours can occur at any time of the year. Average rainfall in the north of Belize is 50ins (127cm) and a much heavier 173ins (439cm) in the extreme south.

When to Visit

Most visitors come to Belize during the winter months of the northern hemisphere – note, though, that this is generally when airfare prices are highest and the hotels book up. Divers, on the other hand, prefer the clearer waters during late spring and summer when the

Caye Caulker weather forecast.

onshore winds die down. December and January are the coolest months, but even so, the temperature rarely falls below 55°F (13°C) at night. In the steamier months, the coastal temperatures usually reach 96°F (06°0), inland can be hotter. The most sweltering part of Belize tends to be on the flatlands around the capital, Belmopan, where it is barely possible to walk the streets during the day; the mountainous area south of San Ignacio, while hot during the day, can actually be quite cool at night, getting down to around 50°F (12°C) in winter.

What to Bring

Belize is all about the great outdoors – no matter what time of year, you'll spend the bulk of your time outside, whether on the beach, or in the jungle or the cool mountains. The heat and year-round humidity dictate lightweight clothing of natural fibers. On the cayes, you can get by in shorts, a T-shirt, and sandals most of the time, or just bare feet and a swimsuit. However, most of the larger resorts maintain a trendy profile after dark, so pack a more formal tropical outfit to wear under the thatched roof at dinner.

Most of the time, you'll need to dress for the weather rather than for style. Don't underestimate the power of the tropical sun: it can burn you in a half hour or less. If you're spending all day in the sun on a fishing charter or day-trip to the cayes, wear a hat and even long sleeves. If visiting the islands in December and January, take a jacket or a sweater as temperatures can be chilly in the evenings at this time of year.

The two absolute essentials that you will use are sunscreen and insect repellent. Bring them with you: sunscreen is surprisingly expensive here. Bring twice as much as you think you'll need: anyone with a fair complexion should be lathered in suntan lotion from dawn until dusk.

As for insect repellent, mild versions that work well at home are next to useless against the swarms in Belize. Nothing less than a high concentration DEET will do the trick. Again, bring twice as much as you think you'll need. Resort gift shops will charge an arm and a leg for a small can of spray.

Also, if you plan to be staying at hostels and hotels with no safety box or with minimal security, it's worth bringing a money belt for carrying passports and valuables.

Hurricanes

Like most of the Caribbean, the cayes and other coastal areas of Belize can suffer from powerful hurricanes. The official hurricane season lasts from June to the end of November, though the worst storms usually occur during September and October – tourist low season. There are superb warning systems in place, and most of the major weather websites, including www.weather.com, adequately cover Belize's weather systems and hurricane forecasts. Precaution is key: if there is a hurricane developing anywhere in the Caribbean, prepare to leave as quickly as possible or postpone plans for a visit.

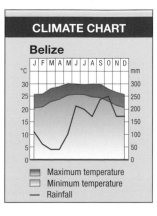

CLIMATE CHART

Belize

■ Maximum temperature
□ Minimum temperature
— Rainfall

Crime and Safety

It's important to take some basic precautions when visiting Belize, but overall it's a fairly safe country – crime against tourists is relatively rare. The city where you'll need to be most careful is Belize City, which has long had a sketchy reputation. While it's generally safe during the day, after dark it's best to take taxis to get around. There are hustlers in Belize City who will try to intimidate you into parting with a dollar, but the threats are seldom serious. Walk on, or speak to the police if you are persistently harassed. Elsewhere, be particularly careful not to leave anything valuable on the beach while swimming, and do not leave valuables in budget hotel rooms or basic beach *cabañas* that are easily broken into. If in doubt, ask hotels to lock up your bag when you go out. Also, make sure that any guide you hire has official credentials – all legal tour guides in Belize are licensed and will have a photo ID. If you have doubts about using a certain guide, trust your instinct and report the incident to the authorities.

Marijuana (called *ganja* in Belize) is illegal throughout the region, as are other drugs. If you get into any trouble with the police, the first thing to do is to contact your embassy (see page 233).

It's always a good idea to stay abreast of current safety in your country by checking the travel advice pages from the US State Department (http://travel.state.gov/) and the UK Foreign and Commonwealth Office (www.gov.uk/foreign-travel-advice).

In addition to its regular police force, Belize has special tourism police, operating from local police stations. Easily identified by their shirts and caps emblazoned with 'Tourism Police,' they patrol Belize City, San Pedro, Caye Caulker, Placencia, and various other tourist destinations around the country.

Customs Regulations

Removal, sale, and exportation of the following are prohibited by law in Belize: any kind of coral without a license, archeological artifacts, orchids; shells, fish, crustaceans, turtles, and materials from turtles.

D

Disabled Travelers

Travelers with disabilities will find it challenging to travel in Belize, though the infrastructure is slowly improving and a number of tour companies now offer services and contingency plans for those with disabilities. Public transportation is not equipped for wheelchairs, however minibus taxis are plentiful and drivers will assist you when asked. Streets in many areas can be difficult to negotiate, as they are mostly unpaved and sidewalks are few and far between. Not many hotels are equipped for travelers with disabilities, so it's imperative to ask about a hotel's accessibility when you call to book; note that the newer and higher-end resorts, particularly in well-touristed areas like Ambergris Caye, are more likely to have facilities for travelers with disabilities.

Resources

A Belizean organization that has been instrumental in increasing the country's awareness of people with disabilities is the non-profit Belize Council for the Visually Impaired (BCVI; tel: 223-2636; www.bcvi.org). Internationally, there are a number of organizations that have information, services, and resources, including the Society for Accessible Travel and Hospitality (SATH; www.sath.org), Disability Rights UK (www.disabilityrightsuk.org), and Accessible Caribbean Vacations (www.accessiblecaribbeanvacations.com).

E

Eating out

What to Eat

Belizean cuisine is a unique mix of Caribbean, Central American, and creole, with rice and beans as its base, often served with stewed chicken or fried fish. Additionally, many of the larger Belizean towns have a range of international restaurants – notably Chinese and Middle Eastern – to add to the mix.

But, Belize's biggest culinary draw is its superb seafood. Feast on everything from red snapper and grouper to lobster, conch, and shrimp, which are served multiple ways – barbecued, grilled, tossed in pastas and salads, and even stuffed into omelets. The creole influence is also evident on menus across Belize, with traditional items like 'johnny cakes,' heavy flour biscuits that got their name from 'journey cakes,' because they hold up well during long trips; and fry jacks, fluffy fried dough. Belize offers an exotic range of tropical fruit, especially in the interior – try a tangy 'soursop' milkshake. In Southern Belize, sample the traditional Garífuna cuisine, which includes cassava, similar to sweet potato, and used to make crispy cassava bread; and hudut, plantains that are mashed into a paste, and then cooked with fresh fish.

Across the country there are countless streetside snack bars and casual eateries serving tasty Central American cuisine, from empanadas to tacos. And, for some added spice to any Belizean meal, there will always be a bottle of the country's signature Marie Sharp's pepper sauce (see page 71).

Where to Eat

Belize's relaxed nature comes through in its restaurants and eateries, which are decidedly casual and pretension-free. In the larger towns, you might find a couple of white-linen spots, but otherwise Belize's restaurants generally consist of a few basic tables topped with the ubiquitous Marie Sharp's pepper sauce, a fan spinning in the corner, music emitting from a crackly speaker, and a simple menu. On the cayes and coast, the added bonus is dining out while tucking your toes into the warm sand. Also, there are Central American-style streetside vendors throughout the country, where you can pick up fast and delicious snacks, like tamales and tacos. Download your free app for restaurant listings, see inside front cover.

Drinking

When it comes to beer, the choice is clear: Belikin, the only brewery

⊘ Emergencies

Police 90 or 911
To report a crime 227-2222 (Belize City)
Ambulance/Fire 90 (Belize City only)

in Belize, produces almost all the beer consumed in the country. Belikin beer comes in several varieties, including regular, a tasty, lager-type beer; a dark, rich stout; and the malty Premium. The legal age for drinking alcohol in Belize is 18. Local rum such as the popular brand Travellers One Barrel Rum is, for quality and price, the best-value alcohol to buy in Belize. Full-bodied cashew nut and berry wines are bottled and sold throughout the country; you can also purchase imported wine, though it's generally quite pricey. Belize also has a wealth of fresh fruit juices, including orange, lime, and pineapple. Tap water in towns, though safe, is highly chlorinated, and most villages have a potable water system. Filtered, bottled, and mineral water are sold almost everywhere.

Embassies and Consulates

Canada: Consulate of Canada, The Renaissance Tower of Belize, 8 Newtown Barracks, Belize City; tel: 223-1060; www.canadainternational.gc.ca
UK: High Commission, North Ring Road/Melhado Parade, PO Box 91, Belmopan; tel: 822-2146; www.gov.uk/world/organisations/british-high-commission-belmopan
US: Floral Park Road, Belmopan; tel: 822-4011; https://bz.usembassy.gov

Etiquette

Politeness and a smile goes a long way while traveling in Belize. And, although Belize is a very casual country – shorts and sandals are the unofficial uniform throughout the cayes and the coast – there are plenty of occasions that call for dressier outfits, such as dining out at an upscale restaurant, attending church, or visiting a local's home for a party.

In general, it's best to avoid being openly critical of the region's problems, including crime and dilapidated houses – Belizeans recognize their country's difficulties, but some are sensitive to criticism. If you have an appointment, get there on time, but don't be too surprised if you have to wait around a while – the definition of punctuality is loose here. If you add some flexibility to your travel plans, and expect the odd delay, you will have a far less frustrating time if you get held up. Perhaps the biggest mistake inexperienced travelers

make is to try to see too much in too short a time. With the inevitable delays, by setting a punishing itinerary you will spend most of your time on buses and in bus stations.

Festivals and Events

As throughout Central America, festivals are popular in Belize – and range from Hispanic-based rituals and colorful Caribbean parades to traditional Garífuna dancing and drumming in the south.

January
New Year's Day (January 1). Celebrations around the country to mark the start of the New Year, including annual horse racing in Burrell Boom, in northern Belize.

February
Sidewalk Arts Festival (mid-February) in Placencia. One of the best arts festivals in the country, with local art, from paintings to photography, as well as cuisine, music, and other performances.

March
La Ruta Maya Belize River Challenge (early March). A boisterous four-day boat race from San Ignacio to Belize City.
Baron Bliss Day (early March). Honors this British Baron, who was one of the country's most generous benefactors, particularly in the arts.

April
Easter Fairs (dates shift yearly). Lively Easter fairs and celebrations, with local food, dance performances, and church services, in San Ignacio and other towns throughout the country.

May
Cashew Festival (first week in May) in Crooked Tree village. A celebration of the cashew nut in all its tasty variations, from cashew jam and fudge to wine.

⏻ Electricity

Belize uses **110 volts** and flat two-pronged plugs.

National Agriculture and Trade Show (early May) in Belmopan. One of the largest public events in Belize, with impressive crop and livestock displays and exhibits.

June
Lobster festivals in San Pedro, Caye Caulker, and Placencia. Lobster season launches in June, which is marked by lobster festivals where you can feast on the famous crustacean every which way.

July
Benque Viejo Fiesta (mid-July) in Cayo District. From fireworks to salsa bands to parades, this festival celebrates Cayo's mestizo culture and history.

August
International Costa Maya Festival (first week of August) in San Pedro. A celebration of Mundo Maya countries (Mexico, Belize, Guatemala, Honduras, and El Salvador), with parades, traditional cuisine, and other cultural rituals from each.

September
Independence Day (September 21). Independence Day celebrations take place nationwide, including a parade and carnival in Belize City.

October
Pan-American Day (mid October). Originally known as Columbus Day, Pan-American Day pays tribute to Belize's ethnic diversity, with festivals, concerts, and parades, from Belize City to the Cayes.

November
Garífuna Settlement Day (November 19). The Garífuna community comes together with great enthusiasm to celebrate the anniversary of their ancestors' arrival in Dangriga in 1823. Dangriga, Hopkins, and other Garífuna communities throw big parties, with Joncunu dancers, masked drumming, traditional cuisine, and more.

Health and Medical Care

Hygiene standards are much better than in many other parts of the developing world, but diarrhea may still strike no matter how careful you are. Stomach upsets are likely to be your main concern, but you should also be inoculated against polio, cholera, tetanus, typhoid, and hepatitis. None of these diseases are at all common Belize – immunization is not a mandatory requirement and the risk is very low – but every year there are cases. Getting bitten by a rabid animal is also statistically extremely unlikely, but if you are bitten you should begin immunization shots immediately.

Mosquitoes are likely to be much more of a concern, and it's imperative to minimize the chances of being bitten, especially in remote, lowland areas. Diligently apply insect repellent with a high DEET content to all exposed areas of skin, especially around your ankles. Burn mosquito coils (available locally) and leave a fan on at night while you sleep.

There is malaria in some parts of Belize. Most travelers visiting the cayes or San Ignacio don't need to worry too much, but if you are heading for extended stays in jungle areas, it is advisable to begin a course of anti-malaria tablets. Your doctor can prescribe the latest version: most courses start one week prior to arrival and continue for four weeks afterward. (Of course, no visitor escapes without bites from regular non-malarial mosquitoes – 'flies' to Belizeans – but there is no need to panic.)

Dengue fever, carried by a daytime mosquito, is on the increase worldwide, and there have been a few outbreaks in and around Belize. It's normally caught as a result of being bitten near pools or puddles of dirty, stagnant water. The symptoms are fever, severe headache, complete loss of energy, and usually a skin rash. There is one rare strain, dengue

☉ Weights and Measures

The British imperial system is generally used, with speed and road signs in miles. However, gas is sold by the American gallon, and some imported goods are weighed using the metric system.

hemorrhagic, that can be very serious, but it is rarely fatal in adults: in most cases the body heals itself within a few days. There's no vaccine for any strain of dengue, so you should take great precaution against being bitten; the only remedy is to take complete rest until the dengue clears, which seriously interrupts your holiday.

Belize has a fairly high number of reported cases of AIDS. The problem is being traced partly to foreign visitors – particularly those from elsewhere in Central America and from the United States. Visitors are advised to practise safe sex; condoms are inexpensive and widely available at pharmacies.

Take high-factor sunscreen, a hat for protection against the sun, and drink plenty of (bottled) water to avoid dehydration, especially at high altitudes.

Those with fair complexions should be careful in the strong sun. Drink plenty of water on walking trips and, like Belizeans, avoid much activity between 11am and 3pm on hot days. Watch out on boat trips to the cayes and use sunscreen on your back and legs when snorkeling.

Divers and snorkelers should be careful to avoid touching the coral, especially when getting from a boat into shallow water. Disturbances to live coral outcroppings can result in their death, while cuts and abrasions from the reef nearly always become painfully infected and take a long time to heal. Once in the water, the various moray eels, barracuda, stingrays, sharks, and so on look menacing but are nothing at all to worry about. Your guide will steer you away from strong currents through cuts in the reef. Those susceptible to motion sickness and planning a live-aboard dive trip with several days on a boat should consider taking Dramamine tablets or patches with them.

The quality of food and its preparation in Belize is good so there is not as great a risk of stomach problems as in neighboring countries. Tap water is potable in most of Belize, but in some parts of the cayes or in the south of Belize, it's not recommended for drinking. Instead, drink bottled water, sold at all gas stations and stores. You

will quickly discover a variety of 'jungle remedies' on sale at many guesthouses for common travelers' ailments. For more serious conditions, your hotel should be able to recommend a doctor.

Medical Services

If you require the services of a physician, your hotel should be able to recommend one nearby. If you need daily medication, bring an ample supply since your brand may be unavailable or extremely expensive in Belize.

Few pharmacies are open late at night or on weekends and, should you need urgent medical attention, be warned: district hospitals are supposed to have doctors on call at night and on weekends, but serious illnesses or injuries are usually referred to the Karl Heusner Memorial Hospital in Belize City. So, if the worst happens and you have the option, your best bet is to go directly there. Belize Medical Associates (tel: 223-0303), next to the hospital in Belize City provides a more rapid service, although it is more expensive.

Public Hospitals
Karl Heusner Memorial Hospital, Belize City
Tel: 223-1548
www.khmh.bz
Corozal Hospital
Tel: 422-2076
Dangriga Hospital
Tel: 522-2078
Orange Walk Hospital
Tel: 322-2072
Punta Gorda Hospital
Tel: 722-2145
San Ignacio Hospital
Tel: 824-2066

L

LGBTQ Travelers

Belize presents no serious difficulties for LGBTQ travelers, but the scene is quite underground, with very few gay and lesbian bars. Few locals, though, will make their disapproval obvious to foreigners, and many openly welcome the gay cruises that visit the country. San Pedro and Caye Caulker are among the best spots to enjoy a hassle-free time.

Media

Newspapers in Belize are all weekly and are either owned by, or connected to, political parties. The main mastheads are *Amandala*, the *Belize Times*, the *Guardian*, and the Reporter. While in San Pedro, try the *San Pedro Sun* and in Placencia there's the *Placencia Breeze* – both provide excellent tourist information.

As for radio, Love FM, with pop tunes, news, and current affairs, has one of the most extensive networks. Another big station is KREM FM, with an emphasis on talk and local music. Also, each major district town has its own local station. The two main TV stations are Channel 5, the country's best broadcaster, with strong news programs. Channel 7 features a mix of American and Belizean programming mixed in with local news and political discussion programs. Cable TV is also big in the country, with a variety of cable channels that broadcast everything from American soaps, talk shows, and CNN to sports and movies.

Money

Debit cards are the most popular way to access money, and credit cards are useful in upscale hotels, restaurants, and stores. Visa and MasterCard are widely recognized. Most towns have an ATM or two for 24-hour withdrawals, but note that some ATMs do not accept five-digit PINs – make arrangements with your bank for a four-digit PIN ahead of your trip. In many places it is possible to arrange a cash advance on your credit card, though this is often time-consuming and you'll usually need to pay a fee. In smaller places, you will likely have to pay cash.

Travelers' checks can be cashed in many banks, but smaller branches may take a long time over it, so try to use city branches instead. Make sure you get your travelers' checks issued in US dollars (other currencies are rarely accepted) and from an established name such as Thomas Cook or American Express. In Belize, US-dollar travelers' checks can be used as currency in some stores.

US dollar bills are accepted almost everywhere, because the Belize dollar is pegged to the US dollar at a rate of Bz$2 to US$1. Some prices are quoted in US dollars, so it is important to check which currency a price is in before agreeing to it.

Currency

Belizean dollars, with notes from Bz$2 to Bz$100, are divided into 100 cents.

Tipping

Tipping is not obligatory but will be appreciated and usually 10–15 percent will be all right.

Opening Hours

Most stores and offices open Mon–Fri 8am–noon, with afternoon hours varying between 1–5pm and 3–8pm. Most banks open Mon–Fri 8am–3 or 4pm; some are also open until noon on Saturdays. Almost everything is closed on public holidays.

Postal Services

Belize City Post Office is on the north side of the Swing Bridge (near the intersection of Queen and North Front streets). Belizean stamps are beautiful, with depictions of native flora and fauna, and are prized by collectors. Belize provides one of the most economical and reliable postal systems in Central America. Allow around 4–7 days for mail to arrive in the US and around two weeks (often less) to Europe, Asia, or Australia. The post office is open 8am–noon and 1–4.30pm.

Public Holidays

January 1 New Year's Day
March 9 Baron Bliss Day
March/April Easter weekend
May 1 Labor Day
May 24 Commonwealth Day
September 10 St George's Caye Day
September 21 Independence Day
October 12 Pan-American Day
November 19 Garífuna Settlement Day
December 25 Christmas Day
December 26 Boxing Day

Religious Services

Nearly 50 percent of the population is Roman Catholic, but as Belize welcomes more and more nationalities into the population, the number of different religious groups also increases. At present the list includes Anglican, Methodist, Mennonite, Baha'i, Hindu, Muslim, Presbyterian, Seventh Day Adventist, and Evangelical Christian.

The Garífuna people practice their own unique religion, which is often incorrectly compared by outsiders to Haitian-style voodoo. The central focus is the concept of a continued communication with ancestors, who are held in great reverence. Their spirits are summoned to assist with problems and provide guidance for the living. The Garifuna Mass is a synthesis of Roman Catholicism and African traditions and is now being openly shared with other Belizeans and visitors, especially around Settlement Day in November.

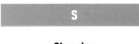

Shopping

Unlike Mexico and Guatemala, Belize has not developed such a strong souvenir industry, although it is growing. A couple of small operations around San Ignacio are teaching old skills like Maya pottery and slate carving.

Many hotels near San Ignacio stock Guatemalan handicrafts but note that they are, of course, much cheaper if bought on the other side of the border.

Local specialty items are always a good bet, with many visitors taking home Marie Sharp's pepper sauce, cashew nuts, coconut rum, berry or cashew wine, or Gallon Jug coffee. Local preserves (chutney and jam) made from mangoes, bananas, papayas, and other tropical fruits also make good gifts. Herbal remedies or bush medicines are sold by individual herbalists.

Look out for the delicate baskets woven from jipijapa plant fibers by Maya women, who also continue the traditions of their grandmothers making beautiful blouses with Maya animal motifs around the neck and sleeves. Groups of Maya women and their daughters set up stalls at the entrance to the archeological sites in the Maya mountains of Toledo district. In the south, towns like Placencia have a variety of small art galleries and crafts shops.

Hammocks made in Guatemala, both the nylon string and cotton cord variety, are sold in the better gift shops, but are much more reasonable from street vendors. Mexican jewelry is sold at better shops, but never purchase black coral or turtle shell souvenirs: it encourages their depletion and is illegal. Download your free app for more detailed information on shopping in Belize, see inside front cover.

T

Telephones

The country's main telephone and cell phone provider is Digi (www.livedigi. com). Cell phone coverage is best in towns and cities. Most North American cell phones should work in Belize, but only tri-band or multi-band European phones will pick up a signal.

Public telephones are available throughout Belize, except in the more remote areas where you will often only find a community phone in someone's house. International phone cards are the cheapest way to make international calls when using a public telephone. Your hotel will also have fixed rates for national and international calls. Check the rate before you make the call and watch out for the service charge some hotels may add to your bill.
Directory Assistance 113
International Call Operator 114

Time Zone

US Central standard time; GMT minus 6 hours

Tourist Information

The official Belize Tourism Board website, www.travelbelize.org, has a broad range of information, from sights and attractions to outdoor adventures to accommodations. There are Belize Tourism offices in Belize City and in main towns around the country, including in Placencia and San Pedro. The Belize Tourism Industry Association (BTIA; www.btia. org) represents many of the tourism-related businesses in the country and produces the annual *Destination Belize* magazine (www.destinationbelize.com), which is filled with helpful information and available free from tourist offices and many hotels. Note also that a number of towns and regions in Belize have developed their own tourism-friendly websites, often focusing on current news and local information – two of these are www.ambergriscaye.com and www.corozal.com. Other helpful websites include www.gov.uk/foreign-travel-advice/belize, the government's own website, which has an overview of current politics and tourism trends; and http://edition.channel5belize.com, the local news station, which covers Belize news and headlines.
Belize Tourism Board
64 Regent Street, Belize City; tel: 227-2420 (toll-free: 1-800-624-0686); www.travelbelize.org; Mon–Fri 8am–noon and 1–5pm.

For further information on Belize's ecology and protected areas, contact:
Belize Audubon Society, 16 North Park Street, Belize City; tel: 223-5004; www.belizeaudubon.org; Mon–Fri 8am–5pm. Belize's oldest conservation organization.
The Belize Zoo and Tropical Education Center, Ladyville GPO, Belize City; tel: 822-8000; www.belizezoo.org.

For more detailed information about Maya archeological sites, or for permission to visit certain sites in the region, contact the **Belize Institute of Archaeology**, Museum Building, Culvert Road, Belmopan; tel: 822-2106; http://nichbelize.org.

Specialist Tours

In addition to the international tour operators, there are a numerous operators that focus on certain themes or activities.
Toledo Ecotourism Association (TEA)
Punta Gorda
Tel: 722-2096
http://belizemayatourism.org
www.teabelize.org

The long-running TEA is one of the country's leading organizations in preserving Maya traditions and culture, with a variety of tours to Maya villages and sites, as well as homestay programs.
Belize Trips
Belize City
Tel: 610-1923 or 1-561 210 7015 (US reservations)
www.belize-trips.com
Belize-based specialist Katie Valk is a font of knowledge on Belize, and can curate specialized itineraries that take in everything from watersports to Maya sites.
S & L Travel and Tours
Belize City
Tel: 227-7593
www.sltravelbelize.com
This top-quality tour operator creates tailored tours that cover a wide range of activities, from kayaking to birding to Maya sites.
Sun Creek Tours
Front Street
Punta Gorda
Tel: 607-6363722-0112 or 600-8773
www.suncreeklodge.de
Personalized tours to Maya sites, nature reserves and cayes throughout Belize, specializing in the Toledo District.

Visas and Passports

Visas are not required by most nationalities, including citizens of the United States, United Kingdom, Canada, Australia, New Zealand, South Africa, and CARICOM (Caribbean Community) countries, as well as most members of the European Union. It is advisable to check with your nearest consulate or embassy before travel as requirements do change. All people from the above countries still need an international passport that is valid for at least six months, and an onward or round-trip air ticket.

All visitors are permitted to stay up to 30 days. To apply for an extension visit any Immigration Office. A moderate fee is charged, and applicants must demonstrate sufficient funds for the remainder of their stay, as well as an onward ticket. Note that there's a departure tax of US$40 to leave the country, by land or sea (payable even if you're on a day trip to Tikal).

Many of the best books written about Belize or by Belizean authors are published in the country and may not be available elsewhere. Cubola Productions (www.cubola.com) is Belize's foremost publisher. Their Explorer series includes textbooks on subjects such as the environment, the history, and the geography of Belize, plus an atlas of Belize, academic literature, and cookbooks. Angelus Press (www.anqeluspress.com) in Belize City also offers a mail-order service for a variety of titles.

GENERAL

Belize 1798, The Road to Glory by Emory King (Tropical Books, 1991). Bombastic, bodice ripping account of the Battle of St. George's Caye, and of Belize's burgeoning society, written by one of Belize's larger-than life American settlers, also the author of *Hey Dad, This is Belize*.
Inside Belize by T. Barry (The Inter-Hemispheric Education Resource Center, 1992). A good rundown of society and politics.
Profile of Belize by Society for the Promotion of Education and Research, Belize City (Cubola Productions/Spear Press). Informative facts and figures about the country.

HISTORY

13 Chapters of a History of Belize by Assad Shoman (Angelus Press). One of the few comprehensive histories of the country written by a Belizean. Designed primarily as a text for high schools, Shoman's impressive credentials – politician, scholar, and diplomat – make this a worthwhile read.

ENVIRONMENT

A Belize Rainforest: The Community Baboon Sanctuary by Horwich and Lyon (Orangutan Press). Everything you wanted to know about howler monkeys and much more.
The Environment of Belize by Kimo Jolly and Ellen McRae (Cubola Productions, 1998). A high school textbook, which will also appeal to visitors. Accessible, well written and informative.

Jaguar: One Man's Struggle to Establish the World's First Jaguar Preserve by Alan Rabinowitz (Island Press, 2000). The personal story of how wildlife biologist Rabinowitz's 1983 study of jaguars in the Cockscomb Basin of south-central Belize led to the creation of the Jaguar Reserve and the displacement of Maya villagers.

MAYA HERITAGE

The Blood of Kings by Linda Schele and Mary Ellen Miller (Thames & Hudson, 1992). The late Linda Schele was one of the greatest

☉ Send us your thoughts

We do our best to ensure the information in our books is as accurate and up-to-date as possible. The books are updated on a regular basis using local contacts, who painstakingly add, amend and correct as required. However, some details (such as telephone numbers and opening times) are liable to change, and we are ultimately reliant on our readers to put us in the picture.

We welcome your feedback, especially your experience of using the book "on the road". Maybe you came across a great bar or new attraction we missed.

We will acknowledge all contributions, and we'll offer an Insight Guide to the best letters received.

Please write to us at:
Insight Guides
PO Box 7910
London SE1 1WE

Or email us at:
hello@insightguides.com

Mayanists of the late 20th century who proved the Maya did not live a peaceful existence governed by priests and astronomers but were warlike and obsessed with blood-letting and sacrifice. Read *with A Forest of Kings*, written by Schele and David Freide (Quill/Morrow, 1990)
Inside Guatemala; Inside Mexico; Inside Belize (Interhemispheric, 1992) all by Tom Barry. Concise and reliable summaries of the Maya countries, with sections on government and politics, religious issues, society, economics, and the environment.
The Lords of Tikal by Peter D. Harrison (Thames & Hudson, 2000). A detailed but readable study of the great Maya city of Tikal and its rulers, incorporating decades of research.
The Maya by Michael D. Coe (Thames & Hudson, 2003). An excellent general introduction to the subject. Well illustrated with maps, drawings, and photographs and written by one of the century's finest archeologists who also wrote the influential *Breaking the Maya Code* (Thames & Hudson, 1993), which confirmed that Maya glyphs were a written language.
Maya Cities and Sacred Caves by Jaime Awe (Cubola Productions, 2007). A short guide to Belize's publicly accessible Maya sites and an excellent summary of ancient Maya history. Expertly described by the Director of Archeology in Belize, and illustrated with color photography and maps of the sites.
The Popol Vuh translated by Dennis Tedlock (Simon & Schuster, 1996). The K'iche 'bible,' the masterful book of creation, that's both one of the most important pre-Columbian texts in the Americas and also an incredibly rich and imaginative read.

The Rise and Fall of the Maya Civilization by J. Eric S. Thompson (University of Oklahoma Press, 1973). Another excellent introduction to the Maya, and, though many of Thompson's more utopian theories have now been overturned, much of the text still reads well. Thompson's Maya History and Religion (Norman, 1970), is another useful study.

Time Among the Maya by Ronald Wright (Weidenfeld & Nicholson, 1989). An entertaining and informative account of the author's journeys around Central America, with insights into Maya culture.

FLORA AND FAUNA

Animals and Plants of the Ancient Maya by Victoria Schlesinger, illustrated by Juan C. Chab (University of Texas Press, 2002). A useful field guide, with personal observations as well as fairly common species, listed by their Maya name in addition to their English and scientific names.

Birds of Belize by H. Lee Jones (University of Texas Press, 2004). By far the best and most comprehensive fully illustrated guide to all species recorded in Belize.

National Geographic Field Guide to the Birds of North America Edited by Jon L. Dunn and Jonathan Alderfer (National Geographic Books, 2011).

The Cockscomb Basin Wildlife Sanctuary by Louise H. Emmons et al (Orang-Utan Press, USA). A beautifully written and comprehensive guide to history, geography, culture, flora, and fauna of the Jaguar Reserve.

The Ecotravellers' Wildlife Guide: Belize and Northern Guatemala by Les Beletsky (Academic Press, 1999). An excellent guide for the general reader, with sumptuous color illustrations of the region's wildlife, as well as descriptions of the ecology and the most popular parks and reserves.

A Guide to the Frogs and Toads of Belize by Carol Farnetti Foster and John R. Meyer (Kreiger, 1999). Covers 33 species of the frogs and toads (anurans) found in Belize. Illustrated in color, with information on distribution, habitat, and breeding.

A Guide to the Reptiles of Belize by Peter J. Stafford and John R. Meyer (Academic Press, 1999). A detailed field guide, written by experts. Well-illustrated with diagrams and color photographs.

The Last Flight of the Scarlet Macaw: One Woman's Fight to Save the World's Most Beautiful Bird by Bruce Barcott (Random House, 2009). Traces the inspiring crusade by environmentalist Sharon Matola, founder of the Belize Zoo, to save the scarlet macaw.

Rainforest Remedies – 100 Healing Herbs of Belize (Lotus Press, 1993) by Rosita Arvigo and Michael Balick. Fascinating guide to the endemic plant life of Belize, illustrated with line drawings. Dr. Arvigo was the founder and director of the acclaimed Ix Chel Tropical Research Station in Cayo District.

LANGUAGE

Creole Proverbs of Belize (Cubola Productions, 1987). The often hilarious and poetic everyday sayings of creole Belizeans, gathered by Dr Colville Young.

Kriol-Inglish Dikshineri (Belize Kriol Project). For help in understanding creole words and their meanings.

OTHER INSIGHT GUIDES

Insight Guides cover nearly 200 destinations, providing information on culture and all the top sights, as well as superb photography. Insight Guide Caribbean covers the Lesser Antilles, while Insight Guide Caribbean Cruises covers ports of call throughout the region. Other guides to the region include Insight Guides Costa Rica; Cuba; Guatemala, Belize and the Yucatán; Mexico and Puerto Rico.

CREDITS

INSIGHT GUIDE CREDITS

Distribution
UK, Ireland and Europe
Apa Publications (UK) Ltd;
sales@insightguides.com
United States and Canada
Ingram Publisher Services;
ips@ingramcontent.com
Australia and New Zealand
Woodslane; info@woodslane.com.au
Southeast Asia
Apa Publications (SN) Pte;
singaporeoffice@insightguides.com
Worldwide
Apa Publications (UK) Ltd;
sales@insightguides.com
Special Sales, Content Licensing and CoPublishing
Insight Guides can be purchased in bulk quantities at discounted prices. We can create special editions, personalised jackets and corporate imprints tailored to your needs.
sales@insightguides.com
www.insightguides.biz

Printed in China by CTPS

First Edition 1995
Sixth Edition 2019

Every effort has been made to provide accurate information in this publication, but changes are inevitable. The publisher cannot be responsible for any resulting loss, inconvenience or injury. We would appreciate it if readers would call our attention to any errors or outdated information. We also welcome your suggestions; please contact us at: hello@insightguides.com

www.insightguides.com

Editor: Tatiana Wilde
Author: AnneLise Sorensen
Head of DTP and Pre-Press: Rebeka Davies
Layout: Aga Bylica
Update Production: Apa Digital
Managing Editor: Carine Tracanelli
Picture Editor: Tom Smyth
Cartography: original cartography Stephen Ramsay, updated by Carte

CONTRIBUTORS

This new edition builds on earlier editions produced by **AnneLise Sorensen, Peter Eltringham, Karla Heusner, Tony Perrottet, Tony Rath, Errol Laborder, Lynn Meisch, Carolyn M. Miller, Joshua Starr, Gerry Tobin,** and **Dr Colville Young.**

ABOUT INSIGHT GUIDES

Insight Guides have more than 45 years' experience of publishing high-quality, visual travel guides. We produce 400 full-colour titles, in both print and digital form, covering more than 200 destinations across the globe, in a variety of formats to meet your different needs.

   Insight Guides are written by local authors, whose expertise is evident in the extensive historical and cultural background features. Each destination is carefully researched by regional experts to ensure our guides provide the very latest information. All the reviews in **Insight Guides** are independent; we strive to maintain an impartial view. Our reviews are carefully selected to guide you to the best places to eat, go out and shop, so you can be confident that when we say a place is special, we really mean it.

Legend

City maps

	Freeway/Highway/Motorway
	Divided Highway
	Main Roads
	Minor Roads
	Pedestrian Roads
	Steps
	Footpath
	Railway
	Funicular Railway
	Cable Car
	Tunnel
	City Wall
	Important Building
	Built Up Area
	Other Land
	Transport Hub
	Park
	Pedestrian Area
	Bus Station
	Tourist Information
	Main Post Office
	Cathedral/Church
	Mosque
	Synagogue
	Statue/Monument
	Beach
	Airport

Regional maps

	Freeway/Highway/Motorway (with junction)
	Freeway/Highway/Motorway (under construction)
	Divided Highway
	Main Road
	Secondary Road
	Minor Road
	Track
	Footpath
	International Boundary
	State/Province Boundary
	National Park/Reserve
	Marine Park
	Ferry Route
	Marshland/Swamp
	Glacier Salt Lake
	Airport/Airfield
	Ancient Site
	Border Control
	Cable Car
	Castle/Castle Ruins
	Cave
	Chateau/Stately Home
	Church/Church Ruins
	Crater
	Lighthouse
	Mountain Peak
	Place of Interest
	Viewpoint

INDEX

MAIN REFERENCES ARE IN BOLD TYPE

INSIGHT ● GUIDES

OFF THE SHELF

Since 1970, INSIGHT GUIDES has provided a unique perspective on the world's best travel destinations by using specially commissioned photography and illuminating text written by local authors.

Whether you're planning a city break, a walking tour or the journey of a lifetime, our superb range of guidebooks and phrasebooks will inspire you to discover more about your chosen destination.

INSIGHT GUIDES

offer a unique combination of stunning photos, absorbing narrative and detailed maps, providing all the inspiration and information you need.

PHRASEBOOKS & DICTIONARIES

help users to feel at home, when away. Pocket-sized with a free app to download, they go where you do.

CITY GUIDES

pack hundreds of great photos into a smaller format with detailed practical information, so you can navigate the world's top cities with confidence.

EXPLORE GUIDES

feature easy-to-follow walks and itineraries in the world's most exciting destinations, with our choice of the best places to eat and drink along the way.

POCKET GUIDES

combine concise information on where to go and what to do in a handy compact format, ideal on the ground. Includes a full-colour, fold-out map.

EXPERIENCE GUIDES

feature offbeat perspectives and secret gems for experienced travellers, with a collection of over 100 ideas for a memorable stay in a city.

www.insightguides.com